MAKING SENSE OF
SECONDARY SCIENCE

MAKING SENSE OF SECONDARY SCIENCE

Research into children's ideas

*Rosalind Driver, Ann Squires,
Peter Rushworth, Valerie Wood-Robinson*

London and New York

First published 1994
by Routledge
11 New Fetter Lane, London EC4P 4EE

Simultaneously published in the USA and Canada
by Routledge
29 West 35th Street, New York, NY 1001

Reprinted 1994, 1995, 1996, 1997, 1999, 2000

Routledge is an imprint of the Taylor & Francis Group

© 1994 Leeds City Council Department of Education and the University of Leeds

Typeset in Baskerville by
J&L Composition Ltd, Filey, North Yorkshire
Printed and bound in Great Britain by
TJ International Ltd, Padstow, Cornwall

British Library Cataloguing in Publication Data
A Catalogue record for this book is available from the British Library

Library of Congress Cataloguing in Publication Data
A catalogue record for this book is available from the Library of Congress

ISBN 0-415-09767-3 (pack)
ISBN 0-415-09765-7 (pbk)

CONTENTS

CONTENTS

FIGURES

TABLES

THE PROJECT

This publication has been produced by the Leeds National Curriculum Science Support Project. This project, which ran from 1988–1992, was a collaborative project between Leeds City Council Department of Education and the Children's Learning in Science Research Group at the University of Leeds. The project materials were written by the project team in collaboration with teachers in Leeds schools and members of the Children's Learning in Science Research Group. They were edited, for publication, by Ann Squires.

Project team
Director: Rosalind Driver.
Project Co-ordinator: Ann Squires.
Seconded Advisory Teachers: Peter Rushworth.
           Valerie Wood-Robinson.
Project Secretary: Gillian Porter.

Schools team

Abbey Grange C. of E. High School
Nicki Albert, Anne Brivonese, Elin Carson, Robin Challinor, Brian Cooke, David Henderson, David Kent, Stephen Naish, Jeff Spencer.

Intake High School
Roger Riley.

John Smeaton Community High School
Ian Armstrong, David Hughes, Chris Johnson, Tony King, Liz Mastin.

John Smeaton Middle School
Susan Cox, Eddie Gardner, Susan Tuff.

Allerton Grange High School
Tony Henshaw, Paul Mansfield, Adrienne Redhead.

Allerton Grange Middle School
Paul Clarke, Colman Folan, Sarah Latham, Tony Livesey, Jackie Paten, John Whittaker.

Archbishop Cranmer C. of E. Middle School
Richard Hudson.

Boston Spa Comprehensive School
Mike Riches, Peter Wells.

Broad Lane Middle School
David Woodruff.

St Michael's College
Jackie Clark, Mick Kearney, Graham Walker.

Silver Royd High School
Joe Carruthers, Dez Cruikshanks, Lynne Gostick, Richard Hodgson.

Thornhill Middle School
David Page.

Advisory Teachers
Richard Dickason, Mick Lawes, Jackie Sparkes, Rod Taylor.

Leeds City Council Department of Education was represented by Rose Godfrey.

Children's Learning in Science Research Group The following people were involved throughout the project as consultants and reviewers of the text: Philip Scott and John Leach (who also contributed 'Teaching science with children's thinking in mind' and 'A note on continuity and progression' to the Introduction, respectively), Brian Holding (who also contributed parts of the summaries of research into children's ideas about materials, chemical change and particles), Hilary Asoko, Daz Twigger and Elin Carson.

ACKNOWLEDGEMENTS

The following people, together with the Project team, served on the Steering Committee and gave valuable support and advice:

John Rawlinson (Chair):   Director (Advisory), Leeds City Council Department of Education.

John Baker: General Adviser, Leeds City Council Department of Education.

Rose Godfrey: General Adviser, Leeds City Council Department of Education.

John Heald: Head Teacher, Rodillian School, Rothwell, Leeds.

Terry Russell: Director, The Centre for Research in Primary Science and Technology (CRIPSAT), University of Liverpool, School of Education.

Thanks are also due to the following people for comments on drafts: John Steel, Head Teacher, Foxwood School, Leeds; John Smith, Science Adviser, Wakefield Education Authority.

ABOUT THIS BOOK

Pupils come to science lessons with ideas about the natural world. Effective science teaching takes account of these ideas and provides activities which enable pupils to make the journey from their current understandings to a more scientific view.

This overview of research, which presents information on the ideas pupils bring to lessons, has been used in the development of the Learning Guides in the companion volume, *Support Materials for Teachers*.

Research into children's ideas in science has been carried out in the UK and elsewhere in the world for many years. Many thousands of studies have been reported and more are still in progress. It is impossible, in this publication, to give a full account of all the research that has been done. We hope, however, that the overview that this book provides will give readers an indication of some of the major results in the domains of relevance to the National Curriculum. References to original studies are given for those readers who wish to refer in more detail to the studies themselves.

INTRODUCTION

CONSTRUCTING SCIENTIFIC IDEAS: IMPLICATIONS FOR TEACHING AND LEARNING

Children develop ideas about natural phenomena before they are taught science in school. In some instances these ideas are in keeping with the science which is taught. In many cases, however, there are significant differences between children's notions and school science.

Children's conceptions as personal constructions

From the earliest days of their lives children have developed ideas or schemes about the natural world around them. They have experiences of what happens when they drop, push, pull or throw objects, and in this way they build up ideas and expectations relating to the way objects feel and move. Similarly, ideas about other aspects of the world around them develop through experiences with, for example, animals, plants, water, light and shadows, fires and toys. A 9-year-old boy noticed that it took a few seconds after a record player was turned off for the sound to die away. 'There must be miles and miles of wire in there', he said, 'for electricity to go through for the sound to take so long to stop.' This boy had received no formal teaching in science and yet had developed the notion that electricity was involved in making the sound, that it flows through wires and it flows very fast!

Many of the conceptions which children develop about natural phenomena derive from their sensory experiences. Some conceptions or knowledge schemes, while influencing children's interaction with their environment, may not be represented explicitly through language. For example, children playing ball have developed a range of knowledge schemes about the trajectories that balls take which enable them to throw and catch the ball successfully. Only much later will students have formal opportunities to represent and analyse such motions: yet a knowledge scheme which enables the child to interact effectively when throwing

1

and catching balls has been in existence since the early years of life.

Surveys undertaken in various countries have identified common features in children's ideas and developmental studies are giving helpful insights into the characteristic ways in which these ideas progress during the childhood years. Investigations have indicated that such ideas are to be seen as more than simply pieces of misinformation; children have ways of construing events and phenomena which are coherent and fit with their domains of experience yet which may differ substantially from the scientific view. Studies also indicate that these notions may persist into adulthood despite formal teaching.

Common features in children's conceptions

Studies of children's conceptions about natural phenomena are indicating that there may be commonly occurring features in children's notions which can be mapped out and described. Moreover, these children's notions appear to evolve as they become adapted to wider experiences.

A topic which has been well studied is that of children's conceptions of light and sight. How do children understand how they come to see things? Do they relate light and sight? If so, how? If you ask young children, 'Where is there light in this room?', you can anticipate what they may say. Typically, 5- and 6-year-olds will identify light as the source or the effect; they might identify it as this light bulb or that bright patch on the wall. Later, children will identify something in between the source and the effect. You turn the light switch on and the room is filled with a bath of light which enables you to see things. Later, during the primary phase, some children begin to use the notion that light does travel. When you consider the speed at which light travels, the fact that children are spontaneously suggesting this, is an interesting point. They will argue that light sets off from a source, travels and strikes an object, and because the object is illuminated, you can see it. However, they are less clear about what goes on between the eye and the object. Some children do make a link in terms of visual rays from the eye going to the object – a model which embodies an active role for the viewer; we 'look at' things or 'cast a glance' at objects.

The typical textbook diagram of light being scattered from an object and some of it going in the direction of the eye is, according to the literature, a view that is held by a relative minority of secondary school-children.

An important feature is the similarity in the conceptual models that children from different countries and backgrounds are using. Children's science conceptions are not idiosyncratic, nor are they in many cases heavily culturally dependent. They are shaped by personal

2

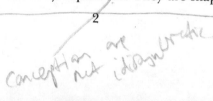

experience with phenomena. In schools which have pupils from a wide range of social and ethnic groups teachers are likely to find that pupils' ideas provide common ground for building good working relationships.

A study by Nussbaum and Novak[1] of children's conceptions of the Earth in space revealed a series of five conceptions or, as they termed them, 'notions'. They progressed from the Earth as a flat surface with an absolute frame of reference for up and down, through intermediate notions, to the scientific notion of the Earth as a sphere and up and down being defined in terms of the Earth as a frame of reference (see Figure I.1). This study was replicated in Nepal[2] and the same sequence of conceptions was identified. Figure I.2 shows the percentage of Nepalese 12-year-olds holding each of the five notions. It is compared with the percentage of American 8-year-olds. As the authors of the article comment, 'the remarkable thing to us is not that the Nepali children are slower in gaining the concept, but that the development of these ideas is similar in such widely divergent cultures'.

The social construction of knowledge

Over the last few years there has been a growing emphasis on the process of interaction in learning. It is recognised that learning about the world does not take place in a social vacuum. Children have available to them through language and culture ways of thinking and imaging. Phrases such as, 'shut the door and keep the cold out', or 'dew is falling', provide, through metaphor, ways of representing aspects of the physical world.

Whether an individual's ideas are affirmed and shared by others in classroom exchanges has a part to play in shaping the knowledge construction process. In the following example a group of 13-year-olds was invited to develop their model to explain the properties of ice, water

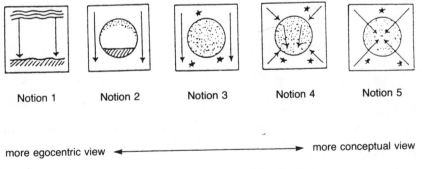

Notion 1   Notion 2   Notion 3   Notion 4   Notion 5

more egocentric view ←————————————→ more conceptual view

Figure I.1 Children's conceptions of the Earth in space

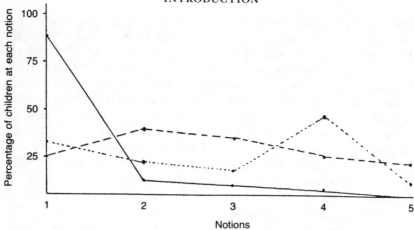

Figure I.2 Percentage of American and Nepalese children holding each notion of the Earth
Key: ―――― American 8-year-olds; .... Nepalese 12-year-olds; ―――― Nepalese 8-year-olds.

and steam following activities relating to change of state. After an initial discussion in which the idea of molecules was introduced by pupils and adopted, a group started paying attention to the question of bonding.

P1: Water turned to ice? I think it probably strengthens the bonding.
P2: Yeah, that one's not too clear really.
P1: 'Cos we didn't really do an experiment similar to that today. We were just on about melting.
P2: We weren't sure, I mean we are more or less clear how things go from solids to liquids to gases, but not from gases to liquids to solids.
P1: The point is, in the gas the bonding has totally gone.
P2: So how does it happen that bonding comes back?
P1: I suppose it works vice versa, when it's heated it destroys the bonding, when it's cold it, you know, re-makes it.
P3: But how does it re-make it? What does it re-make it with?
   [*The question of where the re-made bonds come from continues to exercise the group.*]
P2: If atoms are bonded an atom can't change into a bond to hold the other atoms together, can it?
   [*At this point an observer in the classroom intervenes:*]
 I: How do you imagine bonding?
P4: Sort of like a string between the atoms.
P1: No it isn't. He [*referring to the teacher*] explained to us about magnetic, magnetism. Some sort of force.
P4: Static electricity or something like that.
P2: Yeah. That kept them together. And I suppose if it was hot then

4

it wasn't magnetised as much or something and when it was cold it magnetised more.

[The group seems to have adopted the idea of bonds being due to a kind of magnetic force, and they return to considering how this can account for bonding apparently changing when a substance is heated.]

P4: When they are hot they vibrate more, so that the static isn't strong.

P2: Yeah, I know, but they vibrate more, and break the bonding and then they finally get to a gas and that's as far as they go . . . but how does it get the bonding back?
[emphatically]

P2: When it starts to cool down, they don't vibrate so much.

P1: Ah, yeah. When they cool down, the bonding will be increased so they won't be able to move around as much, that fits in, doesn't it?
[Note the obvious checking for consistency here. The idea being checked appears to be that due to the greater strength of the bonding at lower temperatures the molecules will not be able to vibrate so much due to being constrained. This idea, however, still begs the issue of how the bonding becomes stronger at lower temperatures as the next pupil's comment indicates.]

P2: Yeah, but the point is, how do we get the bonding back?

P4: Slow down the vibrating . . .

P2: Slow down the vibrations.
[One of the pupils at this point has a different insight. He suggests that the force is present all the time.]

P4: I suppose it's ever present there but . . . yeah, it hasn't got a chance to like grip, grip them, you know and keep them together. Well, where it slows down, you know, it might get to grips with the . . .

P3: A bit easier to keep slower things together.

The outcome of this discussion is a considerable achievement. The pupils have brought together their knowledge that particles are in constant motion and that this motion increases with temperature, with the idea of the force between particles being present all the time, to explain the apparent 'making and breaking' of bonds. The example clearly illustrates that pupils, if motivated and given the opportunity, can bring ideas and prior experiences together to take their thinking forward.

Discussion with peers may serve a number of functions in the process of knowledge construction. It provides a forum in which previously implicit ideas can be made explicit and available for reflection and checking. It provides a situation in which individuals have to clarify their own notions in the process of discussion with others. It can also provide an opportunity for individuals to build on each other's ideas in order to reach a solution.

The extent to which children's conceptual understanding in science is promoted by group discussion has been investigated by Howe *et al.*[3] in a number of science contexts. Her work suggests that the progress in understanding is brought about through the opportunity for each individual to reorganise his or her own ideas through talk and listening.

Pupils need ample opportunity to talk and listen to one another if they are to make sense of their experiences in science classes. The atmosphere of learning will not be that of the 'ordered classroom' with pupils working silently; nor will pupils be engaged in practical 'doing' all of the time. Animated talk and argument are likely to be the hallmark of fruitful science lessons.

The nature of science and implications for teaching and learning

The way in which science ideas are constructed by pupils reflects the nature and status of science as public knowledge: it also is personally and socially constructed. Scientific ideas and theories result from the interaction of individuals with phenomena. They then pass through a complex process involving communication and checking by major social institutions of science before being validated by the scientific community. This social dimension to the construction of scientific knowledge has resulted in the scientific community sharing a view of the world involving concepts, models, conventions and procedures. This world is inhabited by entities such as atoms, electrons, ions, forces, genes and species; it is helpfully organised by unifying ideas and procedures of measurement and experimentation.

Science ideas, which are constructed and transmitted through the culture and social institutions of science, will not be discovered by individual learners through their own empirical enquiry: learning science involves being initiated into the culture of science. If learners are to be given access to the knowledge systems of science, the process of knowledge construction must go beyond personal empirical enquiry. Learners need to be given access not only to physical experiences but also to the concepts and models of conventional science. The challenge for teachers lies in helping learners to construct these models for themselves, to appreciate their domains of applicability and, within such domains, to use them. If teaching is to lead pupils towards conventional science ideas, then the teacher's intervention is essential, both through providing appropriate experiential evidence and making the theoretical ideas and conventions of the science community available to pupils.

The relationship between evidence and theory is not only an important facet of the nature of science, it is also a critical issue in children's learning of science. Just as scientific theories serve to organise and explain observations as well as to inform future progress in science, children's ideas about natural phenomena play an organisational role in their construction of new knowledge and their interpretation of new information.

It is important for pupils to know how scientific ideas are developed and evaluated for a number of reasons: so that they can appreciate the significance of sharing and revising ideas; so that they can appreciate the 'provisional' nature of science ideas; and so that they gain confidence in trying and testing ideas. Such aims contrast with the perspectives implicit in those teaching approaches which portray scientific knowledge as 'objective', unproblematic and fixed – often the picture emerging from textbooks or formal lectures – or with those portraying science as 'discovered' through individual empirical enquiries, a perspective which is implicit in naïve process approaches or discovery learning approaches to science teaching.

School classrooms often present students with images of scientific knowledge as impersonal and value-free knowledge. This may be due to the use of certain linguistic devices in science that serve to keep learners 'at a distance' from the science that is being taught. By insisting on talking about science knowledge and classroom activities in the third person, and by removing personification and colloquial language, science can be presented as remote, difficult and authoritative. Scientific thinking can easily be presented as a special sort of thinking that is fundamentally different from common-sense reasoning, and it may therefore be perceived by many pupils as inaccessible.

Teaching and learning based on concern for constructing ideas requires children not only to 'do' laboratory work, but also to think about how their investigations relate to the ideas they are developing. Children need to be aware of the range of different ideas that their classmates may have for explaining the same phenomenon and they should develop the habit of evaluating these explanations.

When children look at phenomena, the sense that is made will be influenced by their existing ideas. Children will focus their observations on what they perceive to be the important factors (which may or may not be those identified by the teacher). Many pupils do not know the purpose of practical activity, thinking that they 'do experiments' in school to see if something works, rather than to reflect on how a theory can explain observations. There is a case for 'letting learners into the secret' of why they are asked to do different types of practical work in school. Rather than seeing themselves as passive absorbers of information, pupils need to see themselves as actively engaged in constructing meaning by bringing their prior ideas to bear on new situations.

Experience by itself is not enough. It is the sense that students make of it that matters. If students' understandings are to be changed towards those of accepted science, then negotiation with an authority, usually the teacher, is essential.

Teaching from this perspective is also a learning process: a characteristic of a teacher working with children's ideas in mind is the ability to listen to the sense that learners are making of their learning experiences and to respond in ways which address this.

TEACHING SCIENCE WITH CHILDREN'S THINKING IN MIND

Teachers need to be aware of pupils' existing ideas, of the learning goals and also of the nature of any difference between the two, when they are planning and implementing teaching. Examples from the teaching of two topics, 'dissolving and melting' and 'rusting', illustrate how this approach might appear in practice.[4]

An example from teaching and learning about dissolving and melting

The teacher of a Year 7 class had completed a unit of work on 'dissolving' and was due to move on to 'change of state' next. During the dissolving work, the teacher had noticed pupils using the terms 'melting' and 'dissolving' interchangeably. This did not surprise her as she had come across the problem before, both in previous teaching and in reading about children's understandings of matter. She decided to find out the extent of the confusion by setting her pupils an activity involving sorting cards. Written on the cards were statements such as: 'soap in bath water'; 'an extra strong mint in the mouth'; 'an ice cube on the kitchen table'.

The pupils worked in pairs, sorted the set of 20 cards into two piles, 'melts' and 'dissolves'. The teacher then collated the responses from each pair in a table on the blackboard. By going through this table of information and asking pupils to justify their choices the teacher was able 'to bring out into the open' some of the pupil thinking in this area and to introduce the science distinction between dissolving and melting. Pupils could then learn to associate the appropriate word with each process and in subsequent lessons pupils prided themselves on not confusing the two.

This brief episode exemplifies an attempt to teach science with children's thinking in mind. The teacher devised an activity which responded directly to a point in her pupils' learning; it allowed insights into those pupils' thinking; it was helpful in developing the pupils' understanding. Furthermore, the card-sort activity and subsequent discussion were greatly enjoyed by the pupils.

Probing children's thinking

A wide range of techniques can be used to explore children's thinking about aspects of science. The following examples have all been
successfully trialled in science classes.

- *Written statements*. Pupils are asked to write down five statements
  including the word 'energy'. They write their statements on strips of
  card and then pool their ideas in small groups. Each group sorts
  through all of their statements and classifies them according to their
  own criteria. (For example, statements relating to movement, to food,
  or to fuels.) They present their ideas to the rest of the class.
- *Posters*. Pupils are asked to make posters to answer the question, 'How
  do plants feed?' They discuss within small groups and make a poster
  to summarise their ideas. They prepare to report back to the rest of
  the class.
- *Card sort*. Pupils are given cards showing examples of dissolving and
  examples of melting. They are asked to sort the cards into two piles:
  'dissolves' and 'melts'.
- *Thought experiment*. Pupils are presented with problems such as, 'I
  release a stone from my hand. It falls. Why?' or 'I stand on the surface
  of the Moon and release a stone from my hand. What happens? Why?'
  They are asked to discuss the questions in small groups and be
  prepared to report back to the rest of the class.
- *Design and make*. Pupils are asked to use whatever materials they
  wish to keep the water in a beaker as hot as possible for as long as
  possible.
- *Explain*. Pupils are asked 'What causes day and night?' They think
  about it and then write down their explanation. They can use
  diagrams if they wish.
- *Checklist/questionnaire*. Pupils are given pictures of objects and living
  things. They are asked 'Which of the following are living? animals?
  plants?'
- *Predict and explain*. Pupils are asked, 'Will a potato float in water?' 'Will
  the apple float in water?' They are asked to explain their predictions
  and try them out.
- *Practical experiments*. Pupils use a 'rollerball' in a plastic channel. They
  can use whatever else they need to set the ball rolling, and they are
  asked to roll it (a) at steady speed, and (b) with an accelerated motion.
  They are asked to make measurements to prove that they have
  achieved each kind of motion and be prepared to demonstrate their
  ideas.

This list is by no means complete. Once the teacher becomes experienced
in probing children's understandings it is soon apparent that there are

many opportunities in teaching to find out what children are thinking, whether through the kinds of activities listed above or simply through more careful questioning and listening. Probing children's thinking is not limited to the start of teaching, it can be an integral and ongoing part of classroom activity and it can be the main purpose of some activities.

Responding to children's thinking

Finding out how children think about the various topics covered in science classes can be very interesting. It is not, however, the end of the story. Science teachers have responsibility for introducing their pupils to the accepted science view of the world. The question therefore arises as to how the teacher might plan to help pupils from their identified starting points to the learning goal of the science viewpoint.

The first thing to do is to consider the nature of any differences between children's prevalent thinking and the science viewpoint. Various possibilities exist and learning science might therefore involve:

- *Developing existing ideas.* For example, from 'guitar strings and cymbals vibrate to make sounds' (where the vibrations are obvious) to 'the air in a simple whistle vibrates to make sounds' (where the vibrations are not obvious).
- *Differentiating existing ideas.* For example, recognising that dissolving and melting are quite separate processes.
- *Integrating existing ideas.* For example, bringing together ideas about materials and living things in explaining the cycling of matter in a biological context.
- *Changing existing ideas.* For example, progression from thinking that drinking straws work by sucking, to thinking in terms of atmospheric pressure.
- *Introducing new ideas.* For example, learning about the particulate model of matter, or thinking of friction as a force.

Once the teacher has identified the nature of any differences between pupils' thinking and the science viewpoint then it becomes easier to plan activities which will support intended learning. Thus, in the first example with which we started, the teacher became aware that her pupils were not differentiating between dissolving and melting and she set the card-sort activity to address that problem directly.

In situations where the science viewpoint is contrary to children's existing ideas it might be expected that learning will prove to be problematic. This is often the case. For example, pupils frequently experience difficulty in coming to terms with Newton's First Law of Motion. The Newtonian view, that no resultant force is needed to maintain a steady motion, is quite contrary to everyday experience of friction-influenced systems, where steady pushes are needed to sustain motion. Teaching in this area will need to acknowledge the fundamental difference in perspective. Time will be needed for pupils to come to terms with the Newtonian view and practical activity is not in itself enough.

An example from teaching and learning about rusting

One teacher planned and implemented some teaching on rusting which explicitly acknowledges pupils' starting points and works towards particular learning goals.

A Year 8 class was working on 'chemical changes' and was about to move on to a section on 'rusting'. The teacher decided that his pupils would certainly have wide experience of the phenomenon of rusting and would probably have some ideas about what causes it. He therefore decided to start the new section by trying to establish what these existing ideas might be.

Two weeks prior to the lessons, just before the half-term holiday, he gave each pupil in the class a bright, shiny iron nail. The pupils were instructed to take the nail home and to 'put it in a place where you think it will go very rusty'. In addition, the pupils were asked to write down answers to these questions:

- Where did you put your nail?
- What is it about that place which made you put it there?
- Why do you think that will make the nail go rusty?
- What do you think rust is?

After two weeks the pupils brought their nails back and set up a display going down the length of the side wall of the lab. The nails were mounted on the display and placed in sequence from most rusty to least rusty.

The display served at least two purposes. It provided the teacher with a wealth of information about his pupils' thinking on rusting and it also offered readily available data on the conditions needed for rusting.

Virtually all of the pupils thought that water was needed for rusting and therefore placed the nail in wet conditions. In addition some mentioned the need for air, others thought that 'cold' helped rusting. A few referred to the action of salt, others thought that acids might help. Some suggested that rust was like a 'mould'.

The teacher set broad learning aims for the topic on rusting. He hoped that by the end of teaching all his pupils would appreciate that:

11

- air and water are essential factors for rusting to occur;
- the rusting process is an example of a chemical change.

In looking at the pupils' ideas on the nail display the teacher recognised that seeing water as an essential factor for rusting was unlikely to present problems to the pupils, whereas the need for air was not so obvious. He also realised that most pupils had not connected rusting to their general work on chemical changes.

The teacher organised groups of pupils to set up controlled experiments to test the various factors they had suggested as being essential for rusting. One group tested to see whether water is needed for rusting to occur, another to see if salt is needed and so on. From the outcomes of these investigations the factors necessary for rusting were established.

The teacher then reminded the pupils of previous work on chemical change, drawing parallels with their observations of rusting. Class discussion focused upon where the rust had come from and agreement was finally reached that it was a new substance formed on the outside of the nail. This was an interesting lesson because some children argued that the rust must already be under the surface of the nail, and that it is simply exposed during rusting. The teacher helped the pupils to consider this view by sawing through a rusty nail and passing the pieces round the class. The sight of the bright shiny metal certainly had an impact on the pupils: the rust was clearly on the outside of the nail. The teacher built on these ideas by explaining that rusting is a chemical change during which iron from the nail combines with oxygen from the air, in the presence of water, to form rust. After further discussion members of the class had to return to the display of nails and use their new ideas, about rusting as a chemical change, to explain the differences in rustiness that could be observed.

A NOTE ON CONTINUITY AND PROGRESSION

Teaching science with children's thinking in mind depends upon careful planning in which continuity of curriculum is designed for progression in pupils' ideas.

The term 'progression' is applied to something that happens inside a learner's head: thinking about experiences and ideas, children develop their ideas. Some aspects of this learning may happen quite quickly and easily, whereas other aspects happen in very small steps, with difficulty and over a number of years.

Continuity, on the other hand, is something organised by the teacher: it describes the relationship between experiences, activities and ideas which pupils meet over a period of time, in a curriculum which is structured to support learning. Curricular continuity cannot guarantee progression. Its role is to structure ideas and experiences for learners in a way that will help them to move their conceptual understanding forward in scientific terms.

In designing a science curriculum, as in designing a lesson, it is important to have children's starting points as well as intended science learning goals in mind. This can be illustrated with reference to teaching about plant nutrition, photosynthesis, respiration and decay, the cycling of matter and the flow of energy in ecosystems.

Several studies have highlighted the problems that learners have in making sense of the role of plant nutrition in photosynthesis, the role of photosynthesis in matter cycling and of energy flow in ecosystems. In particular, pupils tend to use analogies of animal feeding to explain plant nutrition, seeing plant roots as organs to 'ingest food' from the soil. Many pupils also think that carbon dioxide gas and water are 'food' for plants, since they are 'ingested'. One issue in learning about plant nutrition is the specific meaning of the word 'food' in science, since this is different from its everyday meaning. For many pupils up to the age of 16, ideas about the role of 'food' in both plants and animals may not extend beyond a notion of 'helping' processes such as growth and movement. The idea of food as a substrate for respiration, resulting in energy becoming available for life processes, is not evident in most 16-year-olds. Most pupils at Key Stages 1 and 2, and also a significant number of older pupils, think that matter can 'appear' and 'disappear' in processes such as decay.

In planning teaching it is useful for teachers to think in terms of helping pupils to make a number of 'small steps' towards the big ideas. The sequencing of these 'small steps' can be informed by what is known about the progression of children's understanding. However, it is important to bear in mind that some of these 'small steps' may, in themselves, present learners with difficulties. For example, moving from a view of matter where things can appear and disappear to the idea that matter is conserved is not a trivial step.

Teachers should not feel obliged to take explanations too far with younger pupils. The purpose of particular bits of teaching is to help pupils to take small steps towards a greater understanding.

Part I

CHILDREN'S IDEAS ABOUT LIFE AND LIVING PROCESSES

1

LIVING THINGS

THE CONCEPT OF 'LIVING'

Research on children's ideas of 'living' has been in progress since the 1920s. However, we can define 'living' by contrasting living things either with inanimate objects or with dead organisms and these alternatives have not always been distinguished in the research.

The pioneering studies on children's ideas of 'living' were carried out by Piaget[1] who observed that children tend to regard many inanimate objects as capable of sensations, emotions and intentions. He called this view 'animism'. Young children said that such things as the sun, cars, the wind, clocks and fires 'know where they are' and could 'feel a pinprick'. When asked what is and is not alive, they judged these same objects to be alive. Piaget showed that children younger than 10 years old tend to interpret physical phenomena in terms of intention on the part of inanimate objects, saying, for example, 'the sun is hot because it wants to make people warm'. He identified five stages in the development of the 'life concept' in children:

- Stage 0 (age 0–5)   No concept.
- Stage 1 (age 6–7)   Things that are active in any way, including falling or making a noise, are deemed alive.
- Stage 2 (age 8–9)   All things that move, and only those, are deemed alive.
- Stage 3 (age 9–11) Things that appear to move by themselves, including rivers and the sun, are deemed alive.
- Stage 4 (over 11)   Adult concept: only animals are deemed alive, or animals and plants are deemed alive.

Carey[2] suggests that progression in the concept of 'living' is linked to the child's developing conceptual framework about biological processes, given that young children (4–7 years) have little biological knowledge, but there is a marked increase by the ages of 9 and 10. Younger children therefore explain bodily functions of living things and the activity of

17

inanimate objects using a 'naïve psychology' of human behaviour rather than concepts of biological function. This 'naïve psychology' is characterised by intentional causal reasoning in the child's explanations, for example: 'spinach makes Popeye strong because he likes it', 'the sun shines in order to keep us warm'. As the biological knowledge of the child grows, the idea of biological function develops apart from human intentional causality and animistic reasoning declines.

Piaget's work prompted a number of other studies, in various countries and cultures, and an extensive literature on childhood animism. In 1969 Looft and Bartz[3] reviewed the literature from which it emerges that animistic notions are present in populations of all age ranges and great cultural differences. A recent study by Inagaki and Hatano[4] suggests that young children use animism metaphorically as a model to explain phenomena, rather than believing that inanimate objects reason like human beings.

The words 'living' and 'life' may label different concepts. Klingberg, reported by Looft and Bartz,[3] found that the question 'Is (a certain object) living?' produced different responses from the question 'Has it life?'. These semantic distinctions have not always been acknowledged in designing research studies and they have given rise to much discussion of their effect on results.

Research in the 1970s attempted to delve into the biological criteria that children use in deciding whether something is alive. Smeets[5] found that 11-year-old children used biological words in criteria for things that they considered as living, but that they did not distinguish the meanings of these words from similar ones. For example, the majority of children seemed to consider the following pairs of words identical in meaning: destruction and dying, seeing and knowing, contact and feeling, presence of ears and hearing, production of noise and talking, expanding and growing.

Looft[6] reports that although thirty-nine out of fifty-nine 7-year-old children correctly classified sixteen items as living or non-living, this ability is not indicative of a biological grasp of the implications of the life concept. Over half of the thirty-nine understood the need for nutriment, but few applied a concept of breathing or of reproduction in defining living things, even when asked questions such as, 'Does a frog breathe or need air?'.

Bell (formerly Stead)[7][8][9] has pointed out that commonly used words such as 'living', 'dead' and 'animal' may be used to label different concepts by different people. She found that all but one of her sample of 9 to 15-year-olds used biologically accepted characteristics of life to justify their categorisation of examples as living things. Many used a combination of these attributes. However, she reports that only five out of thirty-two pupils had a concept of living similar to that of a biologist, despite up to four years of formal biology teaching. Most children over-extended the scientifically-accepted concept of living: they considered fire, clouds, the sun, a candle, a river and a car to be living. This usually resulted from the use of only one or a few critical attributes; for example, 'A cloud is living because it moves'. Some pupils considered that an item such as a bicycle could be living at some times and non-living at other times. Many pupils acknowledged that they were unsure of their categorisations.

Arnold and Simpson[10] investigated the concept of living things amongst Scottish pupils aged 10–15, including biology and non-biology students. All the pupils could use the term 'living thing' in context and could give appropriate examples, but in classifying eighteen examples and non-examples of living things there was no steady improvement from age 10–15, and non-biology certificate pupils performed better than biology pupils. Of the non-certificate (lower attaining) pupils aged 15, 28 per cent included at least one of the following as living: fire, milk, water, cloud, energy, car. Only 9 per cent correctly classified all eighteen items. The four most popular attributes chosen to identify living things were eating/drinking, moving/walking, breathing, growing. Only 36 per cent of 14- to 15-year-olds included respiration as a criterion of life although many had studied biology. Arnold and Simpson recommend a focus upon the unity of living things through attention to their characteristics. Leach et al. confirm these findings.[11] These researchers found that a few infant children were unfamiliar with the word 'alive'. When they did recognise the word, most children at this age, and many up to 11, did not consider plants to be alive.

The results of Stavy and Wax,[12] from a study of children aged 5–16 in Israel, are similar. They found that almost all children recognised animal examples as living, but only 30 per cent of 6-year-olds, and 70–80 per cent of 12- to 15-year-olds regarded particular plants as living. Almost all the children attributed growth to plants, but apparently did not consider this a prerequisite of life: 100 per cent of 8- to 11-year-olds stated that plants grow but only 69 per cent of them regarded plants as living. Stavy and Wax attribute their results in part to the Hebrew language, where the word for 'life' is similar to that for 'animal', but not to that for 'plant'. Also the words for 'growth' and 'death' in animals are different from those applied to plants.

Tamir et al.,[13] studying 424 Israeli pupils aged 8–14, also found that there was no significant difference with age in children's ability to classify sixteen pictures as living or non-living. Over 99 per cent of the children classified all the animal pictures as living and 82 per cent of the responses correctly classified the plant illustrations as living, with the tree and the mushroom considered alive less frequently than the herbaceous plant. Moreover, 80 per cent of responses classified inanimate examples as non-living, with natural things like a river or the sun more frequently being considered alive than man-made objects. (Overall, 20 per cent of item responses were incorrect and this may represent far more than 20 per cent of individual children failing to classify correctly at least one item.) Responses about embryos were interesting: only half the children considered eggs to be alive whereas 60 per cent classified seeds as alive.

A progression from the ideas of the younger to those of the older students was apparent in the criteria they gave for classifying examples. Overall, the most popular criteria as indicators of life were movement for animals, and growth and development for plants and embryos. About half the reasons were based on life processes with more emphasis on biological processes and less on usefulness to man by the older children. Most of the children who classified inanimate items as alive believed that they have a different kind of life and about half thought that plants have a different kind of life from animals. The differences were related to supposed differences in movement, sensation and consciousness.

Lucas, Linke and Sedgwick[14] [15] used an unfamiliar object, in a photograph, to elicit concepts of life from nearly a thousand Australian children aged 6–14. The object was actually a lump of dough photographed on a sandy background and children were asked to write down how they could find out whether the object was alive, with clues about how to proceed: what would you look for? what would you do to it? what would it do?. The overwhelmingly common response (86–100 per cent, varying with age) was in terms of the behaviour of the object. The behaviour most children chose was some sort of movement, with an increase in this response through the primary grades and a decline through the early secondary years. However, analysis of the children's range of responses revealed that even young children's ideas of life are based on more than movement. Children at all grade levels applied a variety of criteria and consulted expert advice. At all grade levels more than 40 per cent of pupils suggested a criterion based on external structure. An increasing proportion at higher grades used an aspect of internal structure, such as blood or cells; a substantial proportion used physiological functions, such as heartbeat or respiration.

Brumby[16] studied fifty-two British university biology students' perceptions of the concept of life. She set four different problems, one of which was similar to that of Lucas et al. Her stimulus material was a weathered stone, rather than a photograph, and her other questions related to whether fire is alive, to evidence for life on Mars and to explaining the expression 'the web of life'. Most students referred to the criteria used by young children, such as growth and movement. The seven characteristics of life (movement, respiration, sensitivity, growth, reproduction, excretion and nutrition) dominated their explanations but these were applied in an unsophisticated way and without reference to principles of scientific experimentation, suggesting that the seven characteristics had been rote-learned. Some responses included references to cells or organic chemicals, but there was hardly any mention of a self-replicating molecule. Brumby suggests that the 'learning' of fragmentary 'facts' had overwhelmed the curiosity and wonder of children as they became tertiary students and had contributed little towards understanding.

It should be noted that a number of researchers view as simplistic the notion that children classify objects as living or non-living by the systematic use of criteria. Carey[2] and Inagaki and Hatano[4] suggest that factors such as movement may encourage children to view an object as living because children are likely to compare unfamiliar objects with objects known as living or non-living. They suggest that children are more likely to appeal to expert adult knowledge than to particular biological criteria in reaching their decisions.

Children often attribute human characteristics, thoughts, emotions and intentions to non-human things. It is not always clear whether children giving such anthropomorphic responses think that other organisms or objects really think like humans or whether they are speaking metaphorically.

Inagaki and Hatano[4] point out that children distinguish people from other living things and do not readily accept that humans are a kind of animal. However, children appear to recognise degrees of similarity between humans and other things.

A number of studies of children's concept of death, reviewed by Carey,[2] have suggested that children progress to an intuitive biological conceptualisation by the age of 9 or 10. They show that young children consider death in terms of human experience, relating it to notions of sleep and departure, separation and punishment and seeing it as neither final nor inevitable. Around the age of 9 or 10, it seems that children begin to understand death as an inevitable biological process, the body ceasing to function.

A study by Sequiera and Freitas[17] showed the stability of Portuguese primary schoolchildren's concepts of death and decomposition, even after teaching. These children tended to conceptualise death in terms of a human or animal model, referring to tiredness of the body, or the stopping of human or animal organs, mainly the heart. Some children tended to define death using a theological approach or reference to affective causes like sadness or lack of friends. Cell-based explanations were only found amongst those aged 12–13 and then only in 40 per cent of the responses. Few children considered death in relation to all living organisms.

THE CONCEPT OF 'ANIMAL'

Carey[2] points out that very young children appear to have a concept 'animal' that does not include inanimate objects, although the concept is diffent from an adult's concept. Leach et al., however, found some infant school pupils unfamiliar with the word 'animal'.

Stead (Bell)[18] and her colleagues report that to many students animals are only the large land mammals, such as those found as pets, on farms or in zoos: their range of examples of animals is more restricted than that of a scientist. She found that only four out of thirty-nine 15-year-old pupils categorised pictures of animals and non-animals as a biologist would. Only about half the pupils categorised fish, boy, frog, snail, snake and whale as animal. Reasons for identifying something as an animal included: four legs, large size, land habitat, fur and noise production. About half of the children used the criterial attributes of living things to specify items as animals. They did not seem to recognise that these attributes do not distinguish animals from other living things. Some mentioned feeding, but simply as an attribute of living things, rather than emphasising the heterotrophic nature of animal feeding. Pupils', tertiary students' and teachers' understandings of the word 'animal' led to the responses shown in Table 1.1 and Figure 1.1.

Bell and Barker[9] report that traditional teaching about consumers and about animals as consumers did not appreciably affect pupils' understanding of either concept. Pupils tended to believe that only large mammals are consumers. However, teaching activities directed at extending the concept of animal were successful. A parallel class of pupils was taught the biologist's view of animal before they were taught about consumers. After this focused teaching all the children correctly identified a range of creatures as both animals and consumers.

Trowbridge and Mintzes[19] also report a restricted concept of 'animal' in the thinking of school and university students. Asked to name five animals, most students gave large four-legged terrestrial

Table 1.1 Positive responses to the question 'Is it an animal?'

Object	11-year-olds (N = 49) (%)	Primary teacher trainees (N = 34) (%)	Experienced primary teachers (N = 53) (%)	University biology students (N = 67) (%)
Cow	98	100	100	100
Boy	57	94	96	100
Worm	37	77	86	99
Spider	22	65	86	97
Grass	0	0	0	0

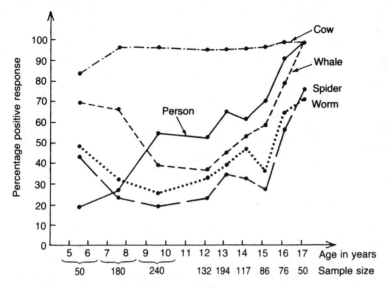

Figure 1.1 Positive responses to the question 'Is it an animal?'

examples. These researchers recommend a teaching stategy including non-examples to develop skills of discrimination and generalisation.

Tema,[20] basing her study on Bell's work, set out to investigate the conceptions of 'animal' held by rural and urban African pupils. Despite their culturally different backgrounds most students showed some similarities with Bell's pupils.

THE CONCEPT OF 'PLANT'

Stead (Bell)[21] established, from interviews with twenty-nine children aged 9–15, that they had a much narrower meaning of the word 'plant' than that of the biologist. Only four children used generalised criteria such as 'grows in the ground', 'has leaves', 'has roots', 'is green', to categorise all the instances of plants. Bell found children, from all age groups, who considered that a tree is not a plant, although they said 'it was a plant when it was little'. Over half did not consider a seed to be a plant. It appears that many pupils view weeds, vegetables and seeds not as sub-sets of the set 'plants' but as comparable sets. The ideas of many 15-year-olds were as restricted as those of 10-year-olds despite science teaching (see Figure 1.2).

Leach *et al.*[11] confirm that pupils choose 'plant', 'tree' and 'flower' as exclusive groups. However, their pupils were willing to assign trees and flowers to the category 'plant' when they were given a restricted number of categories in a classification task.

23

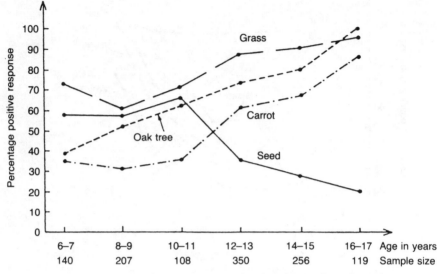

Figure 1.2 Positive responses to the question 'Is it a plant?'

CLASSIFICATION

Leach *et al.*[11] report that most 7-year-olds can assign organisms to groups of their own choice, but their groups are of differing status and are mutually exclusive rather than hierarchical. In assigning organisms, young children could use only two groups at the same time, whereas older children used a number of groups at the same time. By the age of 13 most children, when asked, could use the group 'animals' to include groups such as 'bird', and by the age of 16 most students used hierarchical classification more spontaneously.

Ryman[22] found that English 12-year-olds encountered difficulties in classifying organisms into taxonomic categories, more so with plants than with animals. Pupils appeared to learn a 'school science' way of classifying whilst retaining their intuitive ideas about concepts such as 'flower' and 'animal' for use in everyday life.

The categories 'flowering plant' and 'vertebrate' were found to be used in the scientific sense by less than half of the 13-year-olds surveyed by Schofield *et al.*[23] Even fewer, 18 per cent, of the sample of about 800 children could apply the term 'reptile' correctly.

Askham[24] reports that Californian children aged 9–12 used mixed strategies in classifying plants outdoors in a botanic garden. They focused on individual features of the plants such as the shape of leaves, the flowers or the colour, rather than on the whole plant. Leach *et al.*[11] also note that children of all ages focused on more obvious

24

features such as number of limbs or habitat, rather than on more fundamental differences such as physiology, when classifying living things.

Trowbridge and Mintzes[19] report similar findings to those of Ryman.[22] Groups such as 'insects' were used for animals whose group name was not known. Many students relied on everyday, rather than on the taxonomic, use of class names such that jellyfish and starfish were classified as fish, and turtles with amphibious habits were classified as amphibians. The 'amphibian' classification of turtles and also of penguins was found by Braund in many of the children he studied.[25]

THE CONCEPT OF 'SPECIES'

Leach et al.[11] report that pupils from 5–16 recognised that rottweilers, poodles and alsations should all be put into one group called 'dogs' but that they showed little understanding of the basis of this grouping. At the age of 16 a few pupils referred to genetics, but they showed little knowledge of the genetic basis of the concept 'species'.

CELL THEORY

Arnold[26] has shown that pupils seem to suffer from interference between the concepts of 'cell' and 'molecule'. Scottish pupils aged 11 were asked to draw their view of molecules. Most drawings resembled cells, with features such as nucleus and membranes discernible. Children seemed to have a generalised concept of 'very small units that make up larger things' which Arnold has called the 'Molecell'. Pupils aged 14–15 were asked to indicate whether certain items are made of cells and/or molecules. As well as living organisms themselves, things associated with living organisms were thought, by a large minority of pupils, to be made of cells. It seemed that those items studied in biology lessons, including proteins, carbohydrates and water, were thought to be made of cells. At the same time, an overwhelming majority of pupils indicated that living organisms are not made of molecules, but that energy and heat are. It seems that pupils confined the concept 'molecules' to things encountered in physics and chemistry.

Dreyfus and Jungwirth[27][28] report similar confusion about orders of magnitude and levels of organisation amongst 16-year-old Israeli students. Responses suggested that pupils thought that molecules of protein are bigger than the size of a cell and that single-celled organisms contain intestines and lungs. The pupils had been taught about cells in the previous year and superficially 'knew' a number of correct statements about them. However, over a third of responses revealed 'inadequate' alternative ideas about cells.

ADAPTATION

Pupils tend to see adaptation in a naturalistic or teleological sense: undertaken to satisfy the organism's need or desire to fulfil some future requirement. In Engel Clough and Wood-Robinson's study,[30] two-thirds of 12- to 14-year-olds and half of 16-year-olds gave teleological interpretations of examples of adaptation and only 10 per cent of the whole sample gave scientifically acceptable explanations. Students confused an individual's adaptation during its lifetime with inherited changes in a population over time: they appeared to believe in the inheritance of acquired characteristics. This Lamarckian belief is clear from many surveys of students both before and after instruction in genetics and evolution.[29 30 31 32 33]

Brumby[34] found that only 18 per cent of students, even after studying 'A' level biology, could correctly apply a process of selection to explain evolutionary change. Most gave the Lamarckian interpretation that individuals can adapt to change in the environment if they need to, and that these adaptations are inherited.

ORGANISATION OF THE BODY: STRUCTURE AND FUNCTION

Carey[2] has reviewed a number of studies of children's concepts of the organisation of the body. By the age of 10, but not by the age of 7 or 8, children appear to understand that the body contains numerous organs which function together in maintaining life.

Caravita et al.[35] and Caravita and Tonucci[36] found that young children gave egocentric explanations for parts of the body, as in 'my hair is for washing', but by the end of primary school they explained the functions of organs or apparatus in terms of causal relationships. These authors confirm Carey's contention that a shift in children's thinking occurs between the ages of 7 and 9, from a holistic, human-centred view to a view which recognises different functional parts working together.

2

NUTRITION

FOOD – WHAT IS IT?

Any discussion of 'food' is fraught with the semantic problem of the word 'food' having different meanings in everyday and scientific contexts and there are no ready alternative words to offer pupils in either context. The school science definition of food, as organic compounds which organisms can use as a source of energy for metabolic processes, is not consistently used even by science educators. Moreover, the word 'food', when used in science lessons, is used in a variety of ways both by teachers and in textbooks.

Children appear to consider food as anything useful taken into an organism's body, including water, minerals and, in the case of plants, carbon dioxide or even sunlight. When referring to starch in the context of plant nutrition, a child's typical comment was 'starch is not food because it is made not eaten'.[1] When Eisen and Stavy[2] asked advanced high school and university students 'What does food mean to you?', the responses included the following:

- essential materials   24 per cent;
- energy source   40 per cent;
- materials for building the body   14 per cent;
- both energy and building materials   11 per cent.

Children often gave a non-functional explanation of the importance of food: they said that it is needed to keep animals and plants alive, without reference to the role of food in metabolism. School pupils, aged 13–14, 'do not grasp, or are unaware of, the . . . meaning of the word "food" as a material that serves as a substrate for respiration'.[3] Eisen and Stavy found fewer correct responses among 14-year-olds than among 13-year-olds. After learning science ideas, pupils appeared to revert to their naïve concepts and this was particularly evident among advanced students who had continued with biology.

In New Zealand, Barker[4] investigated students' concepts of food, first

27

by interviewing twenty-eight pupils (aged from 8 to 17) and then by surveying a larger sample of pupils, students, teachers and texts. He concludes that any learner's concept of food is fluid and context-dependent, depending on who is considered the eater, whether materials are considered in isolation or in combination, or whether food is considered metaphorically.

DIETARY COMPONENTS

From an early age children link eating with several consequences: growth, health, strength and energy, but for pupils these are vague concepts. Carey[5] quotes studies, by Wellman and Johnson[6] and by Contento,[7] of children's ideas about nutrition. Pre-school children thought that the consumption of anything, including water, would lead to body weight gain and that differences in height as well as differences in girth are a direct consequence of the amount consumed. These children thought that some diets are more wholesome than others in ensuring health and growth. From the age of 8 most children differentiated different kinds of diet as making people fat or strong.[6] Five-year-olds knew that fruits and milk are good for them but they did not know why. They knew of vitamins as 'pills to make people strong and healthy' but only three out of thirty-four 5- to 11-year-olds realised that ordinary food contains vitamins.

Lucas,[8] in his survey of 1,033 adults, found that they were familiar with the names of dietary components but not with their functions: 37 per cent thought that proteins provide most of the energy needs of the human body and 19 per cent thought vitamins do. Proteins are more frequently identified with food: most of a sample of 1,405 students aged 10–19 selected proteins as the product of photosynthesis, presumably relating these substances to food and to growth.[9] Food was associated with growth, rather than energy. Some pupils referred to plants getting vitamins from the soil.

Following Arnold's suggestion of 'interference' between the concepts of cell and molecule,[10] Simpson[11] studied the ideas about food held by 249 14- to 15-year-old biology students in six schools, who had all been taught about food and digestion. They were asked to identify items on a list as being 'made of atoms and molecules', and/or 'made of cells'. Three-quarters of the pupils accepted that carbohydrates and proteins are made of molecules but a large minority thought that they are also made of cells. Only half of those students also studying chemistry, and a mere third of non-chemistry students, thought that a biscuit is made of molecules and nearly a fifth thought it is made of cells. Pupils appeared to regard those associated with living things as being made of cells but not molecules, whereas those (including energy) which are studied in physics and chemistry are made of molecules and not cells. Proteins and carbohydrates were placed in both categories.

Pupils appear to have difficulty in developing concepts of 'carbohydrate' and 'starch'. Arnold and Simpson in Pascoe[12] found that many pupils (54 per cent of 11-year-olds, 30 per cent of 13-year-olds) think that carbohydrate is a gas.

HUMAN DIGESTION AND ASSIMILATION

Carey's review of a number of studies[5] provides insight into young children's ideas of the human digestive system. Fraiberg[13] found that up to about 9 years old a child imagines his body as a hollow skin bag which is all 'stomach'; a reservoir in which blood, food and wastes are somehow contained. Mintzes[14] found that when the stomach was drawn as an internal organ it was usually shown larger and lower than it really is. Intestines were drawn, but the liver was rarely shown. Many children in Brinkman and Boschhuizen's study[15] drew or described the digestive system as being double with two outlets, one for faeces and one for urine. The youngest children appeared to relate the stomach to breathing, blood, strength and energy, whereas from about 7 years old the idea emerges that the stomach helps to break or digest food, and later that food is transferred elsewhere after being in the stomach.[5] [14]

Gellert[16] found that by the age of 11 most children had a fairly correct view of anatomy and the overall function of systems. Top primary age children said that lumps of food are broken down, juices or acid dissolve food, and that 'goodness' is somehow extracted. Children under 9 thought that food vanishes after it is eaten. Older children suggested that food turns into 'goodness' or 'energy', apparently not conserving energy in this context. Only three of thirty-four subjects, aged 9–11, knew that food is changed in the stomach and that it brings about its effects after being broken down into other substances that are carried to tissues throughout the body.

A very common idea, found by Simpson, is that digestion is the process which releases usable energy from food.[17] This appears to arise from their linking the two acceptable ideas ('energy is obtained from food' and 'digestion is the breakdown of food') to construct an unorthodox idea.[18]

Children's ideas of the sequence of digestion appear to be very confused, both in the anatomical route and the processes. The sequence of processes may start, as shown by Simpson,[17] with breaking into soluble particles and releasing energy, to be followed by swallowing. Clearly, these ideas are not naïve intuitive notions but rather constructions derived from information: pupils having met a lot of unfamiliar words or familiar words with new meanings.

Simpson[17] found that 58 per cent of 13-year-olds thought that enzymes are made of cells.

Top primary children appear to think that defecation is necessary to make room for more food.[5][17] By the age of 13 most children said that some of our food is useless or harmful and so must be eliminated.

PLANT NUTRITION

During the 1980s a considerable amount of research was done on children's ideas of plant feeding, and consistent patterns in children's thinking were noted in several different countries. Several research projects (for example, those based at Aberdeen College of Education, at the Children's Learning in Science Research Group at the University of Leeds, at the Science Education Research Unit at Waikato University, New Zealand, and at the Institute for Research on Teaching at Michigan State University, USA) have developed teaching schemes.

Many researchers note the conceptual demands of the topic of plant nutrition. Arnold and Simpson[21] sum up the demands made by the abstract and complex concept of photosynthesis by pointing out that pupils need to understand that:

> an element, carbon (which is solid in pure form), is present in carbon dioxide (which is a colourless gas in the air) and that this gas is converted by a green plant into sugar (a solid, but in solution) when hydrogen (a gas) from water (a liquid) is added using light energy which is consequently converted to chemical energy.

They suggest that many pupils do not possess the prerequisite concepts of living things, gas, food and energy which are required to build an understanding of photosynthesis.

Barker and Carr[22] comment 'how unlikely and counterintuitive is the concept of photosynthesis'. The sequence of events has the 'makings of a fairy story. How much more plausible is the probability that plants suck up food from the soil.'

Bell[18] reviewed the work of Simpson and Arnold,[23][24] Roth, Smith and Anderson[25] and Driver et al.,[26] as well as her own work within the Children's Learning in Science Project.[27][28] The universal and very persistent intuitive conception, identified in all studies with subjects of all ages, is that plants get their food from their environment, specifically from the soil; and that roots are the organs of feeding (as exemplified by Figure 2.1). Half of Simpson and Arnold's sample of 344 Scottish 12- to 13-year-olds and a third of their 627 14- to 16-year-olds, as well as over 70 per cent of Roth's 229 American 11-year-olds held the view that plants feed in a similar way to animals.

Analysing hundreds of 15-year-old students' responses to questions

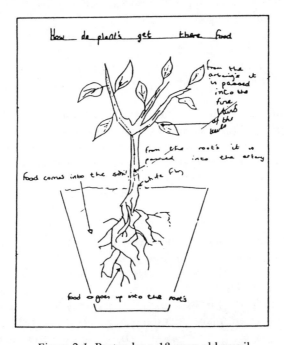

Figure 2.1 Poster by a 13-year-old pupil

Source: B.F. Bell and A. Brook, *Aspects of sceondary students' understanding of plant nutrition*, Children's Learning in Science Project, Centre for Studies in Science and Mathematics Education, University of Leeds, 1984.

administered in the Assessment of Performance Unit surveys, Driver *et al.*[26] and Bell and Brook[28] found that a fifth of the responses attributed the growth of a tree to the food it had taken in, most referring to the soil. Only 8 per cent indicated that a tree makes its own materials from constituents it takes in from its environment.

In other studies large numbers of children claimed that plants take in organic food substances (starch and sugar[29] or protein[9]) from the soil. They appeared to believe that plants have multiple sources of food.[20]

Barker's study[4] shows that the naïve view gives way to the school science view, with teaching. Children appear to hold the heterotrophic view concurrently with taught ideas about photosynthesis.[18] [20] The view that plants' food is the material that they absorb is resistant to change even in the face of continued instruction.

Children, understanding that plants absorb water from the soil and that water is essential to growth, appear to assume that it is the main component of growth material.[30] Having learnt that plants take in carbon dioxide, water and minerals, pupils tend to regard these as the food of plants and when food is associated with energy, these inorganic substances are assumed to contain and supply energy.[4][28] Half of 12- to 13-year-olds, in a sample of 344, knowing that plants absorb carbon dioxide, thought that it is absorbed through the roots.[24] Some pupils thought that water is absorbed through the leaves.[30] Many children thought that water and carbon dioxide support the processes of drinking and plant breathing, respectively, and that they remain unchanged during these processes.[20]

Some children, in Tamir's study,[31] thought that the sunlight absorbed by plants is food. Pupils knew that plants take in minerals from the soil and they thought that these are food for the plant or that they contribute directly to photosynthesis. It is sugggested that everyday reference to fertilisers as 'plant food' may promote this idea.

PHOTOSYNTHESIS

There is evidence that children construct alternative meanings for technical words such as 'photosynthesis' and 'chlorophyll' when these words are introduced during teaching. Children appear to think of photosynthesis as a substance rather than a process,[1] or as the plant's kind of respiration.[31] Pupils appear to have very little understanding of energy transfers in plant metabolism. They thought that the food acquired by a plant accumulates as it grows. There was little understanding of food providing energy for the plant's life processes[24] and Bell[32] found that many pupils do not develop the ideas intended from their practical work in this field.

Barker studied acceptance of the proposition, presented in many school textbooks, that 'during photosynthesis, energy is stored up in food'. He found that 60 per cent of 13-year-olds agreed with the statement, but that less than half of these gave a reason considered to be scientifically valid and many reasons suggested rote learning of the statement. In Barker's study, 54 per cent of 13-year-olds, in free-response writing, described photosynthesis in terms of food-making, 19 per cent in terms of producing carbohydrates and only 3 per cent in terms of storing energy.[4]

Roth and Anderson[20] found that photosynthesis was often seen, not as something important to plants themselves but as something that plants do for the benefit of people and animals, particularly in relation to exchange of gases.

There appears to be an intuitive disbelief in weight increase and growth due mainly to the incorporation of matter from a gas.[3][29] Even 15-year-old students failed to mention carbon dioxide as being the source of increasing weight of growing seedlings, although many knew that carbon dioxide is absorbed.

Children appear to consider chlorophyll either as a food substance, a protection, a storage product, a vital substance like blood, something that makes plants strong or something that breaks down starch. Some children, with a notion of its function in photosynthesis, thought that chlorophyll attracts sunlight or absorbs carbon dioxide. Some held the anthropocentric view that it is just there to make leaves green and attractive.[19] [24] [28] The role of chlorophyll in absorbing light energy was seldom appreciated by students, even after teaching.[4] Only 29 per cent of 12- to 13-year-olds and 46 per cent of 14- to 16-year-olds in Simpson and Arnold's study[24] understood chlorophyll as a converter of light energy to chemical energy.

Sunlight was considered by many children to be a reagent in photosynthesis along with carbon dioxide and water,[22] and light was considered to be made of molecules by well over half of Simpson's sample.[11]

Most children of 11 appear to think that plants always need light to grow and they apply this idea to include germination.[25] This idea persists even in the face of evidence to the contrary from germinating seeds and mature plants kept in the dark.[9] [28] Barker found that 26 of his sample of 28 pupils, when shown a picture including a tree and the sun, said that plants get their energy from the sun. However, the interviews showed that most did not understand the energy transfer, and most used the terms heat and light interchangeably. Nearly 80 per cent of 13-year-olds thought that plants use heat from the sun as the energy for photosynthesis and most pupils considered that the sun is one amongst many sources of energy for plants, others being soil, minerals, water, air and wind. An introduction to photosynthesis, emphasising the origin of sugar, starch and cellulose, and focusing upon wood, was subsequently developed by Barker.[33]

GAS EXCHANGE BY PLANTS

The relationship between photosynthesis and respiration is difficult for children to understand. Children display a much better understanding of what happens to oxygen than of what happens to carbon dioxide.[18] However, oxygen is often equated with air.[34] Interviews with 11-year-olds revealed that they thought either that air is not used by plants, or that plants and animals use air in 'opposite' ways.[24] [35] Instances of gases going into or out of organisms were considered as breathing or respiration, respiration being taken as synonymous with breathing. Barker,[4] interviewing children from the age of 9, confirmed that they hold the 'plant breathing–animal breathing' model: that animals breathe in oxygen and breathe out carbon dioxide, whereas plants breathe in carbon dioxide and breathe out oxygen. Plant breathing was often viewed anthropocentrically: it was thought to take place so that our oxygen supply is replenished. Barker identified age-related trends in ideas about gas exchange in plants: towards specifying gases correctly, towards a focus on leaves rather than on the whole plant and away from a human-centred view.

From their analysis of a large sample of 15-year-olds' responses, Driver et al.[26] found that only a third understood gas exchange in plants, that only half used the idea that oxygen is required for plant respiration and less than a third used the idea that green plants take in carbon dioxide. Even fewer appreciated that this occurred only in light. (A notion evident from several studies is that plants do not respire, or that they respire only in the dark.) Many children suggested that respiration in plants occurs only in the cells of leaves, since only leaves have gas exchange pores.[36]

Simpson and Arnold[37] devised a test for 16-year-old students in order to study interference between the concepts of photosynthesis and respiration. Looking for conceptions relating to gas exchange, they found that 46 per cent of students did not understand that increased photosynthesis would reduce the carbon dioxide in a closed system. The following misconceptions were noted:

• water plants absorb carbon dioxide at night (25 per cent);
• photosynthesising leaves produce high carbon dioxide levels (25 per cent);
• pond weed produces bubbles of carbon dioxide in light (18 per cent).

Children tend to believe that energy is used up by living things and that plants use up energy in growing. Their ideas about energy in living things include the notion that plants make direct use of solar energy for vital processes[30][31] and that energy is created or destroyed in different life processes.[21][38][39]

FOOD CHAINS AND ECOLOGICAL CYCLES

The integration of ideas about feeding and energy into an ecological perspective is not evident in the thinking of many students. Only half of a sample of undergraduate biology students, when asked about the phrases 'life depends on green plants' and 'the web of life', explained in terms of food chains. Only a minority of these mentioned harnessing solar energy or photosynthesis as the reason why green plants are crucial in the food chain. Even at the tertiary stage of education, nearly a quarter of the students expressed views suggesting that other organisms exist for the benefit of humans.[40] A subsequent study of students, from age 13 up to undergraduate level, revealed that most students knew that animals could not exist in a plant-free world, but some thought that carnivores could exist if their prey reproduced plentifully. About half of the students at each age level indicated that animals could not live without plants because of their oxygen need, but only 10 per cent mentioned the oxygen cycle in the context of the sun's part in the origin of life.[3]

A study of Nigerian pupils revealed a range of ideas about pyramids of number and biomass. Several ideas were anthropocentric, 'there are more herbivores than carnivores because people breed them', or implied predestination, 'the number of producers is large to satisfy the consumers'. 'Stronger' organisms were considered to have more energy, which they use in order to feed on weaker organisms with less energy. Some pupils saw energy adding up through an ecosystem, so that a top predator would have all the energy from the producers and other consumers in the chain.[34]

A study of 12- to 13-year-olds' conceptualisation of cycles revealed that they thought in linear terms about food chains, rather than recognising cycles of matter or interdependency with other organisms and systems.[41] In a sample of 15-year-old students 95 per cent interpreted food web dynamics in terms of one food chain only, and 18 per cent of this sample thought that a population higher on a food chain is a predator on all the organisms below it.[42]

Pupils tend to regard food which is eaten and used as a source of energy as belonging to a food chain, whilst the food which is incorporated into the body material of eaters is often seen as something different and not recognised as the material which is the food of the next level. The lack of the concept of conservation of matter underlies many of the conceptual problems in this area.[43]

Pupils' ideas about food chains and food webs were identified by Leach et al.[44]

USING HISTORICAL IDEAS

Many concepts held by children resemble those held by eminent scientists in the past. For example, pupils have prior views about plant materials and activities similar to those held by earlier philosophers and scientists. Barker's teaching strategy, 'Where does the wood come from?', in clarifying reactants and products before introducing energy, parallels historical development.[33] The historical parallel is used yet more explicitly in Eisen, Stavy and Barak-Regev's teaching scheme[45] and Wandersee suggests that diagnostic tests, which mirror historical ideas, may help students to discover their own conceptual weaknesses as a starting point for restructuring.[9 46]

3

GROWTH

GROWTH AS A CRITERION OF LIFE

Carey reports that few children of primary age volunteered growth as a criterion of living things.[1] The studies of Bell,[2] and of Tamir et al.[3] both found that growth and development were volunteered as criteria for life in the case of plant examples much more frequently than in animal examples, possibly because alternative criteria such as movement were available for animals. For example, in Tamir's study, growth featured in 38 per cent of the decisions about plants being alive but in only 7 per cent of the decisions about animals. Seeds and eggs were included in examples chosen to elicit pupils' criteria for designating something as 'living' and 20 per cent of the sample gave the potential for growth as a criterion for deciding that these embryos are alive. However, some children believed that eggs and seeds are not alive even when they held that living things develop only from living things. Growth was suggested as evidence of life in inanimate objects like clouds by a few of the younger children in both studies.

THE MEANING OF 'GROWTH'

Pupils' ideas about growth have been studied from different perspectives: human growth as experienced by the children themselves; the experience of macroscopic observations of other organisms; learning about cell division, and differentiation and the assimilation of organic chemicals.

Carey has reported on several studies of young children's concepts of human growth.[1] For pre-school children it appears that growth just means 'getting bigger' and it is explained in terms of intentional human activities. It is associated with ritual and celebration: 'one gets bigger on one's birthday'; 'eating birthday cake makes one bigger'. Evidence from other domains suggests that children establish a physiological concept around the age of 9 and that before this age the lack of firm concepts of

36

time, or even of personal identity through life, precludes development of biological notions of growth.

Schaefer has shown that young people talk about growth in a variety of ways.[4] He used a word-association technique to investigate the concept of growth held by a sample of 423 subjects, including biology students and biology teachers. The youngest of the subjects were aged 15. Half of the words that the young people offered were related to measures (large, fat or narrow) whereas the older people chose more abstract or technical words. Approximately 20 per cent of the words from the teenagers, unlike those from the adults, related to puberty, adolescence, youth, glands and maturity. Very few in all groups mentioned weight or getting heavier in association with growth.

Barker found that all the pupils he interviewed defined growth, as applied to a tree, in terms of getting larger. Only four of these also mentioned development. Another four used the colloquial meaning of 'growth' as existing or being alive as in 'plants grow in the ground', akin to 'a rabbit lives in a field'.[5]

Okeke and Wood-Robinson studied a sample of 120 Nigerian students aged 16–18.[6] The students' notions of growth tended to be observational only, as in 'getting bigger'. Their English counterparts from a pilot study, however, referred to quantifiable criteria (increased length, volume and mass) as indications of growth. The authors attribute this difference to a cultural difference in technological awareness. This study also notes students' difficulty in assimilating taught concepts: they showed confusion between cell division, cell enlargement and cell differentiation, with a fifth of the sample thinking that cells get smaller with every cell division. Further data on this matter comes from the study of Driver et al.[7] in which 69 per cent of respondents realised that growth was occurring when one cell divides into two. The form of the question could not ascertain the conception of the remaining 31 per cent to account for 'no growth' in dividing cells.[7] Hackling and Treagust[8] found poor understanding of the role of cell division in growth among forty-eight Australian 15-year-olds.

CONDITIONS FOR GROWTH

Children, from an early age, believe that eating or absorbing material is a necessary condition for growth. However, they tend to account for the connection between food and growth by tautologous and non-functional explanations. Children do not appear to recognise that the substances taken in are the material basis for growth, becoming transformed and incorporated into the body and thus making it bigger.[9] Indeed, Russell and Watt[10] found that young children often thought that an animal grows or stretches in order to accommodate the food that it wants to eat.

Pupils appear to believe that the necessary conditions for all stages of plant growth include both food and light. However, prior to instruction they do not understand that light is a requirement for the plant obtaining its food and not a condition for growth itself. Roth, Smith and Anderson[11] found the belief in light, as a requirement for all stages of plant growth, to be very strongly held in the face of contrary evidence from seedlings germinating in the dark and plants growing taller in the dark. In fact, the set of prior concepts about food, light and growth were resistant to change in the sample of 12- to 13-year-old pupils, either by didactic or by discovery teaching. However, many pupils did restructure their concepts towards the proposed scientific goals when taught by a strategy which confronted their prior notions.

Russell and Watt[10] investigated some sixty primary school pupils' ideas about the necessary conditions for growth, focusing on germination as well as vegetative growth. Water was named as a condition for plant growth by 90 per cent of the children, though fewer (40 per cent) associated it with a mechanism of germination or growth. Other researchers have obtained similar responses from older pupils.[5] A few of Russell and Watt's sample mentioned air or gases, 'food' (which included soil nutrients) and sun or light and heat. Soil as a source of plant food, was referred to twice as frequently by older junior pupils as by infants. Unfortunately the idea of soil as a source of plant food is a misconception which would hinder later learning.

THE MATERIALS AND MECHANISMS OF GROWTH

Russell and Watt elicited children's ideas about the material aspects of growth, using the stimulus focus of well-established seedlings. The majority of infants and juniors, believed that the new plant material emerged from the bean seed. To an extent this view might have been encouraged by the focus on germination as well as vegetative growth, with no distinction between the two. Very few suggestions about incorporation of new material were encountered.[10]

Barker included three questions about plant growth in his interviews with twenty-eight 8- to 17-year-old pupils in New Zealand. All the subjects knew that trees are made of wood, but when asked 'How did the plant (in the picture) increase in size over the five years?' none could satisfactorily explain the origin of the new wood.[5] About half, across the age range, answered tautologically (as in, 'the tree gets thicker and taller') and half said that growth occurs because the plant absorbs materials such as water and nutrients. Almost identical proportions of similar responses to a similar question were obtained by Driver et al.[7] who analysed over 700 responses from 15-year-olds. In the interview situation, many of Barker's sample realised that their initial responses were inadequate explanations and tried further ideas including: that the seed is responsible for growth, that plant growth is inexplicably like human growth, or that the plant acts on the absorbed material to create growth. Although the seventeen secondary school students had studied photosynthesis, hardly any related this to growth. Only four of the older students suggested that growth is an outcome of photosynthesis and three of these later listed wood as a product of photosynthesis. Although other questions showed that about a third of Driver's sample understood the component ideas of photosynthesis, only 8 per cent of the sample related this to plant growth by indicating that a tree makes tissue from constituents that it takes from the environment. Only three students out of 759 specified that tree tissue is made from carbon dioxide and water using light energy.[7]

Children's concepts of plant growth in relation to photosynthesis have been studied by Wandersee.[12] Many children in his sample of 1,405 10- to 19-year-olds believed that the soil in a plant pot would lose weight as the plant grows because the soil provides the food for growth. The finding of these surveys, namely that children have no ideas about the mechanism of plant growth, is more significant than the explanations which the children advanced when probed. Barker suggests that these latter were on-the-spot inventions to satisfy the interviewer rather than concepts held with deep conviction. Plants were thought to grow and this was accepted at its face value rather than interpreted in terms of where the additional material comes from.[5]

Many primary schoolchildren in Russell and Watt's sample assumed that growth inside an egg is associated with increase in mass within the (assumed closed) system: that the process of growth created new material.[10]

Leach et al.[13] report that few pupils, even at age 16, have a view of matter which involves conservation in a variety of ecological contexts. This work on progression in conceptual understanding of ecological concepts is summarised on pp. 59–67.

DEVELOPMENT

Many of the children studied by Russell and Watt[10] regarded the mechanism of growth as a rearrangement and unfolding from within the seed. The children showed some notions of pre-formation with suggestions of seeds within seeds, or seeds within potato tubers. Questions about the growth of chicks and caterpillars in their eggs revealed notions about embryonic development. Some children considered that the animal had always been there ready to hatch; others thought that distinct body parts came together in the egg. The majority of children suggested that a structurally complete, pre-formed miniature animal was feeding and growing in the egg. A minority suggested some transformation of the contents of the egg into a structurally refined animal.

The regulation of growth by hereditary information does not appear to be appreciated by children. Dreyfus and Jungwirth found that most children think that hereditary information is transmitted and interpreted only during events related to reproduction.[14]

4

RESPONDING TO THE ENVIRONMENT

BEHAVIOUR AS A CRITERION FOR LIFE

Many studies report that people of all ages identify things as living by the characteristic of movement and particularly that of movement following stimulation. However, the application of the criteria of sensitivity and movement can lead children to categorise as 'alive' certain inanimate objects. Piaget made a study of children's ideas of 'living'; this has been summarised in Chapter 1 (see p. 17).

Using movement and response as criteria of life leads children to exclude plants from the category 'living'. Studies by Bell,[1] Leach et al.[2] and Stavy and Wax[3] show that many children do not consider plants to be alive.

VISION

Research into children's ideas about vision has been conducted in several countries. Some definite patterns have emerged and conceptions of vision similar to those held by the ancient Greeks have been found among students.

Piaget found that very young children often made no connection between the eye and the object, whilst older children often thought of vision as 'a passage from the eye to the object'.[4] This 'passage' was studied by Guesne[5] and by Andersson and Karrqvist.[6][7] Guesne suggests that, whilst for luminous objects children might use a 'light coming to the eye', for non-luminous objects they use an 'active eye' model, although this latter model was used by only a minority of the students questioned. Andersson and Karrqvist, however, found what they called the 'visual ray idea' to be a common one. About 40 per cent of their sample of 12- and 15-year-olds used it in at least one of the three problem situations they were posed, although it was rarely used in a consistent way across the contexts.

Ramadas and Driver[8] report on a written task, in which 456 15-year-olds

Table 4.1 Children's ideas about what happens between a book and the eye of a girl who is looking at the book

Ideas	Students (%)	
	Ramadas and Driver[8] (N = 456)	Andersson and Karrqvist[7] (N = 166)
Rays go from book to eye	31	30
Light simply helps to see better	12	4
The visual system (eye or brain) is active	19	13
Something goes from eye to book	9	4
Something goes back and forth between eye and book	7	5
Light from source to eye (may be reflected to book) helps to see	2	–
An image enters the eye	2	5
Contrast with dark helps to see	2	–
(Sight) goes further out when light is on	1	–
No response	16	29

were asked to explain what happens between a book and the eyes of a girl who is looking at the book. Only 31 per cent of the sample suggested that rays went from the book to the eye, a finding supported by Andersson and Karrqvist[7] who asked a similar question of 15-year-olds in Sweden. A substantial number of students in both studies offered a model in which the visual system was the active component. (The response frequencies in these surveys for the most common ideas offered are shown in Table 4.1.)

Ramadas and Driver also report that many children did not recognise the necessity of light for vision and thought that it was possible to see when it was dark. Having not experienced total darkness, they did not appreciate that light must be present in a room if they could see objects, however faintly.

Fetherstonhaugh and Treagust[9] suggest that about 75 per cent of their sample used a 'visual ray' idea assuming that we see, not by light being reflected to our eyes, but by looking. These researchers also found that a substantial number of children thought that people could see in the dark. Interestingly this idea was more prevalent among those living in the city (22 per cent) than among those from the country (10 per cent). In both groups just over 40 per cent thought that cats are able to see in the dark.

Osborne *et al.*[10] found that 35 per cent of their lower junior sample provided no explanation for vision. They suggest that vision may have

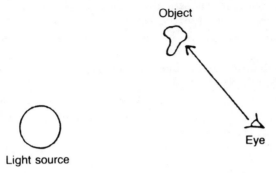

Figure 4.1 Vision represented as an active process

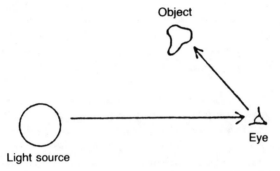

Figure 4.2 Vision represented as an active process involving light

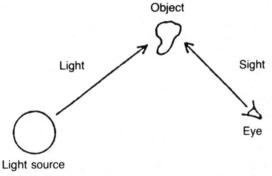

Figure 4.3 Vision represented as light and active eye directed towards object

been non-problematical for these children and that 'we see with our eyes' was for them sufficient to account for the phenomena. More than half the children indicated a link between the eye and the object and often there was a direction to the link, although a large number of these responses suggested vision as an active process and there were very few examples of single links which were directed towards the eye (see Figure 4.1). Some children attempted to reconcile the active eye idea with light

43

being necessary by drawing the line from the light source to the eye and then to the object (see Figure 4.2). Of those responses which indicated direction, most showed both links directed towards the object (see Figure 4.3).

A very small minority of children indicated an explanation consistent with the scientific view. There was some evidence that the numbers increased with age, and that the scientific view was more evident when pupils explained how they saw a torch in a mirror than when they explained how they saw a book.

Jung[11] found that 12- to 14-year-olds had difficulty in interpreting experiences of vision. He notes that no connection was made between seeing an object and receiving light from it into the eyes. Watts[12] found that light was considered as necessary to illuminate objects but it was taken to be local to the scene, with the observer at a distance and detached from it. Shapiro[13] reports on an interview in which a pupil described light as necessary for seeing a building because it illuminates it. However, the pupil did not think of light travelling from the building to the eyes.

Ramadas[14] found that 5 per cent of the students she studied held the notion that light coming from a source to the eye helps vision. In some cases the light was thought to be going to the eye and then to the object. A similar notion was also found by Crookes and Goldby.[15] De Souza Barros[16] has classified the different models of vision used by seventy Brazilian children aged 6–12 and found conceptions similar to those above.

Anderson and Smith's[17] study shows only 6 per cent of their sample holding the scientific view of vision. Over half of their students did not depict any light travelling from the object to the eye: they too tended to the idea that the light simply illuminates the object so that it can be seen.

In contrast, Boyes and Stanisstreet[18] found a sizeable proportion of children holding a scientific view of vision. Their study showed that 10 per cent of 11- to 12-year-olds and 33 per cent of over-14s indicated that the eye is a receptor of light reflected from a non- luminous object. However, in their questionnaire the light source was a lamp (rather than ambient daylight as in previous research) and this highlights the importance of context. Nevertheless, two-thirds of the older students gave inappropriate responses in the case of both non-luminous and luminous objects. The 'general illumination' model, in which light travels from the source to both observer and object but with no link between the two, was the commonest response from 11- to 12-year-olds whether they were considering a non-luminous object or a luminous object. This model was slightly less evident among older students. Some children doubted the need for light in vision: they thought that light facilitates rather than enables vision. The idea of the eye sending out a ray to the object was indicated by nearly one-third of the pupils. The majority of these took the lamp to be the origin of this light, even in the case of viewing a luminous object (a television picture). Very few pupils suggested an active eye giving out rays.

Boyes and Stanisstreet identify a progression in thinking: from the notion that objects are seen because they are bathed in light to the notion of directionality of light (but with light emanating from the eye and travelling to the object).

Although there is no research evidence of pupils relating seeing to brain activity, Johnson and Wellman[19] quote an 11-year-old as saying about brain function: 'You have to think about what you are seeing', apparently recognising that cognition by the brain follows perception by the eyes.

HEARING

Watt and Russell[20] found that although sound reception was frequently associated with the ear it tended to be a more common idea with older children than younger ones. Only one-third of infant children mentioned the ear in connection with hearing.

When thinking about what happens in the ear, one-fifth of upper juniors and one-tenth of lower juniors mentioned the ear drum. One child, in the sample of 57, described bones in the ear. One-tenth of lower and upper juniors mentioned the brain. The need for sound to enter the ear was mentioned by one infant, one-tenth of lower juniors and one-half of upper juniors. Over a quarter of the upper juniors suggested that vibrations enter the ear. Vibrations or sound waves in connection with hearing sound were mentioned by approximately 11 per cent of the whole sample. Few children, mainly upper juniors, included the stage between the ear drum and the brain. Only a very small number suggested that the brain translated the signal that it receives.

Some of the children studied by Watt and Russell[20] (18 per cent at age 11) held an 'active ear' model of hearing, in which the most important factor in hearing is that the listener is concentrating on the source of the sound.

Asoko, Leach and Scott[21] also noted that the part played by the ear in sound reception was mentioned by a large number of children at all ages. They found it described in increasing detail, and more frequently, with increasing age. When asked how they heard a clock ticking, many young children's responses were of the kind 'I heard the clock because it is ticking' or 'I heard the clock because I was listening'. At age 16, most pupils referred to the mechanism of sound transmission in the air and to the vibration of the ear drum.

Boyes and Stanisstreet[18] sought to discover whether children's thinking about hearing converges with their thinking about seeing. The 'scientific' response (with sound travelling from a radio to the hearer) was given by nearly half of 11- to 12-year-olds and nearly 80 per cent of 15- to 16-year-olds. A number of pupils offered explanations in terms of a semi-active ear which taps into the surrounding 'fluid sound', such as 'the ear picks up the sound'. The 'active ear' model in which the ear is presumed to seek the source of the sound, was weakly held and quickly discarded by over-11s, although one 13-year-old referred explicitly to a 'hearing ray' which goes to the radio and back. These researchers found that few children accepted a similarity between light and sound.

THE NERVOUS SYSTEM

Johnson and Wellman[19] questioned about sixty people from age 3, and including adults, about the brain and about activities requiring a brain. By the age of 4 or 5, most children knew that the brain is an internal body part of people but not of dolls. Many knew of the mind and regarded it as an internal organ, additional to the brain. They thought of the brain as a mental organ necessary for thinking, dreaming, remembering and knowing facts. However, they did not think that the brain was needed for overt behaviour, such as physical actions or for telling a story, or that it is concerned with emotions or sensations. From 5 onwards, children considered that feelings related to cognition (such as feeling curious or feeling sure) require the brain, but only older pupils associated the brain with the senses, with voluntary acts such as walking or kicking a ball and with involuntary acts such as coughing. Through the primary years children recognised that the brain is required for all sorts of activities: 'You need a brain to walk because it helps you to know where your feet are going'. They also developed an integrated view of the functioning of the whole body; by age 10, 80 per cent of children understood the brain as helping certain body parts to function. It was not until age 14, however, that the brain was seen as essential for all behaviours.

Gellert[22] found that children below the age of 9 have little knowledge of nerves. About a quarter claimed that they did not have any nerves, and no child under the age of 9 attributed to nerves the functions of carrying messages or controlling activities, whereas many children over the age of 9 assigned one of these roles to nerves. Carey,[23] in her review of work in this field, states that 'coming to see neural processes as part of a system of biological functions is a late achievement'. Johnson and Wellman[19] carried out their study on pupils who had not been taught about the nervous system. However, they tested an additional sample of 11-year-olds from the same school after they had been taught a unit on the brain. The curricular unit appeared to have no effect on the results:

these pupils denied the role of the brain in coughing, sleeping and blinking to the same extent as untaught children. Some could quote the statement 'the brain controls voluntary and involuntary movement' learnt in class, but only one child could apply this to examples.

MUSCLES AND SKELETON

Caravita et al.[24] and Caravita and Tonucci,[25] like other workers, found that children do not relate muscles to meat. They report that young children expressed only the static, supporting function of the skeleton. Older children recognised that the skeleton is necessary for movement, but only 20 per cent could draw muscles appropriately across joints. Verbal discussion and manual tasks with models revealed better understanding than drawings did.

There is no evidence from any studies of pupils' understanding of digestive, circulatory or respiratory systems to suggest that pupils recognise the involvement of muscles in the workings of these systems. Neither is there any evidence of appreciation of regulation of these systems by nervous control.

THE RESPONSES OF PLANTS

In his study of ideas relating to photosynthesis, Wandersee[26] asked secondary school students to draw their predictions for a plant that had been grown in a dark cupboard and another that had been kept on a lighted window-sill. Almost all the students (90 per cent across all ages) drew the plant in the window as being large and healthy. A number also showed the plant growing towards the light, indicating some understanding of phototropism. Of all the students, 85 per cent depicted the plant in the cupboard as being stunted in growth, with only 11 per cent showing it as being tall and etiolated.

5

REPRODUCTION AND INHERITANCE

REPRODUCTION AS A CRITERION OF LIFE

Children's ideas about reproduction as a criterion for life have been studied by a number of researchers. Carey reports that few children of primary age volunteered reproduction as a criterion for life.[1] Some children studied by Tamir et al.[2] believed that eggs and seeds are not alive, although they held that living things develop from living things. Reproduction was used as evidence of life in inanimate objects by a few of the younger children in Bell's study[3] as well as in that of Tamir et al.

HUMAN REPRODUCTION

Studies by several psychologists of children's understanding of human gender and reproduction have been summarised by Carey.[1] To young children under the age of 6, gender is socially determined by hairstyle, clothes, names and behaviour. These young children believe that a person can change gender by changing these outward signs but that it is socially unacceptable to do so. By the age of 7 or 8, gender constancy has become secure in children's thinking: they understand it in a developing biological framework and in relation to their understanding of reproduction.

Studies of concepts of the origin of babies have found the same developmental progression in the thinking of children aged 3–16 in Hungary, North America, England, Australia and Sweden.[1 4 5 6] Pre-school children appear to believe that any baby has always existed: 'in a shop', 'in somebody's tummy', 'in heaven' or 'in hospital'. They don't see questions about origins as meaningful in this or any other context. From the age of about 5 children understand that things are made, and they see the origin of babies as a purposeful human activity involving manufacturing babies from parts. Children may think of babies in a shop or factory, or they may adopt the 'digestive fallacy' idea of the mother eating components from which to make a baby in her stomach.

According to Carey[1] these early concepts represent an understanding of phenomena based on wants and beliefs, before the child develops any physiological understanding. A transitional stage follows as the child tries to make sense of the social relationship between a mother and father, of information about sexual intercourse and of ideas about sperm and eggs. Animistic notions of deliberate actions of sperm and eggs prevail and many children hold a literal interpretation of the 'agricultural model', believing that something like a bean seed is deliberately planted in soil inside the mother or that an egg like a hen's egg is incubated inside the mother. By the age of 11 most children have some idea of the mechanics of sexual intercourse and they understand the role of both parents in getting sperms and eggs together to make babies. Two studies[4] [5] found the following percentages of 11- to 12-year-olds who had reached this stage:

- North American (Californian, middle class), 100 per cent;
- North American (mixed sample), 80 per cent;
- English, 63 per cent;
- Australian, 87 per cent;
- Swedish, 97 per cent.

By the age of 9 few children reached this stage of understanding, although in the Swedish sample 83 per cent had. The Swedish children were several years ahead of their counterparts at all stages and this suggests that social climate as well as psychological development is significant in concept development in this domain. In the absence of any information about genetics, children make sophisticated constructions to explain the production of a new individual from sperm and egg. Of children aged 11 and older, 30 per cent articulated a model of pre-formation: that a miniature baby is folded up inside the sperm or the egg and the other gamete triggers its development. This view parallels historical explanations of reproduction.

CONTINUITY OF LIFE

Tamir et al.[2] investigated the notion of continuity of life in children aged 10–14. Although most could put pictures of seed germination or chick embryology into the correct sequence and 85 per cent said that the seedling was alive, only 66 per cent said that the seed was alive. It appears that 19 per cent did not understand the continuity of life from seed to seedling: they believed in the possibility of living organisms developing from the non-living, stating 'seeds are dead, when we put them in the soil they get food and begin to live' or 'larvae change into pupae which are dead and then we get butterflies'. However, most of the children did have a notion of the continuity of life, explicitly stating

'If the seed were not alive it would not be able to grow' or expressing the idea that living organisms originate from other living organisms. In some cases the latter idea did not prevent children from believing that eggs and seeds are not alive. However, of a class of agricultural school students in the sample, only one classified eggs and seeds as non-living, indicating that agricultural experience had an impact on understanding of the 'life' concept.

BIOLOGICAL PRINCIPLES OF REPRODUCTION

In a group of 120 Nigerian 16- to 18-year-olds,[7] 40 per cent of them, even post-16, did not distinguish between reproduction and the act of copulation in mammals. Moreover, in accordance with this conception of reproduction, these students did not believe that plants are capable of sexual reproduction, yet asexual reproduction was thought to be restricted to micro-organisms. (The study did not probe the students' ideas about how plants produce offspring with neither sexual nor asexual reproduction available to them! Perhaps it was perceived by students as a matter of no interest, just as plant growth evoked no firm concepts amongst pupils studied by Barker.[8])

Relatively small percentages of the Nigerian students displayed some other misconceptions: notably 36 per cent thought that a human ovum contains yolk on the same scale as a bird's egg. This may relate to the 'incubation theory' of young children noted in Carey's work, or it may derive from using the same word 'egg' in a technical and an everyday sense. Some 18 per cent showed confusion between the concepts of male gamete and seminal fluid. This may arise from use of the word 'sperm', in the singular form, for both of these concepts.

Gott et al.,[9] in analysing about 800 responses to the questions in their age 15 survey, found that pupils more often correctly identified examples of sexual reproduction in animals, than examples of its occurrence in plants. This finding corresponds with the findings in Nigerian and Hampshire studies,[7][10] that many pupils do not believe that flowering plants reproduce sexually. This view is very resistant to change by teaching: biology tuition appears to have little effect in changing 'folklore' concepts of reproduction but it does affect performance in the context of formal aspects of sex education, such as recognising unrealistic anatomical diagrams or knowledge of hormonal control and the site of fertilisation. The teachers [10] who undertook an investigation of ideas about reproduction amongst 516 11- to 13-year-olds reached similar conclusions. Their report documents 'misconceptions' revealed by the pilot questionnaire given to 150 children. These include the notions that:

- 'sexual reproduction must involve mating';
- 'male animals are always bigger and stronger than females';
- 'animals consciously plan their reproductive strategies';
- 'asexual reproduction results in weakness and sexual reproduction always produces stronger individuals';
- 'hermaphroditism is the same as asexual reproduction'.

This group also examined many alternative conceptions about twins which are familiar to teachers and which have been documented by Engel Clough and Wood-Robinson,[11] such as: 'twins can be formed from one egg and two sperms', and 'identical twins can be of opposite sexes'.

VARIATION AND RESEMBLANCE

Most research studies in this area assume that the subjects hold the concepts of variation within a species and of offspring resembling their parents. Hackling and Treagust[12] did investigate 15-year-old students' understanding of these concepts and found that 94 per cent understood that one's characteristics come from parents, 50 per cent understood that inheritance and reproduction occur together and 44 per cent understood that one gets a mixture of features from both parents. Deadman and Kelly[13] found that students in their sample of fifty-two 11- to 14-year-olds recognised that variation between species occurs, but that they regarded it as a response to environmental conditions rather than due to inheritance. Pupils had firm ideas of transmission of characteristics from generation to generation. The boys believed in blending inheritance and they regarded characteristics from the male parent as being stronger in their expression. Other studies have found similar notions regarding lack of equality of parental contribution.[10 11 14] Engel Clough and Wood-Robinson[11] and Kargbo et al.[14] found a tendency to favour the mother as providing the main contribution, or to support same-sex inheritance – daughters inheriting from mothers and sons from fathers.

THE MECHANISM OF INHERITANCE

In Kargbo's study[14] of children aged 7–13, half gave naturalistic explanations of the mechanism of inheritance: 'nature makes offspring resemble parents'. Some referred to environmental factors, some to somatic factors such as the brain or blood, and only four subjects (amongst older children) implied any genetic principle. These children's responses to the nineteen questions convinced Kargbo and his colleagues that the pupils were not giving insignificant, unconsidered answers, but that they had established frameworks to make sense of their observations of inheritance.

Several researchers[11] [12] [13] have found that pupils, even before specific teaching, know the word 'gene' and less frequently 'chromosome'. However, pupils appear to understand little of the nature or function of genes and chromosomes, not appreciating that there is a chemical basis to inheritance. Lucas[15] studying adults' understanding of scientific concepts, found that half the respondents volunteered that genes are responsible for the similarities between parents and offspring, but one-third could not offer any explanation of the phenomenon. People who had studied science had no more knowledge of this topic than other people of the same educational level. Half of Lucas's sample chose a correct explanation of the mechanism of sex determination, compared to a quarter incorrect and a quarter 'don't knows'. A science education background made no difference to responses but gender did, with more women than men choosing correctly.

SOURCES OF VARIATION

Lack of a precise concept distinguishing sexual reproduction from asexual reproduction appears to preclude an understanding of the origins of variation.[7] [9] [10]

Several studies, involving students of all ages, point to very persistent alternative conceptions about the source of variation. Students invariably attribute observable variation to environmental factors alone. Sexual reproduction is not recognised as the source of variation in a population. Two questions were used by Gott et al.[9] to probe the concept of variation among 15-year-olds, many of whom were studying biology. On one of the questions, only 14 per cent mentioned sexual reproduction or natural variation, even though the question said that environmental conditions were kept constant. On the other question, only 1 per cent gave an accurate explanation of variation, correctly involving reproduction. Hackling and Treagust[12] found that the influence of environmental factors was more frequently acknowledged by Australian 15-year-olds (in 56 per cent of responses) than the influence of genes (in 30 per cent of responses). Studies involving advanced high school and college students have shown that large proportions do not understand the interaction of genes and environment.[16]

ADAPTATION

Most pupils appear to regard adaptation in terms of individuals changing in major ways in response to their environment in order to survive. In the study by Deadman and Kelly[13] students saw adaptation in a naturalistic or teleological sense, as satisfying the organism's need or desire to fulfil some future requirement. Engel Clough and Wood-Robinson[17] found two-thirds of 12- to 14-year-olds and half of 16-year-olds giving teleological interpretations of examples of adaptation. Only 10 per cent of the whole sample gave scientifically acceptable explanations and the rest merely restated the questions in some tautological form.

Students appear to show confusion between an individual's adaptation during its lifetime and inherited changes in a population over time. They tend to believe in the Lamarckian theory of inheritance of acquired characteristics. This belief is evident in many surveys of students both before and after instruction in genetics and evolution.[11] [13] [14] [18] [19] Brumby[20] found, among Australian and English higher education students, that only 18 per cent of students, even after studying 'A' level biology, could correctly apply a process of selection to evolutionary change. Most gave the Larmarckian interpretation that individuals can adapt to change in the environment if they need to, and that these adaptations are inherited. Brumby considers that pre-existing Larmarckian ideas can block the understanding of a Darwinian explanation.

CHANCE IN INHERITANCE

Pupils have some idea of the randomness of inheritance – that sometimes offspring are like their mother, sometimes like their father, sometimes both – as found by Kargbo et al.[14] However, pupils rarely showed evidence of applying the concept of chance and probability to inheritance and evolution.[12] [13] [16] The concepts of randomness and probability are not held by many students even after advanced courses. Hickman et al.[16] found that many could predict mathematical probabilities of outcomes in isolated theoretical examples but could not do this with examples of situations in human families.

6

MICROBES

THE WORDS AND THE CONCEPT

The word 'microbe' or 'micro-organism' was not used spontaneously by the children in Maxted's study.[1] Most frequently the word 'germ' was used to label the concept, with 'bug' as an alternative. Different usages were found among children of different nationalities but the labels all indicated a generalised concept. The words 'bacteria' and 'viruses' were used as alternatives to 'germs' but there was little evidence of these being distinct concepts, although some pupils used 'germ' to subsume 'bacteria' and 'viruses'. Only 9 per cent of English 15-year-olds studied by Prout[2] recognised that viruses and bacteria are different sorts of organism. When the word 'bacteria' is used it is often as a singular noun, with no lexical distinction between the singular and the plural form. This compounds the problem of distinguishing the concept of an individual bacterial cell from the idea of a bacterial colony, or distinguishing between an individual and a species. Portuguese 8- to 13-year-olds used the word 'mould' to identify fungal growth on bread but regarded it as akin to rust rather than to microbes.[3]

ORIGIN AND REPRODUCTION OF MICROBES

Maxted's study of a class of English pupils suggests that concepts of germs do not appear to arise from immediate experience but from folklore, TV, dentists and health education information.[1]

MICROBES AS LIVING THINGS

Nagy's 370 British and American subjects,[4] aged 5–11, referred to a single kind of germ and were unaware that each disease has a specific pathogen, whereas half of Maxted's subjects, aged 12–13, volunteered that different diseases are caused by different kinds of germ. The data is insufficient to decide whether this is a progression with age of child or date of study.

Nagy's subjects were asked to draw germs. Half of the youngest group, aged 5–7, drew nothing. Older children produced abstract dots or stars, progressing with age to representations similar to insects or spiders. Orally they identified germs with flies or other insects, possibly by confusion with vectors shown on health education posters.

The term 'bug' appears to be applied to both microbes and insects as 'nasty, creepy things'. Some of Nagy's children drew scenes of dirty places or sick-rooms to represent germs and they spoke of dust, dirt and poison. In a brainstorming exercise Wallace[5] found that the words connected with disease and insanitary conditions were strongly associated with the notion of microbes by 11- and 12-year-olds, whereas 12- and 13-year-olds gave fewer such instances and included more specific references to very small size, fungi, bacteria and food making. (The latter may have been due to teaching received six months previously.) Maxted's 12- and 13-year-olds mostly suggested that germs are microscopically small, light and floating in the air. Some referred to different shapes and sizes. They mentioned a range of places where bacteria occur but only two pupils referred to a living host. All these children said that bacteria are living but, although some could recall some characteristics of life taught in the previous year's lessons, none could satisfactorily use these as criteria to define the characteristics of bacterial life. Difficulties in explaining colony size revealed that pupils possessed ideas about growth which differ from the scientific concept.

THE EFFECTS OF MICROBES

Research suggests that children often think of disease and decay as properties of the objects affected. They do not appear to hold a concept of microbes as agents of change.

MICROBES AND DISEASE

In the representation of germs by British and American children investigated in 1953 by Nagy,[4] children attributed all illnesses to germs with no distinction between contagious and non-contagious disease and with no reference to organic, functional or dietary diseases. This was not the pattern emerging from studies where the focus was health.[6 7 8 9] In one study, health and illness were seen by pupils as two different concepts with different causal factors, rather than as a continuum.[8] Another sample of pupils saw illness as the negative end of a health continuum and in terms of lifestyle diseases with no mention of infectious diseases.[9]

Degree of infection and resistance to infection were not recognised, nor were predispositioning factors in infection or cure. When Barenholz and Tamir[10] studied sixteen classes of Israeli 15- to 17-year-olds, the students could not differentiate between prevention and curing of disease. The concept of automatic infection and healing was prevalent, in which any germ or medicine is seen as producing instantaneous change.[4] The route of entry and exit of germs in and out of the body was thought to be mainly through the mouth but also through the nose and through the skin. Children thought that inside the body germs make us ill by walking about, eating, breeding and by poisoning us.

Evidence of conflicting ideas held concurrently, as in 'all diseases are caused by germs' and 'you can catch a cold by getting cold and wet' was found by Maxted.[1] Of Prout's sample, 59 per cent thought that there were different kinds of cold with alternative causes, germ and non-germ. A further 11 per cent held a non-germ theory, 9 per cent a germ-only theory and 23 per cent a germ-plus-predisposition notion in which germs were seen as dormant within the body or ready to invade if cold or wet conditions allow.

The folklore of the common cold is very tenacious. The condition is not regarded as a disease and the name 'cold' helps to reinforce the connection with environmental causes. One child, in defining illness in Campbell's study, stated 'if I just have cold, I am not sick'.[6] Prout[2] maintains that much school biology propagates the germ theory of infection in a simplistic way, as a dogma which may be both inaccurate and also weak in relation to the more robust folk beliefs.

Exposure to TV and publicity on AIDS and other diseases might influence modern children's ideas as compared to a 1953 sample. A study undertaken by Helman in the 1970s[11] found that people born after the 1940s are more likely than older people to hold a germ theory of infection for colds and fevers. The author contends, however, that biomedical knowledge has not displaced folk knowledge, but that each has accommodated to the other: biomedical terminology becomes familiar but the concepts are confused.

Antibiotics appear to be mysterious to the general public,[12] to pupils[2] [10] and even to first-year medical students.[13] Half of Brumby's medical student sample thought that the human body itself is the primary target for antibiotic reaction, with the body becoming resistant to the effect. Some of these students, and many of the samples of 15-year-olds of Prout[2] and Barenholz and Tamir,[10] thought that antibiotics are power-ful medicine for serious disease and they would be wasted on everyday illnesses. In all of these sample groups, most were ignorant of the fact that antibiotics act only on bacteria and not on viruses. Many people appear to confuse antibiotics with antibodies and this is not just confu-sion between similar words; people speaking a language which had more distinction between the words were also confused about the respective concepts.[10]

DECAY AND RECYCLING

Studies of children's ideas about the role of microbes in decay and recycling are summarised in the context of ideas about ecosystems in Chapter 7.

Children studied by Brinkman and Boschhuizen[14] associated food decay with microbial contamination in the household hygiene context. However, pupils generally appear unaware of the role that micro-organisms play in nature, especially as decomposers and as recyclers of carbon, nitrogen, water and minerals.[15] Even after tuition they do not appear to conceive of the fundamental importance of microbes to all life: 30 per cent of a sample of Israeli teenagers[10] said they would eliminate all micro-organisms from the earth if it were possible; another 3 per cent would have let them stay but only in deference to their being part of God's creation, although without any apparent part in the master plan.

BIOTECHNOLOGY

Although there have been a number of initiatives to develop biotechnology teaching in schools, none of them appears to have examined children's prior concepts of the subject. Although it is unlikely that children would create biotechnological concepts intuitively, they may have concepts derived from folk science, advertising or early tuition.

A few of Maxted's pupils[1] thought that bacteria could be useful when dead, for making medicines or vaccines, but there was little evidence of notions about the technological potential of living microbes. Conceptual frameworks are crucial for pupils to make sense of experimental work and the focus of Maxted's work is the interaction of pupil's prior beliefs about bacteria with their understanding of experimental procedures. Prior beliefs were found to be the major influence in a pupil's understanding of the experiments, such that the use of the sterile control plate in a bacteriological experiment could not be understood if a child's concepts of living, size, growth and reproduction in bacteria are not established. The appearance of bacterial colonies as the dependent variable would be meaningless without these concepts, although the same pupil may well be able to cope with the use of controls and the manipulation of variables in other more directly observable situations.

There are implications for the use of bacteriological experiments in the assessment of experimental design skills. Although to the adult scientist batches of agar plates lend themselves ideally to small-scale 'agricultural' experimental design, the physical details of unfamiliar apparatus may 'overload' the pupils, as Maxted found. The notion that bacteria might 'get in round the gap' was a more powerful explanation of colonies than bacteria becoming visible due to reproduction and population growth of those already in the sealed dish. Maxted's pupils could describe colonies and say that a colony consisted of many individuals but they could not explain why sizes varied. The time element in the experiments was not appreciated: pupils expected to see instant results.

Children seemed to be able to focus only on the bacteria intended to be studied (from the air or hands): they did not recognise the possibility of bacterial contamination on unsterilised equipment. Even if the presence of bacteria on the glassware was acknowledged, they were not identified as living organisms, since in that situation they were neither visible nor causing disease. In these circumstances, the notion of sterilisation made no sense to the pupils.

7

ECOSYSTEMS

PROGRESSION IN REASONING ABOUT ECOSYSTEMS

Leach *et al.*[1] describe pupils' reasoning about ecological phenomena from age 5–16. These findings corroborate descriptions of children's thinking in a number of domains reported by Piaget[2] and other researchers. There is a trend from the egocentric (self-centred) thinking of very young children, through anthropocentric (human-centred) reasoning, to the reasoning which includes a wider range of factors shown by older students. Teleological reasoning is common in young children who assume that an event is predetermined in order to fulfil a need, as in 'there are a lot of rabbits so that foxes will not get hungry'. With age it becomes less pronounced but it persists to some extent in senior school students.

Progression in children's thinking in relation to ecosystems has been identified by Leach *et al.*[1] Younger children, aged 5–7, tend to think only in terms of individual organisms which people keep and which need humans for their survival (pets, zoo animals, houseplants). Older junior pupils, aged 7–11, extend their thinking to wild organisms as individuals, although some may think that these are fed and cared for by people. Most pupils over the age of 13 have a concept of populations of organisms in the wild but their 'explanations' of relationships are merely descriptions of nature as in 'birds live in trees' or 'foxes eat rabbits'. It is not until much later that students think in terms of populations or organisms in the wild competing for scarce resources. Distinct stages of reasoning in the conceptual development of any one child or group of children are not evident and a child may use different types of reasoning in different contexts.

NUTRITION AND ENERGY FLOW

Research into pupils' ideas about food and nutrition is summarised in Chapter 2.

Many children associate the word 'food' only with what they identify as being edible.[3] Few pupils associate substances such as starch with food.[4] Although pupils of all ages identify food as necessary to promote growth and health, many do not recognise that it is the source of material which becomes either part of their bodies in growth and repair, or the source of energy. When they do relate food to energy, many 11- or 12-year-olds consider that food is converted directly into 'goodness' or 'energy' and that it vanishes completely in the process.[5]

A universal and very persistent conception amongst children and adults is that plants get their food from the soil. Many pupils think that 'food' for plants is anything taken in from the environment, including water, minerals, fertilisers, carbon dioxide and even sunlight.[3] [4] [6] [7] [8] Even when students have accepted taught ideas about photosynthesis they still believe that plants obtain some food from the environment. They believe that plants have multiple sources of food and few pupils have the understanding that photosynthesis makes food which provides energy and body material for the plant.

Roth and Anderson[9] found many children expressing the teleological idea that plants make food for the benefit of animals and people rather than for the plants themselves. Children did not appear to recognise that photosynthesis is the process by which energy from the environment becomes available to plants and then to animals.

Many children think of light as 'food' for plants or as a reagent in photosynthesis. Indeed, over half of Simpson's sample of secondary school children thought that light is made of molecules.[10] Most of the children did not understand energy transfers in living things: they believed that plants get the energy for all their processes directly from the Sun, and they use the words 'heat' and 'light' interchangeably in this context. Nearly 80 per cent of a sample of 13-year-olds thought that plants use heat from the Sun as an energy source for photosynthesis. Most considered that the Sun is one amongst many sources of energy for plants, others being soil, minerals, air and water.

Gayford[11] reports that 17- and 18-year-old biology students considered that energy flows (or is transported) from place to place in biological systems and that it can be stored like a material. They thought in terms of energy 'formed' or 'used' in biological processes rather than in terms of energy conversions.

FOOD CHAINS AND WEBS

Research into children's ideas about food chains and food webs is summarised in Chapter 2.

Senior[12] analysed the responses of 15-year-old students to questions about populations of organisms in food webs. He found that students were not comfortable with the arrow notation used in school science to indicate a trophic relationship. Hence they failed to understand the underlying principles of the relationship and to complete the activities correctly. Schollum[13] identified a similar difficulty for pupils dealing with food chains: they were better able to answer problems about food chains if lines rather than arrows were used to link populations.

Few students appear to relate their ideas about feeding and energy to a framework of ideas about interactions of organisms. Only half of a sample of undergraduate biology students, when asked about the statements 'life depends on green plants' and 'the web of life', explained these statements in terms of food chains. Only a minority of these mentioned harnessing solar energy or photosynthesis as the reason why green plants are crucial in the food chain. Even at tertiary level many students still think teleologically: nearly a quarter of the students expressed views suggesting that other organisms exist for the benefit of humans.[14] A subsequent study by Eisen and Stavy[15], of students from age 13 up to undergraduate level, revealed that most students knew that animals could not exist in a plant-free world. However, only 25 per cent of biology students and 7 per cent of non-biologists suggested that this is because animals cannot make their own food and some thought that carnivores could exist if their prey reproduced plentifully.

Students' understanding of ecological relationships depends on their concepts of 'plant' and 'animal', and also on their knowledge of habitats and use of physical principles. Adeniyi[16] found that, even after teaching, 13- to 15-year-old Nigerian students were not convinced that producers exist in aquatic habitats. These students had little experience of specific habitats with plants living under water. Pupils studied by Leach *et al.*[1] recognised the existence of aquatic plants but some said that sunlight and carbon dioxide could not get through the water to the plants and hence they did not acknowledge these plants as producers.

Bell and Barker found that pupils' limited recognition of 'producer' and 'consumer' was tied to their understanding of 'plant' and 'animal'. Once the scientific meaning of the words 'plant' and 'animal' was established by teaching, pupils could apply the terms 'producer' and 'consumer' appropriately.[17]

Several studies,[18 19 20] involving subjects ranging from 12-year-olds to undergraduate zoology students, have found that most students interpret food web problems in a limited way, focusing on isolated food chains. This focus on linear food chains, rather than on cycles of matter, interdependency or systems, appears to predominate in thinking about ecosystems.

Smith and Anderson[5] noted that many of the 11- and 12-year-olds who accept that populations in a food web are related may still see predation as a 'specific eating event' for the benefit of the eater alone. Pupils tended to regard food which is eaten and used for energy as belonging to a food chain. Food which is incorporated into the body material of eaters was seen as something different and it was not recognised as the material which is the food of the next level.

COMMUNITIES, POPULATIONS AND COMPETITION BETWEEN ORGANISMS

Adeniyi[16] found that students' meanings of ecological terms were related to everyday usage rather than to scientific definitions. For example, a quarter of the students used the term 'community' to mean a group of people living together with similar ideas. Another quarter did not distinguish between the meaning of 'community' and 'population'. Amongst his Nigerian students, Adeniyi found a range of ideas about pyramids of numbers and biomass. Several ideas were anthropocentric, as in 'there are more herbivores than carnivores because people breed them'. Others implied teleological predestination, as in 'the number of producers is large to satisfy the consumers'. 'Stronger' organisms were considered to have more energy, which they use to feed on weaker organisms with less energy. Some students saw energy adding up through an ecosystem, such that a top predator would have all the energy from the producers and other consumers in the chain.

Leach et al.[1] found that, although nearly half of children at all ages between 5 and 16 could select pictures of organisms to construct a balanced community which contained a producer and primary and secondary consumers, few at any age used the idea of interdependence to explain their selection. Most based their choices on their description of the status quo in nature or used teleological reasoning. The pupils were asked to predict which population of organisms would be largest, and why. Although most pupils at all ages chose producers, a significant number chose primary or secondary consumers. Again, most explanations for the choice were either descriptions of nature, as in 'rabbits have many babies', or teleological. There was little evidence of reasoning about interdependence or energy flow, although there was some progression in reasoning with age. In the context of seasonal change, children made some links between populations, ranging from simple food or shelter links at age 11 to sophisticated energy flows in food webs by some students at age 16. To questions based on changes to food webs, children responded differently according to which organisms were 'removed' from the hypothetical web. Pupils made fewest links between the removal of a top predator and the rest of the food web, and most links between the removal of predators and the rest of the food web. They seemed more able to trace links up through the trophic levels than down.

Griffiths and Grant[20] reported that a fifth of 15-year-olds they studied thought that a population higher on a food chain is a predator on all the organisms below it. Many pupils thought that a change in the population of one species would affect only those species related to it directly as predator or prey, while others thought that a change in the size of prey population would have no effect on its predator population. These authors suggest that the introduction of the food chain ideas as a prelude to food webs is a reason for children failing to use ideas about interdependency to explain relationships in complex ecosystems.

ENVIRONMENTS

Leach et al.[1] investigated children's ideas about what various organisms need to stay alive and healthy, and ideas about the source of these requirements in the environment. Most children recognised plants' need for soil, water and sunlight in their habitat. The need for air, oxygen or carbon dioxide was identified by a small minority of pupils: less than a third of 16-year-olds noted the need for carbon dioxide or oxygen. Consumers were thought to need water, food and shelter. Many pupils at all ages identified food and shelter links between organisms in communities. However, younger children (up to 13) seemed to think in terms of the needs of individual organisms rather than of populations. Many pupils at all ages seemed unable to think of organisms and their environments without human involvement and many younger pupils thought that all organisms are fed by people.

Most pupils, at ages 11–16, were able to mention some features of organisms that are related to a specific habitat, and some were able to predict the habitat of organisms with particular features.

Several studies of children's ideas of adaptation have suggested that students use teleological and anthropomorphic reasoning to explain the relationship between an organism and its environment.[21 22 23 24]

DECAY

Recent research in Portugal,[25] USA[5] and England[1] identifies common notions in children's explanations of decay. The research questions related to the 'disappearance' of dead animals or fruits on the surface of the soil. The youngest children thought that dead things just disappear, or they had human-centred notions which did not allow for ideas about conservation of matter after death. These studies found that most children think of decomposition as the total or partial disappearance of matter. In the sample studied by Leach et al.,[1] 70 per cent of 11- to 13-year-olds gave responses implying a lack of conservation of matter, even after teaching about the topic. Younger pupils were not aware that material from dead organisms becomes part of the non-living environment nor that microbes initiate the process of decay. They tended to think that insects break up material once it has started to rot

63

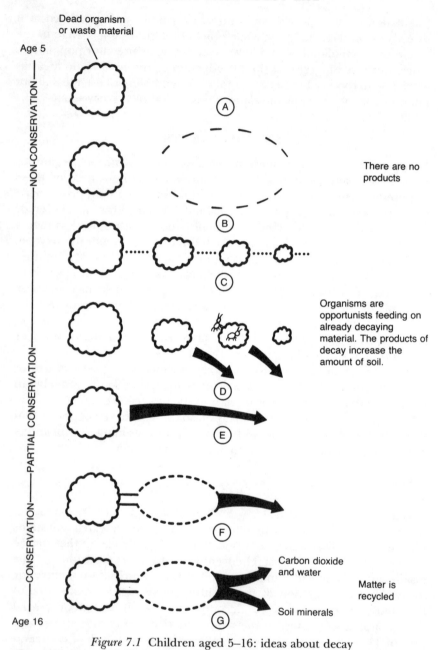

Figure 7.1 Children aged 5–16: ideas about decay

Key: A: No ideas. B: It disappears. C: In time it goes, by natural processes. D: It rots and birds/mice/bugs/insects eat it; it enriches the soil/fertilises the ground. E: Organisms/germs cause it to decay; it produces soil minerals. F: It is decomposed by bacteria and fungi; it produces soil minerals. G: Decomposers use it as food; it produces soil minerals, carbon dioxide and water.

of its own accord. A common idea was that bugs or germs eat the partly rotted matter. Pupils thought that rotted material 'enriches' or 'fertilises' the soil but they did not identify it as part of the soil. After tuition, up to 65 per cent of 15- to 16-year-olds used the words 'bacteria' and 'fungi' or 'decomposers' but they were not sure about their role. Although older pupils tended to offer more factors to explain decay, there was little evidence that pupils at 15 or 16 have an understanding of how various physical factors relate to the action of microbes.[1].

Figure 7.1, based on the findings of Leach *et al.*[1] and of Smith and Anderson,[5] summarises the ideas identified across the age range.

Some Swedish children in Helden's study[26] expressed the belief that all dead material decays to form soil and that the Earth is thus getting bigger all the time. This idea recapitulates historical notions. Very few children in the study by Sequeira and Freitas[25] had ideas about organic matter changing to mineral matter during decay, or about any other recycling.

Generally, pupils were unaware of the role that micro-organisms play in nature, especially of their role as decomposers and as recyclers of carbon, nitrogen, water and minerals.[1]

CYCLING OF MATTER THROUGH THE ECOSYSTEM

Smith and Anderson[5] found that almost all of their 12-year-old sample were aware that some kind of cyclical process takes place in ecosystems. However, most pupils tended to think in terms of sequences of cause and effect events, with matter being created or destroyed in these events, and then the sequence starting again. Some recognised a form of recycling through soil minerals, but they did not incorporate water, oxygen and carbon dioxide into the cycles. Pupils saw no connection between the oxygen/carbon dioxide cycle and other processes involving the production, consumption and use of food. Their understanding of the matter cycling process remained fragmented. Following instruction there was little change, with only 4 per cent of pupils achieving the 'goal conception' that matter is converted back and forth between organisms' bodies and substances (carbon dioxide, water and minerals) in the environment. A few pupils had picked up the idea of food being converted but they thought of it being converted into energy.

Leach *et al.*[1] report that, even at age 16, few pupils have a view of matter that involves conservation in a variety of contexts such as photosynthesis, assimilation of food, decay and respiration. Moreover, pupils did not appear to distinguish between food, matter and energy. No pupils in this study presented an integrated view of a consistent amount of matter cycling, though a few older pupils showed evidence of conserving matter in decay and in photosynthesis.

GAS EXCHANGE AND BALANCE

Various studies suggest that children from 9–16 think that air is not used by plants, or that plants and animals use air in opposite ways. (Studies of ideas about gas exchange by plants are summarised in Chapter 2.)

Eisen and Stavy[15] and Stavy *et al.*[27] investigated students' understanding of the importance of photosynthesis in the ecosystem in maintaining oxygen levels. Most (82 per cent) of the 13- to 15-year-olds studied knew that plants release oxygen in photosynthesis and that this oxygen supports a range of living things. However, only about half of the students at each age level indicated that animals, because of their oxygen need, could not live without plants. The same questions posed to older students produced similar proportions of responses from 'non-biologists', although those who had studied advanced courses in biology were able to give more satisfactory explanations. Nevertheless, only 25 per cent of the 'biologists', and 7 per cent of the 'non-biologists', suggested that animals could not exist in a plant-free world because they were not autotrophic.

Wandersee[28] tested 1,405 students aged 10–18 by a written test. When asked about the flow of gases during photosynthesis, 62 per cent of the youngest children and 85 per cent of the college students knew that carbon dioxide flows into the leaf during photosynthesis. There was a similar awareness of oxygen flow out of leaves, except that only 51 per cent of the youngest knew the correct direction. Most students seemed to think that the two gases always flow in opposite directions. However, questions set in relation to diagrammatic replication of Priestley's experiment (where a mouse and an illuminated plant are placed in a sealed container) indicated that many students had difficulty in applying their knowledge of gas exchange to an 'ecosystem'. Although an increasing proportion through the age groups (38 per cent to 67 per cent) suggested that both the plant and the mouse would live, many thought that both would die or that only the plant would live. In explaining their answers, the percentage of students who used the word 'air' decreased with age (26 per cent to 4 per cent) while there was a corresponding rise in the proportion using 'carbon dioxide' and 'oxygen' (18 per cent to 58 per cent) to justify their choice of answer.

RESPIRATION

Although pupils have notions about gas exchange and usually consider it as a kind of breathing, few at any age have an understanding of respiration. Respiration and breathing were thought, by most students in Haslam and Treagust's study,[29] to be synonymous.

Adeniyi[16] found that children learned from an early age that they breathe oxygen and that oxygen was often equated with air. Gellert[30] and Nagy[31] found that, although young children know that air is necessary for life, they appear to have a limited idea of what happens to inhaled air, often thinking that it remains in the head. Both these researchers found that half of 9- and 10-year-olds associated lungs with breathing, and some pupils recognised that an exchange of gases with the air is important to all parts of the body. However, it seems that young secondary pupils are unlikely to relate the need for oxygen with the use of food.

Leach et al.[1] note an absence of ideas about the physiological role of the gases. By age 11 pupils recognised that animals need air or oxygen. Pupils mentioning oxygen said that it was needed for breathing or to keep an animal alive. However, no pupils mentioned the release of energy from food in connection with the need for oxygen. Responses indicated that pupils had no ideas about the physiological role of breathing, seeing the process as an end in itself. Arnaudin and Mintzes[32] found one-third of schoolchildren and one-quarter of college students in their sample thinking of 'air tubes' connecting the lungs and heart. Up to a third of all their sample suggested that air is simply inhaled into the lungs and then exhaled without links to the heart and circulatory system.

Asked explicitly 'What is respiration?', the 13- to 15-year-olds studied by Stavy et al.[27] referred only to gas exchange by the inhaling and exhaling of air. Most merely said 'we breathe in order to live'. A few had ideas about oxygen: 'oxygen revives the cells', 'oxygen activates the heart and causes blood to circulate'.

Anderson and Sheldon[33] studied the ideas about respiration held by American college non-biology majors. The students identified oxygen as a need of animals and carbon dioxide as a need of plants. They used everyday language to identify respiration with breathing and they did not link food, oxygen, carbon dioxide and energy into any coherent view about respiration. They exhibited a lack of ideas about respiration, as opposed to the range of alternative ideas which they offered about photosynthesis.

A notion identified by several studies is that plants do not respire, or that they respire only in the dark.[27][29][34][35] Pupils who refer to respiration in plants do not appear to perceive it as an energy-conversion process: many think that photosynthesis is the energy-providing process for plants. Many of the children studied by Haslam and Treagust[29] believed that, since only leaves have gas exchange pores, respiration in plants occurs only in the cells of leaves.

Children tend to believe that energy is used up by living things in general and that plants use up energy in growing. They appear to think that energy is created or destroyed in different life processes.[11][27][36]

Even advanced biology students aged 17–18 tend not to think in terms of energy transfer. Of Gayford's sample,[11] 79 per cent did not consider that biological processes such as respiration involve energy conversions. They thought that respiration actually forms energy which is used in synthesis reactions. The view that 'ATP has high energy bonds which release energy', a view probably arising from the teaching, was held by 74 per cent.

POLLUTION

An American study by Brody[37] indicates few changes in knowledge about ecological crises between the ages of 9 and 16. However, this study identified changes in children's ideas of pollution. Nine-year-olds regarded pollution as something which is directly sensed by people and which affects people or other animals. They did not consider that harm to plants constitutes an environmental problem. They thought that air can somehow circulate pollution. Pupils aged 13 had a more conceptual understanding of ecological crises, including a concept of cumulative ecological effects. They did not have to sense a material for it to be included in their thinking, and unseen materials like acid rain were considered pollutants. These students' responses included the idea that pollution kills (rather than harms) animals, particularly fish but also plants. Human populations, factories and cars were considered to be possible sources of ecological crises. By the age of 16, students had a greater number of relevant concepts and also meaningful connections between them. They believed that pollution can affect everything. Biodegradable materials were considered less harmful to life than non-biodegradable ones, and the concentration of pollutants was considered to be important. At this age, the students recognised that environmental issues are complex and they related economic concepts to cause and effects in ecological crises.

Several important 'misconceptions' were held by at least half of the large sample of students interviewed by Brody. They included:

- anything natural is not pollution;
- biodegradable materials are not pollutants;
- the oceans are a limitless resource;
- solid waste in dumps is safe;
- the human race is indestructible as a species.

There was little evidence that pupils used science concepts learnt elsewhere in the curriculum to inform their understanding of ecological issues.

Boyes and Stanisstreet[38 39] and Francis et al.[40] found some scientifically acceptable ideas about global warming already present amongst

11-year-olds. These included the notion that an increase in the greenhouse effect will cause changes in weather patterns. The ideas generally held by the science community, such as the retention of solar energy, took time to become established over the period of secondary schooling. A number of 'misconceptions' were identified amongst 11- to 16-year-old pupils and some of these persisted in the oldest school students and among undergraduate students. The idea that the use of lead-free petrol will reduce global warming was one example. Confusion between ozone layer depletion and the greenhouse effect was common in children's thinking and it seems that students are aware of a range of environmentally 'friendly' and 'unfriendly' actions, and that they know about a range of environmental problems. However, they tend not to link particular causes with particular consequences. Rather, they appear to think that all environmentally 'friendly' actions help all problems.

In a study of primary schoolchildren, Boyes and Stanisstreet[39] found that most children were aware that generating electricity from renewable sources, using recycled paper and replacing trees would reduce global warming. Although the majority of children realised that a reduction in the use of cars would diminish the greenhouse effect, this idea was less prevalent among older primary schoolchildren. More than half of the children thought that keeping beaches clean or protecting wild species would reduce the greenhouse effect, although the frequency of these ideas was lower among the older children. The most common misconception, held by 87 per cent of the pupils, was that the use of lead-free petrol would reduce global warming and children confused global warming, ozone layer depletion and atmospheric lead pollution. The researchers suggest that it required specific efforts to disentangle these important environmental issues in the minds of children, especially since the problems are not readily open to experiential learning.

Part II

CHILDREN'S IDEAS ABOUT MATERIALS AND THEIR PROPERTIES

8

MATERIALS

OBJECTS AND THE MATERIALS OF WHICH THEY ARE MADE

Children sometimes confuse the name of an object with the name of the material from which it is made.[1] Jones and Lynch[2] found that pupils often perceived samples of materials (such as wood, wax or glass) as objects. Vogelezang[3] has suggested that teachers should help children to discriminate between an object and the materials of which it is made. Unfortunately, the everyday use of some words (for example, 'glass') confuses the issue: sometimes the word 'glass' denotes an object such as a drinking glass and at other times the same word 'glass' denotes the material from which drinking glasses are made.

Smith *et al.*[1] made a study of 32 children aged between 4 and 9 years to find the extent to which they made the distinction between an object and the material of which it is made. Children were shown objects such as paper cups and metal spoons and then asked what they were and what they were made of: these objects were then cut up and the questions were repeated. The responses showed that children as young as 4 have some notion of material that is different from their notion of object. From ages 4–7 they relied on qualities, such as lustre or transparency, of the cut-up pieces to explain why it is still the same material. Older pupils stated explicit principles such as 'cutting does not affect the material' and 'it's still paper because the cup was made of paper'.

MATERIALS AND MATTER/'STUFF'

Although in science the word 'material' is used to designate any kind of matter or 'stuff' that can be observed or detected in the world around us, children may initially use the word to mean those things that are required to make objects – for example, fabrics for clothing or bricks for buildings.

Bouma *et al.*[4] studied the meanings pupils gave to the word 'matter'. They showed that at age 13 only 20 per cent of pupils explained it as something that could be handled and takes up space. At age 16, this proportion was 66 per cent. The remainder either gave the word a non-tangible meaning, no explanation or a confused one. These researchers also found that pupils' first meaning of the word 'material' was a fabric for making clothes. Other meanings offered included 'drawing materials' and 'building materials'.

Although the word 'stuff' may not be accepted as a scientific word, it has tangible connotations for pupils and, therefore, it is useful for developing the idea that there are different kinds of 'stuff' and that they are recognised by their different properties.[4]

Several studies of pupils' initial conception of an atom show that they perceive it either as 'a small piece of a material' or as 'the ultimate bit of material obtained when a portion of material is progressively sub-divided'.[5][6][7] Such 'bits' are thought to vary in size and shape, to have no space between them, and to possess properties similar to the parent material. Thus, for instance, children frequently consider atoms of a solid to have all or most of the macro-properties that they associate with the solid. Consequently, children often attribute to atoms properties such as hardness, hotness/coldness, colour and physical state.[5][6][7] Their view contrasts with a school science one of atoms as the 'preformed building blocks' of material substance.

MIXTURES OF SUBSTANCES

Most of the materials children encounter in everyday life are mixtures and therefore, from a science viewpoint, cannot be regarded as 'pure'. However, some materials (such as air, water, honey, yoghurt and other foods) are frequently labelled 'pure', although they are really mixtures of substances. Consequently, conflict of meaning can arise for pupils[4][8] and student teachers[9] alike.

The tendency for pupils to regard everyday materials as single substances was evident in an interview study where many 15-year-olds were unable to give examples of mixtures or explain them.[10] Children could more readily recognise heterogeneous mixtures, such as granite, than homogeneous ones, such as solutions.

Unlike a pure substance which has constant properties (under given conditions), a mixture has properties that depend on the relative amounts of its component substances. Children do not always appreciate that their statements about the properties of a mixture are of little value unless they state the composition of the mixture too. Cosgrove[11] has suggested ways in which children can develop a science conception of mixtures.

When Meheut et al.[12] allowed 11- to 12-year-old French children to observe and comment on the burning of several different materials in air, most of the children came to the view that air is a mixture of gases of which oxygen is only a part.

PURE (SINGLE) SUBSTANCES

Some 60 to 70 per cent of a sample population of Belgian and Dutch pupils (aged 13) were found to understand the term 'pure substance' as 'not a mixture'. However, for some 13 to 17 per cent of them, the meaning was 'without harmful contents'.[4] When the meaning of the word 'pure' itself was explored, only 45 per cent had the idea of unmixed or clear and 48 per cent had ideas that included 'clean', 'bright', 'beautiful', 'as it should be' and 'accurate'.

Whereas, in science, the word 'material' is very broad in its scope, the word '(chemical) substance' has the specific meaning of a homogeneous kind of matter having a definite composition. Briggs and Holding[10] recommend the early use of the term 'pure substance' or 'single substance' to help children to develop the science meaning of 'chemical substance'.

Vogelezang[3] has pointed out that the concept of 'chemical substance' occupies a central position among chemistry concepts and suggests that careful attention should be given to its development when teaching children. He pleads for careful use of words relating to objects, to materials and to single substances, with an early distinction between 'object' and 'substance'; then a progression from the idea of 'substance' to 'homogeneous substance' and, later, to 'chemical substance'. He argues that when talking to children it is easy to use the word 'substance' ambiguously. A teacher might say 'here are a number of everyday substances: a piece of marble, a brick, a jar of sugar ...' and such a statement leaves pupils in some doubt about the focus of attention – objects? materials? or chemical substances? – although the teacher may be clear on the intended focus of attention.[3]

COMPOUND SUBSTANCES

Although, in science, chemical compounds are regarded as single substances containing two or more elements chemically combined in a fixed proportion by mass, several studies have found that children frequently describe compounds as though they are mixtures of elements.[4 10 13] This may be because they have not formed a science conception of chemical combination of the elements included in a compound's name. Ben-Zvi et al.[14 15] found that children's thinking about compounds at the micro-level is similar to that at the macro-level, namely that component atoms are regarded as 'mixed' or 'joined by glue'. Briggs and Holding[10] found that many 15-year-olds, despite experience of several related science tasks, appeared to be unaware that in most compounds the proportions of combining elements are fixed.

ELEMENTS

Well before being introduced to the idea that a chemical element contains atoms of only one kind (that is, having the same atomic number), children are generally presented with the operational idea that a chemical element is a substance that cannot be decomposed. Although this conception is generally introduced at age 11 or 12, Briggs and Holding[10] have shown that only about 25 per cent of a sample population of about 300 British 15-year-olds were able to apply it. Herron *et al.*[16] suggest that pupils find this conception a difficult one to apply because it is based on prior knowledge of the behaviour of substances rather than on directly observable qualities such as physical state, colour or melting point. As might be expected, some children apply perceptible rather than behaviour criteria, and thereby generate alternative conceptions such as: 'an element is a solid' and 'salt is an element'.

The prevalence among 15-year-olds of the idea that an element is made up of only one kind of atom was explored by Briggs and Holding.[10] About 75 per cent of the sample were able to recognise a diagrammatic representation of a gaseous element. However, some children experienced difficulty in understanding that both polymorphic and polyatomic forms of an element have 'element' status. Difficulties appear to arise because different individuals have different conceptions of an element as the 'simplest type of substance'.

Pupils can readily recognise metals from their perceptible attributes such as the ability to reflect light, to be drawn into wire, to be pounded into thin sheets, to conduct heat and electricity well, to exhibit high strength when pulled, and (after melting) to remain liquid over a wide temperature range. However, Ben-Zvi *et al.*[5] have shown that pupils do not always appreciate that these 'metallic' properties are attributes of the state of aggregation of atoms of particular elements rather than attributes of the atoms themselves. In a diagnostic task concerned with metals, Israeli children were given the physical properties of a piece of copper wire and then asked which of these properties a single atom of copper would possess (if that atom was imagined to be isolated from the copper wire). Similarly, given the properties of the vaporised metal, they were asked which of these properties a single atom of vaporised copper would possess. Almost 50 per cent of the sample population of 288 15-year-olds attributed the same properties to a single atom of copper as they did to a copper wire: they appeared to regard an atom as having the same characteristics as a small piece of metal. Also, 66 per cent of the sample stated that an atom of copper vapour has different properties from an atom of the solid copper: they appeared to regard a change in the physical state of a metal as due to a change within atoms rather than a change in the organisation of the atoms.

Many children appear to have difficulty in restricting the use of the term 'non-metal' to its scientific sense of elements only. When asked to give examples of non-metals, children frequently offer examples such as sugar and wood.[5]

As part of an exploration of 530 Israeli 15- to 16-year-olds' understanding of stoichiometry, Ben-Zvi et al.[14] asked them, 'What is the mass of one atom of hydrogen?' Just under 40 per cent answered, 'One gram'.

CONSERVATION OF MATTER

Several studies have shown that the way in which pupils perceive a chemical or physical change may determine whether or not they regard material substance as being conserved during that change.[6][17][18] For example, if their view of a particular change is dominated by the apparent disappearance of some material(s), then pupils are unlikely to conserve the mass. Further, pupils' ideas about the physical state of a material are found to influence how they interpret a change. If, for example, they regard gases as weightless, then they are unlikely to conserve overall weight or mass in reactions that involve gases.

Pupils' ideas about conservation also appear to be influenced by whether they view materials as continuous or as discontinuous.[6][19] Holding[6] found that, although pupils may be able to conserve when they have an initial continuous view of matter, newly constructed atomistic views can, for a period of time, undermine their ability to conserve mass through a change. For example, in changes where a pupil imagines a material dispersed as very small particles, such particles may be regarded as having a negligible individual weight or as more spread out and seemingly less dense (heavy).

MASS

Researchers have found that, from an early age, children notice how objects differ in the way they appear to 'press down' on the hands, shoulder or head: they learn to 'feel the weight' of objects. Children compare objects by their 'felt weight' and, over time, generate an idea that 'felt weight' is a characteristic property of an object.[6][20]

Holding[6] investigated the development of the idea of an object being pulled down by a force (rather than actually pressing downwards), and also the development of the concept of mass. Both conceptual changes appeared to develop slowly. Mass often became associated with the phonetically similar word 'massive' and, in that way, was conflated with size or volume. In that event pupils often estimated the mass of a material from its bulk appearance.

DENSITY

Smith *et al.*[1] found that children's earliest notion of density may be described by the phrase 'heavy for size'. This notion begins to appear between the ages of 5 and 7. Prior to that age children seemed to have separate conceptions of weight (that is 'felt weight') and size. For example, when deciding which blocks would cause a bridge to collapse, young children judged 'weight' by lifting the objects rather than by observing their size. For them, size was not yet part of their weight concept; they could selectively focus on size – ignoring 'felt weight' – and vice versa, but they did not bring the two together. However, between the ages of 5 and 7 the notion of density ('heavy for size') appears to be added to the child's notion of 'weight' such that 'weight' and 'density' are not differentiated but included in a general notion of 'heaviness'.

Piaget[21] found that notions of weight and density develop as children begin to take account of viewpoints other than their own. Initially, children may judge that a pebble is 'light', but sometime later may express the view that the pebble is 'light for them' but 'heavy for water'. At ages 9 and 10 they begin to relate the density of one material to that of another. For example, children say that a material floats because it is 'lighter than the water'.

Investigating the application of a particle model of density, Hewson[22] showed that, although some students aged 14–22 relate the density of materials to denseness in the packing of particles, explanations may be inadequate or incomplete: their conceptions of mass and volume depend on their conceptions of the arrangement, the concentration and the mass of the particles.

Rowell *et al.*,[23] in their study of sixty Australian 11-year-old pupils, found that over 80 per cent had misconceptions about volume which could present serious difficulties for understanding density.

CLASSIFYING MATERIALS

In the study of materials, pupils are expected to develop skills in classifying not only several types of materials encountered daily but also the changes that materials undergo. James and Nelson[24] suggest that pupils need to recognise items which fit into more than one class or which cannot satisfactorily be fitted into any recognised class.

9

SOLIDS, LIQUIDS AND GASES

THE SOLID STATE

Several researchers have investigated pupils' ideas about solids.[1][2][3] For example, Stavy and Stachel[1] studied the developing ideas about solid materials held by Israeli children aged 5–13. Their research indicates that younger children tend to regard any rigid material as a solid, any powder as a liquid and any non-rigid material (for example, plasticine, sponge and cloth) as intermediate between a solid and a liquid. Pupils explained that powders are liquids because they 'can be poured' and that non-rigid materials are neither solid nor liquid because they are 'soft' or 'crumble' or 'can be torn'. Thus children decided the state of a material according to its appearance and behaviour with the result that they associated solidity with hardness, strength and non-malleability.

By the age of 11, pupils tended to regard a powder as being in an intermediate state rather than as a liquid. The researchers suggest that, at age 11, teachers might encourage the development of the idea that a powder is composed of small pieces of solid. (Although this is a useful development of ideas, these researchers warn that, when subsequently learning the particulate theory of solids, pupils may wrongly infer that the theoretical particles are 'powder grains'. It is suggested, therefore, that, before they learn particulate theory, pupils should be capable of classifying materials according to a science view of the states of matter.)

From a child's viewpoint, the conversion of a bulk solid to a powdered solid or to a liquid is likely to result in a decrease in mass.[1][4]

THE LIQUID STATE

Stavy and Stachel[1] found that children appear to identify a liquid as a material that is 'runny' or 'can be poured'. Consequently, their view of liquids includes materials, such as powders, outside the accepted science classification. Further, because in a child's view, the exemplary liquid is water, all liquids may be regarded as 'watery', or 'made of water', or

79

'containing water'. Jones and Lynch[2] noticed that some children found the task of classifying more viscous liquids such as paste, honey and tomato sauce to be more problematic than classifying 'runny' ones.

Children may regard the liquid form of a material as having less weight (or, occasionally, more weight) than the same mass of its solid form. Similarly, they may regard the liquid form of a material as having more weight than the same mass of its gaseous form.[1,4]

THE GASEOUS STATE

Several researchers[5,6,7,8,9,10] have studied pupils' conception of 'gas' and found that they do not appear initially to be aware that air and other gases possess material character. For example, although young children may have said that air and smoke exist, they regarded such materials as having transient character similar to that of 'thoughts'. In many children's thinking, air and gas appear to have contrasting affective connotations: air is 'good' and it is used for breathing and for life; gas is 'bad' because it may be poisonous, dangerous or inflammable.

Later, pupils develop an awareness of the material character of gases. They come to regard gases as materials which spread and they recognise that some gases can be seen even though most are colourless, odourless and transparent. However, pupils may not regard 'gas' as having weight or mass. Leboutet-Barrell[11] suggests that this is because children's most common related experience is that gases tend to rise or float. This view is supported by studies which show that children aged 9–13 tend to predict that gases have the property of negative weight and hence that the more gas that is added to a container, the lighter the container becomes.[5,10] Until they construct the idea that gases have mass, pupils are unlikely to conserve mass when describing chemical changes that involve gases as either reactants or products.[8]

MELTING

When they observe a solid changing to liquid, pupils may think that it loses weight or mass.[1,4,12] Stavy[12] presented pupils with two samples of ice having identical weights. She melted one sample of ice and then interviewed pupils about the relative weights of the two samples. The proportion of the sample who conserved weight (or mass) was 5 per cent at ages 5 and 6, 50 per cent at age 7 and 75 per cent at age 10.

Young children do not always discriminate between melting and dissolving. Although two materials are required for the dissolving process, children tend to focus only on the solid and they regard the process as 'melting'.[13,14,17,22] Cosgrove and Osborne[15] found that many children in their sample of 8- to 17-year-olds regarded melting as similar to dissolving in that it is a gradual process and, in their view, almost unconnected with a particular temperature.

FREEZING

Throughout their interview studies concerning changes of state, Cosgrove and Osborne[15] noticed that pupils generally do not regard a change of state as being related to a specific temperature.

EVAPORATION

Several researchers have attempted to trace the development of a conception of evaporation.[16 17 18 19 20 21 22] For example Bar[17] found that children at ages 5 and 6 are impressed by the disappearance of material, accept that it happens and offer no explanation. It is not until ages 8–10 that they are likely to attempt to conserve the vaporised substance when they suggest that the disappearing liquid must go to some place. Such a place, in their view, has the character of a receptacle but at this age the only 'receptacle' they can think of is a solid container or a supporting surface: both of which they may regard as porous. Later, when they developed a concept of 'static air', pupils suggested that bits of water go into the (receptacle) 'air'. Not surprisingly, the evaporation concept appears to be dependent on the development of notions of conservation, atomism and (invisible) air, and a conception of evaporation which links these three notions is quite prevalent by the age of 12–14.

When children observe a liquid changing to a gas or vapour, they may construct the idea that, because material substance seems to disappear, weight or mass is lost. Moreover, those who conserve substance may generate the idea that a gas is lighter than the same amount of liquid. Both of these ideas were noted by Stavy[12] in a study where Israeli children were shown two sealed tubes containing identical masses of acetone. She heated one of them until the acetone completely evaporated and asked individuals to estimate the relative weights of the acetone samples. At age 9, the proportion who conserved weight was about 5 per cent – this proportion increased steadily to 80 per cent by age 14. In general, the younger pupils suggested that the gaseous form of acetone has no weight whereas the older pupils suggested that liquid acetone is heavier than the gaseous form.

Bar and Travis[16] found that pupils' understanding of boiling precedes that of the evaporation of liquids from surfaces such as floors, saucers and roads. They found that 70 per cent of a sample of 6- to 8-year-olds understood that when water is boiling vapour comes from it, that the quantity of water decreases and that the vapour is made of water.

However, the same children said that when a solid object, such as a wet saucer, dries then water just disappears or else it penetrates the solid object.

BOILING

Andersson[23] investigated Swedish pupils' understanding of the idea that the boiling point of a pure substance (at a particular pressure) is definite and does not vary with either the time of boiling or with the energy supplied. He set children two problems regarding what would happen if the water continued to be heated for a further five minutes. Of 12-year-olds, 40 per cent responded that the temperature would be greater than 100°C, with the majority of this group explaining that water gets hotter the longer it is heated. The number of children offering this answer fell with age but 16 per cent of 15-year-olds still felt that the temperature would be greater than 100°C. Of those children suggesting that the temperature would remain at 100°C, 25 per cent of 12- and 13-year-olds explained their answer in terms of the switch number of the stove determining the temperature of the water. The proportion of children offering this explanation was 35 per cent in 14-year-olds and 32 per cent in 15-year-olds. Andersson's second problem required the children to suggest what would happen if the setting of the stove were increased. Here 80 per cent of children aged 12 thought that the temperature would increase above 100°C. This response was also given by 63 per cent of 13-year-olds, 60 per cent of 14-year-olds and 54 per cent of 15-year-olds. Even by age 15 only 31 per cent gave correct answers and appropriate explanations of both problems. Thus some children's logic had led them to think that time of boiling and energy supply could influence the boiling point of a pure liquid. Much of the confusion arises from the child's view that heat and temperature are the same thing and so, they argue, if you increase the amount of heat you will increase the temperature.

CONDENSATION

Ideas concerning the condensation of water on a vessel containing ice have been explored among Israeli children by Bar and Travis[16] and among New Zealand children by Osborne and Cosgrove.[4] Both groups of researchers used a multiple choice procedure in which the alternative choices were based on previously obtained interview responses. Israeli children aged 10–14 chose most frequently the responses 'the coldness changed into water' and 'cold caused hydrogen and oxygen to change into water'. (Approximately 40 per cent chose each alternative.) Less than 20 per cent chose the response 'the water condensed from water vapour in the air'. As a result of comparing these with other responses by the same pupils, the researchers conclude that, although pupils know that vapour can be changed to water, applying that knowledge appeared to cause some difficulty. New Zealand 12- to 17-year-olds most frequently chose the response 'the coldness caused oxygen and hydrogen in the air to form water'. (Around 60 per cent did so between ages 12 and 15, and 30 per cent at age 17.) Less than 15 per cent chose 'the coldness comes through the glass and turns to water'. The proportion who expressed the view that the condensation results from water in the air increased with age from 10 per cent to 55 per cent between ages 12 and 17.

The same Israeli pupils were asked to explain how a hand can become wet when held above boiling water.[16] There was an almost even distribution of two responses: 'the vapour changes into water' and 'the hand became wet from the vapour'. The frequency of the former response increased with age between ages 10 and 14, from 20 per cent to 55 per cent respectively. Only a small proportion of the sample chose the responses 'the hand sweats' and 'hydrogen and oxygen changed to water'.

SUBLIMATION

When pupils observe a solid changing to a gas, they may construct the idea that weight or mass is lost. Stavy[22] showed children two sealed tubes containing identical masses of iodine, then heated one of them (thereby filling that tube with purple gas). She asked pupils to estimate the relative weights of the iodine in the two tubes. At age 9 the proportion who conserve weight was about 30 per cent. This increased with age to around 50 per cent at age 11–13 and then to 80 per cent by age 15.

DISSOLVING

Ideas about dissolving and solution

Several researchers[14 15 24 25 26 27] have found that, from an early age through to adulthood, there are several conceptions of 'dissolving'. Some of these are revealed by the words used to describe what happens to sugar placed in water. Up to age 8, there is a tendency to focus on the solute only and say it 'just goes', 'disappears', 'melts away', 'dissolves away' or 'turns into water'.[25] When the response 'melts' is probed, many children tend to describe it as similar to ice 'going runny'. Frequently, older pupils imagine that as sugar dissolves 'it goes into tiny little bits'. Later on some say that 'sugar molecules fill spaces between water molecules' or else 'mix with water molecules'.

Some researchers[25 28 29 30 31] have explored the conservation aspect of dissolving. Holding[25] investigated pupils' ideas about conservation (of substance, weight/mass and volume) by using interviews about practical tasks, together with surveys of written tasks and children's diagrams. About 67 per cent of 8-year-olds thought that the substance dissolved is preserved in some form. However, when probed about the weight of the solution, only about 50 per cent of those who said the sugar is 'there' also say that 'it weighs something'. It seems the reason for this apparent discrepancy was that some children thought the weight of the sugar was now 'up in the water', that is in a 'suspended' state, so that, in their view, sugar was not 'pressing down' on the bottom of a container. The gap between the proportion of pupils who conserve substance and those who conserve weight widens through ages 9–11 but then narrows in later school years. Initially a steadily increasing proportion, with age, conserve substance but a decreasing proportion conserve weight. However, after age 8, pupils increasingly generate more ideas about the kind of changes that they imagine the solute undergoes (they refer to 'bits' of solute, 'liquid' solute, 'atoms' of solute). However, they do not regard weight as a gravitational force acting on the 'bits', 'liquid', or other imagined forms of solute. After age 12, many pupils begin to develop a gravitational view of weight and also a science conception of mass so that eventually many, but by no means all, conserve both weight and mass of solute.

In school science pupils are expected to regard a solution as a homogeneous mixture of two or more substances. However, several studies have shown that they hold a variety of ideas about solutions.[15 25 32 33 34 35] Holding[25] found that in the early school years, some children did not regard a sugar solution as a single phase but, instead, held the idea that invisible gross particles of sugar remain. Children suggested that the particles can be filtered out or may settle out from the solution. Other children, because they did not see a boundary between solute and solvent, regarded a solution as a single substance rather than as a homogeneous mixture.

Gaseous solution

In addition to constructing the idea of a solution in the liquid state, pupils are expected to develop a conception of a solution in the gaseous state, as exemplified by air. Meheut et al.[36] report that young children often hold to the idea that a mixture such as air is one substance.

10

CHEMICAL CHANGE

MIXTURES OF SUBSTANCES

Most of the materials children encounter in everyday life are mixtures which, from a science viewpoint, cannot be regarded as pure. Consequently, conflict of meaning may arise when these materials are labelled 'pure'.[1] [2] [3] Not only pupils but also student teachers suffer confusion.[4] Although about 60 to 70 per cent of a sample population of Belgian and Dutch pupils (aged 13) were found to understand that 'pure substance' meant 'not a mixture', for some 13 to 17 per cent the meaning was 'without harmful contents'. When the meaning of the word 'pure' itself was explored, just 45 per cent had the idea of unmixed but 48 per cent had ideas that included 'clean', 'bright', 'beautiful', 'as it should be' and 'accurate'.[1]

CHEMICAL CHANGE

Although in science the term 'chemical change' is reserved for processes in which the reacting chemical substances disappear and other (new) substances appear, several studies have found that children often use the term 'chemical change' to encompass changes in physical state and other physical transformations, particularly so when the colour of a substance alters.[3] [5] [6]

Some educators do not distinguish between physical and chemical changes on theoretical grounds but others find such a distinction useful for the development of science ideas.[7] [8] [9] How well pupils make such a distinction depends partly on their conception of 'substance'. For instance, if they regard ice as a different substance from water, then they are likely to classify the melting of ice as a chemical change. Vogelezang[10] has suggested that substances should be regarded as identical if their properties are identical when compared under the same conditions.

Andersson[11] [12] and Pfundt[13] have investigated children's notions of chemical changes. They appear to fall into six main types:

85

- no conception other than 'it just happens like that';
- matter just disappears: when petrol is used as a fuel 'it just vanishes';
- product materials, though unseen, must somehow be contained in the starting materials (for example, some think that the water which results from the distillation of wood must already have existed as such in wood);
- the product material is just a modified form of the starting material: 'as the alcohol burns it turns into alcohol vapour';
- the starting material undergoes transmutation to the product material: 'the steel wool that burnt has turned into carbon';
- starting materials interact and form a different product: 'oxygen reacts with copper and forms copper oxide'.[5] [14] [16]

Pupils tend to identify a chemical reaction by unusual and unexpected happenings: fizz, explosion or change of colour. Consequently, it is doubtful whether, initially, they interpret such happenings as indicators of changes of substances into other substances.[1] From a science viewpoint, evidence for chemical change is obtained by ascertaining differences in properties, that is, by observing whether individual products have different densities, crystalline forms, melting points or boiling points, from the reactants. Briggs and Holding[3] found that 75 per cent of their sample suggested that an apparent change in overall mass could provide evidence for a chemical change. Clearly, pupils' ideas of both chemical change and conservation of mass needed attention.

Stavridou and Solomonidou[14] explored the conceptions of eighteen daily phenomena held by fifteen Greek pupils aged between 8 and 17 years. From a science viewpoint, nine of those phenomena were regarded as physical and nine as chemical changes. The researchers' general conclusion was that children who used the reversibility criterion were able to distinguish between physical and chemical changes, whereas those who used other criteria failed to do so. Pupils who used the reversibility criterion considered a reversible change to be non-radical and therefore physical. Unlike science teachers, who consider most chemical reactions to be reversible, such children consider chemical changes to be irreversible. All the criteria offered in pupils' responses were macroscopic in character; they made no reference to microscopic ideas about substances.

In general, pupils find difficulty in developing an adequate conception of the chemical combination of elements until they can interpret 'combination' at the molecular level. Furthermore, the science idea of a chemical compound depends upon an understanding of chemical combination. Novick and Nussbaum[15] explored the particle models held by 13- to 14-year-old Israelis by asking them to explain the formation of 'white smoke' from the gases ammonia and hydrogen chloride. Of those who held a particulate view, 55 per cent thought there was a combination of the gases and 30 per cent thought that gases simply form a mixture where they meet. The corresponding percentages for those holding a continuous view of matter were 18 per cent and 51 per cent respectively.

Laverty and McGarvey[16] investigated pupils' particulate representations of chemical combination by asking groups of children first to discuss the reaction between magnesium and oxygen in terms of what happens to their component particles and then to represent their ideas diagrammatically. The types of representation of chemical combination included:

- a random mixture of particles;
- oxygen particles surrounding the magnesium particles;
- two magnesium and one oxygen particle, or one magnesium and two oxygen particles, joined;
- an assembly of joined magnesium and oxygen particles arranged alternately and described as 'being the same all the way through'.

COMBUSTION

Pupils' ideas about combustion and other combination reactions have been the subject of several studies.[13 17 18 19 20 21 22 23 24] Studies of 11- and 12-year-olds' ideas about the role of air in burning suggest that most of them appreciate that air (or oxygen) is needed for burning, although the function of air is not generally understood.[23 24]

Meheut et al.[23] explored the ideas about combustion held by 400 French 11- to 12-year-olds and found that the pupils' ideas were 'far removed' from the concept of a chemical reaction between a substance and oxygen. For example, although oxygen was perceived as necessary for combustion, it was not regarded as interacting with the combustible material. Some combustibles were said to be unable to burn: they were said to have merely 'melted' or 'evaporated'. Some pupils appeared to hold the view that a combustible substance is made up of the substances that eventually appear as combustion products.

Pfundt[13] interviewed ten children aged 8–13 as they observed the burning of alcohol. Their main conception of reaction was that alcohol ceases to exist (is irreversibly destroyed) and gases come into existence. Another idea was that 'burning is similar to evaporation, except that it is faster due to the heat'. Consequently, it was thought that the alcohol could be recovered from the gases.

Andersson and Renstrom[17] and Donnelly and Welford[18] investigated the ideas of 15-year-olds about changes of mass on combustion. They found that quite large proportions (60 per cent) of those having above average ability predicted loss of mass on the combustion of iron wool. Their reasons included: that iron is lost through burning; that air or moisture is lost from the wool; and that powder weighs less. Ideas about the combustion of phosphorus were also explored. Only 34 per cent expected mass to be conserved and again the idea that air or phosphorus was lost accounted for the large proportion of predictions of a decrease in mass.

DECOMPOSITION

Ideas about decomposition reactions have been explored by Pfundt[13] and de Vos and Verdonk.[25] Pfundt interviewed ten German 8- to 13-year-olds as they observed the heating of copper sulphate in an open crucible. Their ideas about decomposition included: drying (two pupils), bleaching (two pupils), the formation of ash – 'white and crumbly' (six pupils). Some thought that only the appearance changed, a 'drying idea', while others thought that the substance itself changed, an 'ashing idea'. When they dripped water on to the 'ash', those with the 'ashing' conception changed their view to the idea that the copper sulphate 'must have stayed'. After observing the reversibility of the process, all the children concluded that copper sulphate must have remained the same: it had only changed its properties.

INTERACTION

It appears difficult for pupils to appreciate that, in a physical or chemical change involving two or more materials, there is a mutual interaction. Pupils tend to focus their attention on one of the participating materials and then regard that one material as the cause of an observed change. In the context of dissolving they tend to regard water as solely responsible for dissolving sugar, as though the sugar does not participate[26] and Meheut et al.[23] found that some pupils view a chemical reaction in a similar way. For example, oxygen, although regarded as necessary for combustion, may not be regarded as a reacting substance.

CONSERVATION OF MATTER THROUGH CHANGE

Despite several years' experience of school science, many pupils do not appear to appreciate the quantitative aspects of chemical change, particularly the fixed masses of reacting substances and the conservation of overall mass. Briggs and Holding,[3] in their study of a sample population of about 300 British 15-year-olds, found that only 30 per cent of them understood that fixed masses of reacting substances participate in chemical reactions.

Several studies have shown that the way in which pupils perceive a chemical or physical change may determine whether or not they regard material substance as being conserved during that change.[24] [26] [27] For example, if their view of a particular change is dominated by the apparent disappearance of some material(s), then pupils are unlikely to conserve the mass. Further, pupils' ideas about the physical state of the material are found to influence how they interpret a change. If, for example, they regard gases as weightless, then they are unlikely to conserve overall weight or mass in reactions that involve gases.

Pupils' ideas about conservation also appear to be influenced by whether they view materials as either continuous or particulate.[26] [28] Holding [26] found that, although pupils may be able to conserve when they have a continuous view of matter, newly constructed atomistic views can, for a period of time, undermine their ability to conserve mass through a change. For example, in changes where a pupil imagines that a material substance is dispersed as very small fragments, such fragments may be regarded as each having a negligible weight or as more spread out and seemingly less dense (heavy).

ENERGY AND CHEMICAL CHANGE

Children have difficulty in classifying the burning of a candle as 'exothermic': they point out that heat is needed to light it. Researchers de Vos and Verdonk[29] suggest that pupils are unable to estimate and compare the amounts of energy involved in the (supposed) two stages. Pupils applied similar reasoning to the reaction of copper with oxygen: they said, 'Copper oxide is only formed when a copper sheet is heated in a gas flame'. In the light of pupils' difficulty, these researchers decided to teach energy changes by using reactions which show a spontaneous rise or fall in temperature. They chose the reaction of steel wool with copper sulphate solution because, not only could the new substances be readily identified, but the temperature change could be felt. Most pupils recognised that there was some relationship between the temperature rise and the reaction. Some regarded the rise in temperature as a result or a product of the reaction whereas others regarded it as part of the reaction itself.

In the second reaction studied by de Vos and Verdonk students added 2 ml portions of 2M hydrochloric acid to 10 ml of 2M sodium hydroxide solution. They recorded the temperature after each addition of acid until 16 ml had been added. They were encouraged to graph the data and discuss many aspects of the observed results: the reasons for the shape of the curve; the effect of interchanging the reagents, and of adding more base at the end of the experiment. Some students suggested that five reactions had taken place – perhaps their substance concept had not lost its quantitative aspect. Some overlooked the physical effect of excess reagent and said that the reaction was accompanied by a negative heat effect.

De Vos and Verdonk[29] have also shown that, when describing a chemical change, children often fail to distinguish between heat and temperature. When pupils observed that the temperature of a candle flame remains constant, many suggested that no more heat was being given out.

In order to help children make sense of their experiences. Holman[30] has suggested that teachers should develop five conceptual areas: the meaning of energy; energy transformation; the storage of energy in chemicals; the degradation of energy; the conservation of energy during transformation.

'NEW' SUBSTANCES

A chemical change is recognised by the disappearance of the reacting (old) substances and the appearance of other (new) substances. Pupils are expected to make this recognition by comparing the physical and chemical properties of the 'old' substances with those of the 'new' substances.[10] However, in daily life 'property' means something that is owned by someone. Consequently, pupils often find it difficult to use the word 'property' in science where it means a characteristic feature of a material – a feature that may be used to identify it and/or distinguish it from another material. Johnston[31] obtained a better classroom response among 12- to 13-year-olds by asking 'What things about this material make it different from that material?' than by requiring pupils to describe the 'properties' of a material.

Several researchers have shown that children appear to have difficulty distinguishing physical and chemical changes.[6] [9] [14] [15] [32] However, pupils eventually learn to relate properties to the (internal) structure of a particular material and to its uses.

ACIDS AND BASES

Carr[33] has suggested that pupils' ideas about acids are derived from sensory experiences such as tasting sour milk, lemons and vinegar, and from the crime stories about acid baths, advertisements for anti-acid remedies, and news about the effects of acid rain.

Hand and Treagust[34] interviewed seventy-eight pupils, aged 15, about their conceptions of acids. They found that the two major conceptions were 'acids eat material away' and 'acids can burn you'. Further probing revealed two other widely held ideas: that 'the only test for an acid is to see whether it eats something away' and that 'strong acids eat away material faster than weak acids'. Hand and Treagust then tried out a 'conflict' teaching strategy in an attempt to enhance student learning of acids and bases. However, one-third of the students still did not perceive the reactions of acids with either metals or calcium carbonate as 'properties of an acid'. Instead, they regarded them as further examples of 'acids eating something away'.

Hand[35] tested 17-year-olds some two years after they had been taught (and given a repeat of the same test) about the characteristics of acids. He found that they scored less well the second time on those tasks related to defining the term 'acid' and testing for an acid. However, they scored better on describing the difference between 'acid strength' and 'acid concentration'. Hand interprets these findings in the light of several factors such as other subjects studied, the construction of ideas, motivation and attitude.

Carr[33] found evidence that students are often confused by the several science models of acids and bases because, although words and ideas change their meaning from one model to another, students are not always made aware of this. He recommends that teachers and texts give clear indications of when a new model is being introduced or used, how the new model differs from previous ones and why the new model works better.

Because the term 'base', as used in chemistry, is less prevalent in daily life than 'acid', pupils are less likely to form preconceptions of bases before they are taught about them. Usually, pupils are made aware of bases when, after being introduced to acids, teachers provide sensory experiences of soluble bases. (For example, their soapy feel and their effect on dyes.) Hand and Treagust[34] found that the only idea about bases held by 15-year-olds was the erroneous one that 'a base is something that makes up an acid'. The continuing difficulty individuals have with bases is illustrated by a study of 400 first-year university students when Cros et al.[36] found that 43 per cent of them were unable to name more than two bases.

11

PARTICLES

DEVELOPMENT OF PARTICLE IDEAS ABOUT MATERIALS

When Piaget[1] interviewed children about the behaviour of several different materials, he concluded that some children spontaneously generate the idea that materials are composed of 'small bits' or 'particles' or 'atoms'. However, further research has shown that children attribute to such 'atoms' characteristics that are quite different from those attributed by scientists. Pupils often regard 'atoms' as 'small bits of solid' (or as 'small drops of liquid') that are static, non-uniform and without cohesive force.[2][3][4] Such ideas might be regarded as intermediate models along the 'journey' from a continuous (non- particulate) view of matter to a science atomistic view of it.[5][6]

Pfundt and other researchers have found that children's initial conception of an atom is 'a small piece of material substance' or 'the ultimate bit of material substance obtained by progressively sub-dividing material'.[2][3][4] Children appear to think that such 'bits' vary in size and shape, having no space between them, and that they possess similar properties to the parent material. Children frequently consider atoms of a solid to have all or most of the macro-properties that they associate with the solid. Consequently, children often attribute to atoms (rather than to assemblies of atoms) properties such as hardness, hotness/coldness, colour, physical state and so on.[2][3][4] Researchers de Vos and Verdonk[7] have reported on a classroom exercise designed to follow children's thinking as they begin to construct an idea of 'molecules' of substance.

Particle ideas about solids

Dow et al.,[8] in exploring secondary school pupils' particle ideas, found that although they could depict the solid state as an ordered arrangement of molecules, they gave no reason why the structure should hold together, nor were they able to explain the incompressibility of solids. When prompted to adjust their model to account for incompressibility, they could not explain the vibration of molecules. These researchers concluded that the pupils understood most attributes of the particle model 'one at a time' but were 'not able to pull all these attributes together as a single conception of molecular behaviour within a solid'.

Holding's study[3] of nearly 600 pupils' pictorial representations of the inside of a sugar crystal showed that, at each of the ages 8, 10, 12, 15 and 17, ideas ranged from continuous, through continuous-bits to taught science representations of particles. The proportion of the latter increased with age. Indeed, about 20 per cent of pupils still had a continuous (non-particulate) view at age 17. Other tendencies that increased with age were: for random structures to be replaced by more ordered ones; for non- uniform 'atoms' to be replaced by uniform ones; and for non-bonded structures to be replaced by bonded ones.

Particle ideas about liquids

Children's ideas about liquids are quite different from the science idea that liquids are composed of tiny invisible particles in constant motion which roll over one another. Before instruction children tend to regard liquids as continuous (non-particulate) and static, but Novick and Nussbaum[9] found that, even after instruction in the kinetic theory, over 10 per cent of a sample of 13- to 14-year-olds depicted the particles of air as changed to continuous liquid air when sufficiently cooled. These pupils did not appear to apply the particle model to liquids. Dow et al.,[8] investigating the particle ideas of liquids held by secondary school pupils, found that children's misconceptions arose mainly from regarding the liquid state as a halfway state between solid and gas. As a result, pupils held ideas that greatly over-estimated the spacing and speed of the particles of a liquid. Often their idea of random motion did not include speed, but only direction. Further, they expected the molecules to slow down over time. These researchers suggest that a liquid based on the pupils' particulate conceptions of a liquid would not have a fixed volume. The molecules would just move apart from each other. The liquid would also be compressible. Moreover, the pupil's model would not allow explanation of the process of evaporation.

Particle ideas about gases

Several research studies of particle ideas concerning the gaseous state, held by students and teachers, have been reported.[8,9,10,11,12,13] Novick and Nussbaum[9] studied the conceptions of the gaseous state held by 13- to 14-year-olds who had already been instructed in the particulate theory of matter. Pupils were shown a Buchner flask, containing air. A hand pump was attached and then operated to remove some of the air. Subsequently, children were asked to depict what the air would look like (imagining that they could see it) before and after operating the pump. They were also asked several questions: 'Which in your view is the best of several pictures of air drawn by other pupils?', 'What is between the dots in the particle pictures?' and 'Why don't particles fall to the bottom of the flask?'. About 60 per cent of the sample population indicated that gas is composed of particles; 46 per cent said there is empty space between particles; and 50 per cent said that intrinsic motion accounts for the distribution of particles in space. These researchers report a similar study of older students[14] and they propose the use of a conceptual-conflict-based teaching strategy for particle theory.[15]

Ben-Zvi et al.[16] explored the way in which 337 Israeli 15-year-olds visualised the symbol $O_2(g)$. They found that only 10 per cent represented it as many scattered molecules of oxygen, although 68 per cent of the same sample population had, in another task, satisfactorily depicted an element in the gaseous state.

PARTICLE IDEAS ABOUT CHANGE OF STATE

Particle ideas about melting

Osborne and Cosgrove[17] interviewed forty-three Australian 13- to 17-year-olds about what happens to a block of ice held on a teaspoon. Only eight of them described the melting of ice in particle terms. Generally, pupils held the view that heat makes the particles move further apart. They appeared to use the underlying model that 'the volume of substance increases as its temperature rises', when unfortunately this model does not apply to melting ice.

Particle ideas about freezing

Osborne and Cosgrove[17] found that, across the age range 8–17, pupils' explanations of the freezing process were expressed in terms of particles becoming more packed together. ('They go more compact.') That idea may lead them on to reason that 'ice doesn't take up as much room as when it is a liquid or gas'. Although eight of the older pupils interviewed had been taught about latent heat and hydrogen bonding, none of them mentioned these concepts in explaining freezing.

Particle ideas about evaporation and condensation

Osborne and Cosgrove[17] also report that, of the forty-three Australian 13- to 17-year-olds interviewed, only eight mentioned particles or molecules when describing what happened to water evaporating from a plate. At least one was aware that the particles were 'getting energy from somewhere and flying off'. The possible sources of energy mentioned were: 'what they've got' or 'each other' or 'the air around'. Although the majority of the 13- to 17-year-olds gave macroscopic descriptions of condensation, a few suggested that 'water molecules moved closer together'. Just one student, a 17-year-old, said that 'the molecules lose energy and become water . . . they form up with links between each molecule'.

Novick and Nussbaum[9] asked 13- to 14-year-olds to draw the particles in a flask containing air which had been cooled and liquified. About 70 per cent drew closely located particles on the bottom and on the walls of the container. Just over 10 per cent drew a continuous representation of the liquid despite having been given a particle picture of 'the gas before cooling'. It appears that these students regarded the liquid state as continuous and the gaseous one as particulate.

Particle ideas about solution

Holding[3] investigated the use of a particle view of dissolving among pupils aged 8–17. He asked five groups of pupils (each of over 100 pupils aged 8, 10, 12, 15 and 17 respectively) to place some sugar in water and stir the mixture until the sugar could no longer be seen. He then asked them to draw their idea of what was 'there', assuming they could see the resulting liquid with 'super' eyes. The majority of children depicted 'bits of sugar' distributed in several ways without drawing the water. This representation reached a peak close to age 12 at about 65 per cent. The next most prevalent picture of a solution was 'continuous' shading throughout. This apparently non-particulate view reached a peak between ages 10 and 12 at just over 20 per cent. Molecules were rarely mentioned in the earlier years but later an appreciable proportion depicted 'molecular particles' of sugar – at age 15 (30 per cent) and age 17 (50 per cent) – but only half of these pupils also depicted molecules of water. It would appear that a continuous view of water is still quite prevalent in older pupils' thinking about solutions.

Pfundt[4] interviewed forty-nine German 13- to 15-year-olds about the crystallisation of copper sulphate from a solution a few days after dissolving that salt in water. She found only four of them expressing a particle view of the crystallising process.

ATTRIBUTES OF PARTICLES

Conceptions of atomic size and mass

In a study of children's explanations of what happens to a dissolved substance, Holding[3] found that although many pupils eventually construct the idea that an atom or molecule is the smallest structural unit of a substance they often have difficulty appreciating the minuteness of atoms and molecules. At a later stage, when some appreciation of the minuteness of atoms and molecules began to emerge, pupils reasoned that, because atoms and molecules are so small, they have zero or negligible mass.

From an exploration of 530 Israeli 15- to 16-year-olds' understanding of the combination of elements in compounds, Ben-Zvi et al.[18] suggest that pupils have difficulty in coping with the early emphasis on concrete ball and stick models of single interacting particles and, at the same time, holding the idea of millions and millions of particles involved in any observed change.

Conceptions of the internal structure of molecules

When Ben-Zvi et al.[18] studied more than 300 Israeli 15-year-olds' diagrams of molecules of a compound, they found that one-third of them represented N_2O_4 either as two connected, or as two disconnected, fragments of N_2 and O_4. This additive type of representation was given consistently with similar questions in different situations. When asked to draw diagrams of molecules in the gaseous state, pupils depicted the distance between the atoms in the molecule as being much greater. This is perhaps the result of misapplying learned particulate representations of the kinetic theory.

PARTICLE MODELS OF ELEMENTS AND COMPOUNDS

As a result of school science studies, pupils are expected, eventually, to abandon a continuous (non-particulate) view of chemical substances and to understand that each element or compound can be represented as a structure or pattern of its component units – whether these units are atoms, molecules or ions. In addition, they are expected to appreciate that such units are held together by forces (chemical bonds) and that they are not merely mixed and/or 'glued' together. Against the background of these goals many studies have shown that, in their several individual journeys towards the science view, pupils may generate a variety of 'intermediate' mental pictures of the structure of materials.[1 4 5 8 9 10 14] Nussbaum and Novick[15] have developed a teaching strategy in which such journeys are taken into account.

The prevalence of the idea that an element is made up of one kind of atom was explored by Briggs and Holding.[19] They found that about 75 per cent of the sample of about 300 British 15-year-olds were able to recognise a particulate representation of a gaseous element.

Selley[20] has argued that, in textbooks and classroom discourse, chemical substances and their molecular particles are frequently confused. Two of the examples he quotes are: 'the synthesis of complicated molecules from simpler substances', and 'hydrogen ions are reduced to hydrogen gas'.

In general, pupils find difficulty in developing an adequate conception of the chemical combination of elements until they can interpret 'combination' at the particle level. However, a particulate view does not ensure an understanding of chemical combination, as Novick and Nussbaum[9] found when they explored the particle models held by 13- to 14-year-old Israelis. Pupils were asked to explain the formation of 'white smoke' from the gases ammonia and hydrogen chloride. Of those who held a particulate view, 55 per cent thought that there was a combination of the gases and 30 per cent thought simply that a mixture is formed where the gases meet. (The corresponding percentages for those holding a continuous view were 18 per cent and 51 per cent respectively.)

Laverty and McGarvey[21] investigated children's particulate representations of the chemical combination of magnesium and oxygen. The types of chemical combination depicted included:

- a random mixture of particles;
- oxygen particles surrounding the magnesium particles;
- two magnesium and one oxygen particle, or one magnesium and two oxygen particles joined;
- an assembly of joined magnesium and oxygen particles arranged alternately and described as 'being the same all the way through'.

PARTICLE MODELS OF GIANT IONIC LATTICES

Conceptions about ionic lattices have been explored by Butts and Smith[22] and Peterson et al.[23] Butts and Smith interviewed twenty-eight Australian 17-year-olds drawn from ten schools. The interview focused on the formation of sodium chloride and on ball and stick models of it. Although pupils could describe the electron transfer process involved in ionic bond formation, ten of them referred to 'molecules' of sodium chloride, and two of them said that ionic bonds between sodium chloride 'molecules' produced the crystalline structure. Confusion arose in the use of that kind of model for ionic substances: the six 'sticks' around each ball were interpreted as 'one ionic and five physical bonds'; only two students said that the sticks merely supported the balls in place.

12

WATER

WATER AS A LIQUID

Research into children's ideas about water is often in the context of research into ideas about solids, liquids and gases in general. However, from a child's view water is the exemplary liquid and all liquids tend to be regarded as 'watery', 'made of water' or 'containing water'.[1]

Dow et al.[2] studied pupils' application of a particle model to water and liquids. They found that pupils tended to think of the particles, not as being closely packed and simply rolling over one another, but rather as moving freely away from one another. As a result of holding this view, pupils saw no reason why a liquid sample should have a fixed volume and they also expected a liquid to be compressible.

FREEZING WATER AND MELTING ICE

Osborne and Cosgrove,[3] studying children's ideas about freezing, found that pupils generally do not regard freezing as taking place at a specific temperature. Those pupils who tried to apply a particle model to the process of freezing tended to think in terms of the particles of water becoming more packed together. Consequently they reasoned that 'ice doesn't take up as much room as when it's liquid'.

Pupils are inclined to think of a loss of mass when ice changes to water. Stavy[4] presented pupils with two samples of ice having identical weights. She melted one sample of ice and interviewed pupils about the relative weights of the two samples. Mass was conserved by 5 per cent at ages 5 and 6, by about 50 per cent at age 7 and 75 per cent at age 10.

BOILING WATER

Andersson[5] investigated Swedish pupils' ideas about the temperature of a pan of water boiling on a stove. When asked what would happen if the water continued to be heated for a further five minutes, 40 per cent of 12-year-olds responded that the temperature would be greater than 100°C, with the majority of the group explaining that the water gets hotter the longer it is heated. The number of children offering this answer fell with age, but 16 per cent of 15-year-olds still felt that the temperature would be greater than 100°C. Of those children suggesting that the temperature would remain at 100°C, 25 per cent of 12- and 13-year-olds explained their answer in terms of the switch number of the stove determining the temperature of the water. The percentage of children offering this explanation was 35 per cent in 14-year-olds and 32 per cent in 15-year-olds.

Andersson then asked pupils to suggest what would happen if the setting of the stove were increased. Here 90 per cent of children aged 12 thought that the temperature would increase above 100°C. This response was also given by 63 per cent of 13-year-olds, 60 per cent of 14-year-olds and 54 per cent of 15-year-olds.

Even by age 15 only 31 per cent gave correct answers and appropriate explanations to both problems. Children appear to consider heat and temperature to be the same thing, arguing that if you increase the amount of heat you will increase the temperature.

Bar and Travis[6] found that pupils' understanding of boiling precedes that of the evaporation of water from surfaces such as floors, saucers and roads. They found that 70 per cent of a sample of 6- to 8-year-olds understood that when water is boiling vapour comes from it, that the quantity of water decreases and that the vapour is made of water. However, the same children said that when a solid object, such as a wet saucer, dries, then water just disappears or else it penetrates the solid object.

EVAPORATION

Several researchers have attempted to trace the development of a conception of evaporation.[6 7 8 9 10 11 12] For example, Bar[7] found that at ages 5 and 6, children are impressed by the disappearance of material, accept that it just happens and offer no explanation. It is not until ages 8–10 that they are likely to attempt to conserve the vaporised substance by suggesting that the disappearing liquid must go to some place. Such a place, in their view, has the character of a receptacle but at this age the only 'receptacle' they can think of is a container or a supporting surface, both of which they may regard as porous. Later, when they developed a concept of 'static air', pupils suggested that bits of water go into the (receptacle) 'air'. By the ages of 12–14, a conception of evaporation which links conservation of matter, a particle view and awareness of air is quite prevalent.

However, Osborne and Cosgrove[3] report that, of forty-three Australian

99

13- to 17-year-olds, only eight mentioned particles or molecules when describing what happened to water evaporating from a plate. At least one was aware that the particles were 'getting energy from somewhere and flying off'. The possible sources of energy mentioned were: 'what they've got', or 'each other' or 'the air around'.

CONDENSATION

Ideas concerning the condensation of water on a vessel containing ice have been explored among Israeli children by Bar and Travis[6] and among New Zealand children by Osborne and Cosgrove.[3] Israeli children aged 10–14 chose most frequently the responses 'the coldness changed into water' and 'cold caused hydrogen and oxygen to change into water'. The researchers conclude that, although pupils know that vapour can be changed to water, applying that knowledge appears to cause some difficulty. New Zealand 12- to 17-year-olds most frequently chose the response 'the coldness caused oxygen and hydrogen in the air to form water'. The proportion who expressed the view that the condensation results from water in the air increased with age from 10 per cent to 55 per cent between ages 12 and 17.

The same Israeli pupils were asked to explain how a hand can become wet when held above boiling water. There was an almost even distribution of the two responses: 'the vapour changes into water' and 'the hand became wet from the vapour'.

DISSOLVING SUBSTANCES IN WATER

Several researchers[2] [13] [15] [16] [17] have found that, from an early age through to adulthood, individuals hold several conceptions of 'dissolving'. Some of these are revealed by words they use to describe what happens to sugar placed in water. Up to age 8, there is a tendency to focus on the sugar only and say 'it just goes', 'disappears', 'melts away', 'dissolves away' or 'turns into water'.[15]

Some researchers[15] [18] [19] [20] [21] have explored pupils' conservation of matter and mass in the context of dissolving. Holding[15] found that about two-thirds of the 8-year-olds studied thought that dissolved sugar is preserved in some form. However, only about half of those who said the sugar is 'there' also say that 'it weighs something'. It seems that some children think the weight of the sugar is now 'up in the water', in a 'suspended' state and not 'pressing down' on the bottom of a container.

In school science, pupils are expected to regard a solution as a homogeneous mixture of two or more substances. However, several studies have shown that they hold a variety of ideas about solutions.[14] [15] [22] [23] [24] [25] Holding[15] found that in the early school years, some children did not regard a solution as a single phase but as gross particles of sugar that can be filtered out from the water. Other children regarded a solution as a single substance. The majority, in a sample of 500 between the ages of 8 and 17, depicted 'bits of sugar' without drawing the water. (This representation peaked close to age 12 at about 65 per cent.) The next most prevalent picture of a solution was 'continuous' shading throughout. (This apparently non-particulate view peaked between ages 10 and 12 at just over 20 per cent.) Molecules were rarely mentioned in the earlier years but later an appreciable proportion depicted 'molecular particles' of sugar – at age 15 (30 per cent) and age 17 (50 per cent) – but only half of these pupils also depicted molecules of water. It would appear that a continuous view of water is still quite prevalent among older pupils.

THE WATER CYCLE

Bar[7] concludes that in order to understand the water cycle pupils need to understand not only the concepts of evaporation and condensation but also that water vapour and drops of water have weight and undergo free-fall. Sample populations of pupils from each of the ages between 5 and 15 were interviewed about aspects of the water cycle. The questions used were as follows: 'Where do clouds come from?', 'How do they start?', 'What are clouds made of?', 'Can you tell me how rain falls?' and 'How does it start?'. The responses indicated that particular ideas were prevalent in certain age ranges.

- At ages 5–7 the most common idea was that rain falls when somebody, possibly God, opens water reservoirs. Children also said that clouds are made of smoke or cotton wool: it follows that clouds and rain are unrelated in their thinking. An alternative view was that clouds, regarded as bags of water, are kept above or in the sky. (When clouds collide, they may explode, or open, or get torn, or split, so that rain falls out.)
- At ages 6–8 the clouds were thought to go into the sea and collect ('drink') water; then they move on to other places and give rain.
- At ages 6–9 clouds were considered to be made of vapour created when the sea is heated by the sun, or to be made of vapour from kettles. (Eventually the clouds open to give rain.) The sun was thought to go into the water, thereby heating it to a high temperature. (Water vapour so created enters the clouds; later, the clouds open to give rain.)
- At ages 7–10 a cloud was visualised as a sponge having drops of water within it. (When it rains the drops fall through little holes in the cloud; this happens when the cloud is shaken by the wind.) Alternatively, some held that rain falls when clouds get cold or become hot.

- At ages 9–10 clouds were said to be made of water evaporated from puddles. (Rain falls when clouds become cold or heavy.)
- At ages 11–15 clouds were thought to be created when the vapour becomes cold. (The rain falls when the water drops become big and heavy.) None of the sample population explained how the clouds became cold.
- Above the age range 11–15 weight was attributed to vapour and to small drops of water.

WATER AND LIVING THINGS

Wood-Robinson[26] has summarised the findings of several studies concerning children's ideas about plants. Many of the children studied thought plants take in water as a food. Many thought that the plants' leaves took in water, the leaf's main function being to capture rain, water or dew. Some thought that water vapour moves into the leaf during photosynthesis.

In their study of children's ideas of nutrition, Wellman and Johnson[27] found that pre-school children thought that the consumption of water, as well as food, would lead to body-weight gain.

FLOATING AND SINKING

Biddulph and Osborne[28] surveyed 7- to 14-year-olds' understanding of the term 'floating'. When they considered objects which floated with a sizeable proportion above the surface most children described them as 'floating'. When only a small portion of the object was above the surface, however, some pupils took a different view: they thought that it was partly floating and partly sinking. Others suggested that it might be starting to sink and would eventually go down. Some pupils, considering objects which appeared to be on top of the water, thought that the objects were not floating because they were held up by the water's skin. Many children thought that objects which were completely submerged but freely suspended, such as fish or submarines, were not floating.

When pupils were asked for one reason why some things floated the most frequent suggestion was that things floated because they were light. Only three children qualified their answer by saying 'light for their size'. The majority of the children in the sample could not offer one single reason why objects float but resorted to giving different reasons for different objects.

The same study asked children aged 8–12 how a longer piece of candle would float compared with a shorter piece. The survey showed that with increasing age an increasing percentage considered the longer candle would float at the same level as the smaller candle and a decreasing percentage considered the longer candle would sink or float lower. However, at age 12, there was still a sizeable proportion of children (about 40 per cent) who thought length would affect floating.

Although by age 9–10 the majority of children considered that the depth of water would not affect the level at which an object floated, even at age 11–12 up to 35 per cent of the children surveyed thought that the depth of water would affect the level of a floating object. Few children correctly predicted the amount of water which would be displaced by floating objects.

Grimellini Tomasini et al.[29] studied children's ideas about buoyancy and found, among their sample of pupils, four 'ways of looking'. The children offered ideas in terms of:

- the role played by material and weight;
- the role played by shape, cavities and holes;
- the role played by air;
- the role played by water.

Many children thought that holes in objects affected their ability to float. Despite teaching, this idea was firmly held by some children. The part envisaged for water varied: some children thought that water made objects heavier if it went inside them; others offered ideas involving water pressure pushing either upwards or downwards.

13

AIR

EXISTENCE OF AIR

Research into children's ideas about air is often in the context of research into ideas about solids, liquids and gases in general.

From a study of French students aged 11–13 years, Séré[1] reports that by the age of 11 the idea that air exists in open containers was well established. Many pupils made reference to the ability of air to get into and out of containers. However, she found that some children were less sure that air was contained inside a sealed vessel, and some associated the existence of air only with the sensation felt when it moved.

A study conducted by Miller *et al.*[2] involved students aged 11–15 years in answering open-ended written questions concerning the properties of air. More than half of the 11-year-olds in the sample spontaneously used ideas about air to explain phenomena such as drinking through a straw and by age 15 three-quarters of the students gave explanations involving air.

Several researchers[1 3 4 5 6 7] have studied pupils' conception of 'gas' and found that, initially, they do not appear to be aware that air and other gases possess material character. For example, although young children may have said that air and smoke exist, they regard such materials as having transient character similar to that of 'thoughts'.

Pupils who have developed an awareness of the material character of gases may not regard 'gas' as having weight or mass. Leboutet-Barrell[8] suggests that this is because children's most common related experience is that gases tend to rise or float. Until they construct the idea that gases have mass, pupils are unlikely to conserve mass when describing chemical changes that involve gases as either reactants or products.

Stavy[7] conducted a study of 9- to 15-year-old Israeli students which focused on their ideas about the substantive nature of gas (in this case carbon dioxide) before and after they had received instruction about the nature of gases. Tasks involved students in predicting what would happen to the weight of a carbon dioxide cartridge before and after it

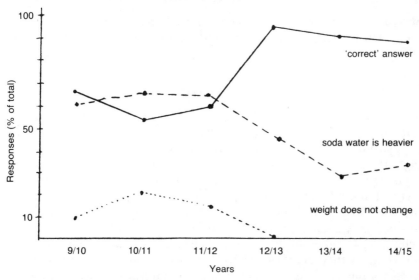

Figure 13.1 Pupils' predictions about change in weight in soda water after bubbles of carbon dioxide have escaped

was used to make soda water and predicting the weight of a cup of soda water before and after the bubbles had escaped from it. Students aged 10–12 years produced fewer accepted predictions than both younger and older students and this 'dip in the curve' was accounted for by the growth of a 'gas is light' notion in students between the ages of 9 and 10 years (see Figure 13.1).

The development of the 'air is light' notion at the age of 9–11 was also reported by Brook and Driver.[4] Nearly all the 5-year-olds in their sample appeared not to differentiate weight and volume and they used the apparent size of a container for air as an indicator of its weight. By the age of 8 the idea of weight was linked more strongly with the notion of falling objects and air seemed to 'float around' rather than 'press down'. About three-quarters of 8-year-olds and half of 12-year-olds in the sample, considered that air has 'negative weight' or no weight. The idea that air has 'positive weight' was held by a quarter of 16-year-olds in the sample Séré[1] suggests that, although some students between the ages of 11 and 13 think that air has negative mass (that is, the property of 'lightness'), the concept of air having mass is easily acquired when taught at the age of 13.

An interesting study carried out by Ruggiero *et al.*[9] investigated 12- and 13-year-old students' understanding of the relationship between air and gravity. They found that for some students air and gravity are inseparable: that 'things do not fall in space because there is no atmosphere and, in the absence of air, weight becomes zero'.

PARTICLE IDEAS ABOUT AIR

Several research studies have been reported on the particle ideas about the gaseous state held by students and teachers. These are summarised in Chapter 11.

AIR PRESSURE

Séré, working with eleven French 11- to 13-year-olds, found pupils thinking that only wind, and not still air, has pressure.[10] Working with eighty-four 12-, 14- and 16-year-olds, Engel Clough and Driver[11] found high percentages (67 per cent, 80 per cent and 87 per cent respectively) thinking that pressure increases with depth. However, pupils were less inclined to think in terms of pressure acting equally in all directions (13 per cent, 19 per cent and 34 per cent respectively): they were inclined to think of a greater pressure downwards. This study found frequent references to either air or a vacuum 'sucking', in pupils' explanations of the changes they experienced with straws and syringes. Atmospheric pressure pushing was mentioned but few pupils explained changes in terms of balancing pressures.

Studying 600 French 11- to 13-year-olds and their ideas about air pressure differences and consequent movement of air, Séré[3] found 85 per cent accurately describing the extent to which air is squashed in a ball before and after blowing it up. However, only 63 per cent of the pupils accurately compared air pressure inside the ball with the air outside. Pupils did not readily make pressure comparisons. An important finding in Séré's study is that pupils tend to associate pressure in gases with moving air, assuming pressure acting in the direction of motion. There was less tendency to associate pressure with static gases.

Séré investigated children's understanding of air pressure using a range of syringes. She found that forces in air are considered by most students to act only when an external force produces movement, and then only in the direction of movement. Thus, in the equilibrium state (when no movement is perceived), students said that air was 'doing nothing'. When students were asked to predict and explain phenomena where pressure clearly acted in a direction other than that of the external force, they maintained that the main force of the air would be in the direction of the external force (see Figure 13.2).

Séré also reports that students experienced difficulty in coming to terms with atmospheric pressure. When asked to interpret situations involving atmospheric pressure, although pressure difference was perceivable, only one-fifth of students referred to it in accounting for the phenomena and about half of the sample referred only to what was happening inside a container. Explanations tended to be in terms of a

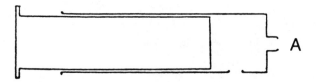

Figure 13.2 Given a syringe with a hole in the side of the barrel, pupils said that most of the air came out of the end hole A

vacuum inside the container 'sucking', pressure inside the container sucking or pulling, or an idea that spaces tend to be filled (that is, that a vacuum is difficult to maintain in nature). Other students used the idea of atmosphere pressing down on surfaces but did not extend this to an explanation in terms of pressure difference. Séré concluded that, in general, gases are seen as transmitters of motion rather than exerters of pressure.

Students' understandings of atmospheric pressure were also reported by Brook and Driver,[4] and by Engel Clough and Driver.[11] The former study reports that questions involving atmospheric pressure explanations appeared difficult for pupils to answer: most students referred only to events inside the containers, in terms either of a vacuum sucking or of pressure inside pulling. A difference was noted, however, between phenomena where atmospheric pressure was greater than the pressure inside the container (where more than half of the 15-year-old students explained in terms of atmospheric pressure) and phenomena where pressure inside the container was greater (where less than one-fifth of 15-year-old students referred to atmospheric pressure). The study conducted by Engel Clough and Driver involved responses to similar written questions by 12-, 14- and 16-year-old students. Again, the study reported that responses tended to be in terms of 'vacuum sucking' (even in the case of a question involving drinking through a straw where the statement 'use the idea of atmospheric pressure' was included in the question) or in terms only of atmospheric pressure acting on surfaces. Few students used the idea of pressure difference in their explanations.

SUMMARY OF IDEAS ABOUT THE PHYSICAL PROPERTIES OF AIR

Figure 13.3 from Brook and Driver,[4] summarises the ideas about the physical properties of air which researchers have found in 5-, 8-, 12- and 16-year-olds. It shows the way in which particular ideas tend to become more common or less common with age.

A curriculum scheme for teaching about air as a material and air pressure, based upon research into pupils' prior ideas, is proposed by

	Existence of air	Components of air and life processes	Air occupies space
5-yr-old	• All used word 'air' • Air indentified with movement (i.e. breeze, draught, wind)	• Some identify air as being involved in breathing	• A third appreciate that air takes up space
8-yr-old	• Air identified as existing even in static situations	• Air involved in breathing • Some recognise that 'breathed in' air is different from 'breathed out' air	• Two-thirds appreciate that air takes up space
12-yr-old	• Air identified in static situations • Some recognise the existence of an atmosphere	• Majority recognise that air contains oxygen – stating it comes from plants/trees • Half acknowledge that 'breathed in' air contains more oxygen and 'breathed out' air more carbon dioxide	• Two-thirds appreciate that air takes up space and that it can be compressed
16-yr-old	• Air identified in static situations • A third appreciate that the Earth's atmosphere changes with distance from the Earth's surface	• Majority recognise that air contains oxygen • Half recognise that air is a mixture of components • Most recognise that breathing involves gas exchange • A third link oxygen with the process of respiration and energy requirements of living things	• Nearly all recognise that air takes up space and that its volume can be changed

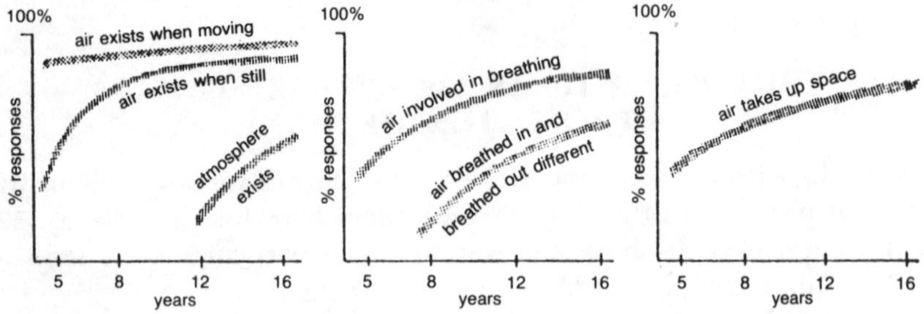

Figure 13.3 The development of pupils' ideas about the physical properties of air.[4]

Transmitting forces	Air and weight	Air and pressure differences
• Three-quarters recognise that air can push against things	• Nearly all compare 'weight' of containers of air in terms of their volumes	• Majority identify 'sucking action' with human activity or cannot explain pressure difference phenomena • A third identify 'air' inside partially evacuated container as pulling
• Nearly all recognise that air can push against things	• Three-quarters compare 'weight' of containers of air in terms of their volumes • A quarter consider air has negative weight or weighs nothing – has a tendency to go upwards	• Two-thirds identify 'air' inside partially evacuated container as pulling • A tenth beginning to use a vacuum idea – space where there is no air
• Nearly all recognise that air pushes against things • Half identify air as resisting movement • A quarter recognise that air transmits force forwards • A fifth recognise both forwards and resisting forces • A few recognise that forces in air are transmitted in all directions	• A few compare 'weight' of containers of air in terms of their volumes • Over three-quarters consider air has negative weight or no weight	• Half identify 'air' inside partially evacuated container as pulling • A third use vacuum idea • Few beginning to use idea of external air pressure or pressure difference
• Nearly all recognise that air pushes against things • A fifth identify it as resisting movement • A third recognise that air transmits force forwards and backwards • A third recognise that forces in air are transmitted in all directions	• A few compare 'weight' of containers of air in terms of volumes • Two-thirds consider that air has negative weight or no weight • Less that a quarter consider that air has weight	• A third identify 'air' inside partially evacuated container as pulling • A third use vacuum idea • A third use idea of external pressure or pressure difference

Table 13.1 A curriculum scheme for teaching about air

Age	Conceptual aspect	Contexts
5–7	Air exists and moves naturally	Windy days
	Air is all around	Effects of moving air (streamers, parachutes)
	We can make air move	Sucking and blowing
	We use air in our bodies	
	Air occupies space	Balloons
	Air can be squashed	Squeezy bottles
7–11	Air occupies space	Bubbles in water
	Air can be squashed	Pneumatic syringes
	Air pushes out in all directions	Balloons, tyres
	Air has weight	Inflation increases weight
11–14	Air can be compressed and expanded	Phenomena including: collapsing can
	Air pushes out in all directions	pneumatic syringes
	Pressure differences tend to equalise	vacuum pump
		sink plunger
		breathing/lungs
	Atmospheric pressure	Supports column of water

Source: Brook and Driver.[4]

Brook and Driver.[4] They propose a focus on different concepts for different ages as shown in Table 13.1.

COMPOSITION OF AIR AND CHEMICAL INTERACTIONS OF AIR

A study by Meheut *et al.*[12] reports that pupils often hold to the idea that air is one substance. However, many studies appear to have focused upon pupils' ideas about particular component gases rather than upon the overall composition of air.

Several studies of 11- to 12-year-olds' ideas about the role of air in burning have shown that most of them appreciate that air (or oxygen) is needed for burning, although its function is not generally understood.[12] [13] Meheut *et al.*[12] found that, although some view oxygen as necessary for combustion, pupils may not regard it as a reacting substance.

GASES INVOLVED IN LIFE PROCESSES

Gellert[14] and Nagy[15] report that although young children know that air is necessary for life, they appear to have a limited idea of what happens to inhaled air, often thinking it remains in the head. It appears that younger secondary pupils are unlikely to relate the need for air or oxygen to the use of food. Arnaudin and Mintzes[16] found up to one-third of their sample of 495 students suggesting that air is simply inhaled into the lungs and then exhaled, without links with the heart and circulatory system.

In the context of photosynthesis, and the use by plants of gases in the air, pupils appear to have an intuitive disbelief that a plant's growth and increase in mass could be due mainly to the incorporation of matter in the form of gases. This may be due to pupils' difficulties in accepting a gas as a substance.[17] Pupils appear to show a better understanding of the role of oxygen than of the role of carbon dioxide in plant metabolism,[18] although oxygen was often not distinguished from air.[19] Wandersee found that there is an increasing tendency with age to specify 'carbon dioxide' or 'oxygen' rather than referring only to air, although those using the names of gases did not exceed 58 per cent.[20]

Arnold and Simpson,[21] interviewing 11-year-olds, found that pupils thought either that air is not used by plants or that plants and animals use air in 'opposite' ways.

Driver et al.[22] found that processes involving oxygen appeared to be better understood by 15-year-olds than processes involving carbon dioxide.

Eisen and Stavy[23] investigated the understanding of photosynthesis shown by high school and university students in a sample of sixty-two 'biologists' and 126 'non-biologists'. They found that 90 per cent of 'biologists' could account for the constant proportion of oxygen in air in spite of its use by living things, whereas only 50 per cent of 'non-biologists' could similarly explain.

(Studies of ideas about photosynthesis and gas exchange in plants are summarised in Chapter 2; studies of ideas about gas exchange and respiration are summarised in Chapter 7.)

WIND

With a focus on ideas about weather, Moyle[24] studied the ideas about wind held by pupils up to the age of 16. In this study, pupils often appeared to account for winds in terms of visible moving objects such as cars, clouds or tides. Some pupils accounted for winds in terms of the movement of the Earth or the coldness of the poles. There was a tendency to relate wind speed to temperature, linking a high speed with cold winds and assuming a warm wind to be gentle or slower. Pupils rarely accounted for wind in terms of pressure differences between regions of the atmosphere.

14

ROCKS

ROCK

Most of the research which has been carried out on children's prior ideas on this topic has been done in New Zealand. The presence of volcanoes there may explain the frequency with which children classified rocks (and the minerals of which they are composed) as volcanic.

Children recognise rocks by their weight, hardness, colour and jaggedness. They tend to apply the word 'rock' intuitively and often to mineral samples.[1] [2] To the children studied, rocks had to be large, heavy and jagged. Smaller fragments were described as stones. Rock was at first regarded as being made of only one substance, with consequent difficulty in recognising granite as rock. Children were also confused when deciding whether a sample was natural or not,[1] [3] house brick being regarded as rock because it contains some natural material. The opposite view was also taken: that a cut and polished piece of marble is not a rock and is not natural because to be natural it must be 'untouched by mankind'. Children may classify rock specimens as 'crystal rocks' and 'normal rocks' and the word 'crystal' is used to describe both rock and mineral specimens, but only if the sample is thought to be attractive in appearance.

MINERAL

Most children in Happs's studies[1] [2] did not associate 'mineral' with rocks. They were more likely to think of mineral water, minerals and vitamins or mineral resources. Occasionally, it was suggested that minerals are 'small stones or precious things'. After a particular teaching programme, minerals were treated as being the same as rocks and both words were used indiscriminately in classifying rock samples as 'volcanic' (regardless of whether they were sedimentary, metamorphic or igneous).

SEDIMENTARY ROCKS

Very few children in Happs's study[1] appreciated the relationship between sedimentary rocks and the sedimentary processes by which they are formed. Such rocks were described as 'volcanic' and this included the notion that heat is involved in their formation. Happs[3] reports that additional confusion arises when children confuse the layers apparent in sedimentary rocks with the cleavage planes often associated with metamorphic rocks.

IGNEOUS ROCKS

Most children in Happs's sample,[1] when confronted with specimens of igneous rocks, had no ideas on formation to offer and merely described their appearance. A small minority associated igneous rocks with fire or volcanoes.

METAMORPHIC ROCKS

Happs found that the word 'metamorphic' was associated by most children with metamorphosis in animals and they linked metamorphic rocks with butterflies and plants in general.

SIZE OF FRAGMENTS

The words 'boulder', 'gravel', 'sand' and 'clay' have specific scientific meanings relating to the average size of fragments. Children in Happs's study[3] did not have this awareness and they used the words in an everyday way:

- 'boulder': children usually saw a boulder as a larger, rounded piece of material which has rolled down a hillside;
- 'gravel': this word was usually used only to describe the loose material at the sides of roads;
- 'sand': children associated sand with beaches or desert;
- 'clay': this was thought of as sticky, orange stuff found underground.

MOUNTAINS AND VOLCANOES

Mountains, in Happs's study,[4] were described by children as 'high rocks' or as 'clumps of dirt or soil'. A few children thought that mountains are made of molten rock or 'rock pushed up' while others thought that all mountains are volcanoes (either extinct, dormant or active). The term 'a range of mountains' only rarely meant a row of mountains to children and most associated it with cowboy movies or paddocks and feeding grounds.

113

Some children had ideas that imply that volcanoes occur on fault lines or over weak spots and 'stuff just comes up there'. In some cases, the build up of pressure under the crust was mentioned: in others, earthquakes shaking the region around the volcano were supposed to account for volcanic eruptions. An idiosyncratic view was that 'heat builds up and has to get out'.

Happs found that most of the children studied were unable to relate in any way to a theory of mountain building which involves plate tectonics.

WEATHERING

Cosgrove and Osborne[6] found that the idea of water expanding on freezing appears to be a difficult one for children to accept: the most common idea held was that volume increases as temperature rises. Pupils holding this view of freezing would have difficulty in accounting for the breaking of rocks when water freezes within them.

SOIL

Among the common misconceptions Happs[5] found about the nature of soil was that soil is 'just dirt' or 'any stuff in the ground'. It was nearly always agreed by children that soil is a medium which is useful for plant growth. They were aware that there are living organisms in the soil and these were assumed to be 'eating the soil'. Children seemed to be largely unaware of the role of the living organisms, or of the identity of these organisms in soil. In some cases, children distinguished 'dirt' from soil by saying that 'soil has more goodness in it'. The formation of soil was strongly associated with deposition by rivers, although there was an alternative view that soil has 'always been there ever since the Earth was formed'. Idiosyncratic ideas about the origin of soil included the suggestion that soil is 'dinosaur manure', or that it results from volcanic action.

Children's ideas about the age of soil were varied. Some thought it was quite young – 'years or so'. Others held the view that soil was as old as the Earth. A notion widely held was that soil is the precursor of rock and that it changes to rock in the sequence: soil–clay–rock.

Recent research in Portugal, the USA and England identifies common notions in pupils' explanations of decay of dead organisms in soil. This work is summarised in Chapter 7.

Part III

CHILDREN'S IDEAS ABOUT PHYSICAL PROCESSES

15

ELECTRICITY

MAKING A COMPLETE CLOSED CIRCUIT

Most pupils' introduction to learning about electricity the world over involves using a battery, wire, and a 1.25V bulb to make the bulb light. Pupils generally tackle this with enthusiasm and also with certain established ideas about how batteries and bulbs work. Several researchers[1] [2] [3] [4] [5] have investigated pupils' earliest ideas about electricity and they report that these ideas generally indicate a source–consumer model in which the battery gives something to the bulb. In practice this model underlies the common examples of circuits which are built by children in the 8–12 age range in their initial attempts to light a bulb. Common arrangements of a battery and a bulb, identified by Shipstone, are shown in Figure 15.1.

It seems that many strategies designed to help pupils to understand electricity actually introduce and reinforce problems.

PUPILS' IDEAS ABOUT A SIMPLE CIRCUIT

Solomon *et al.*[6] and Licht[7] have pointed to the importance of pupils' background awareness of, and interest in, electricity. Licht found, among 207 pupils studied, that danger/safety, sound and video apparatus and electronics were the contexts in which pupils were most interested. This of course leaves the teacher with the difficult task of maintaining pupils' interest in the modest DC circuits which will help them to begin to understand the phenomena.

Pupils' mental models of a DC circuit

The models which are used by children to explain the phenomenon of a simple circuit have been studied in several countries: New Zealand, Australia, the USA, Sweden, Greece, France, and Germany as well as the UK. Osborne and Freyberg's work in New Zealand[8] identified four

Figure 15.1 Examples of attempts to light a bulb
Source: D. Shipstone, 'Electricity in simple circuits', pp. 33–51 in R. Driver, E. Guesne and A. Tiberghien (eds), *Children's Ideas in Science*, Open University Press, Milton Keynes, 1985.

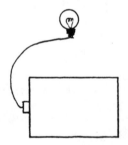

Figure 15.2 The unipolar model (A)

explanatory models (see Figures 15.2–15.5) which have since been found by other researchers world-wide.[2] [5] [9] [10] [11] Some of these alternative models are very firmly held, not only by young pupils but by physics and engineering students who are regularly involved in practical work and calculations relating to circuits.

The first of these models is illustrated in Figure 15.2. Here, pupils regard only one wire as active and, whilst most come to recognise the practical requirement for a complete circuit, they nevertheless think that the second wire doesn't play an active part. It is sometimes regarded as a safety wire.

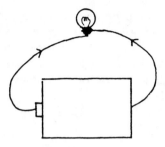

Figure 15.3 The clashing currents model (B)

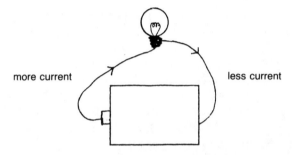

more current   less current

Figure 15.4 The current consumed model (C)

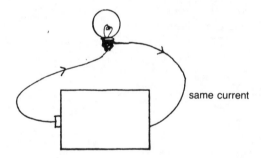

same current

Figure 15.5 The scientists' model with current conserved (D)

A second model is shown in Figure 15.3. Pupils think of current flowing from both terminals of the battery to the bulb. They sometimes explain the light in terms of the 'clash' of the two currents.

In the third model (Figure 15.4) current is seen as 'used up' by the bulb and so there is less in the wire 'going back' to the battery. Some pupils expect a second bulb to be less bright than the first when two bulbs are in the circuit: others imagine components sharing the current equally but in either case current is 'used up' by the bulbs.

The fourth model (Figure 15.5) shows the magnitude or value of the current unchanged in the return wire.

119

It is notable that all the prevalent alternative models are 'sequential' models in which something from the battery travels around the circuit, meeting wires and components in sequence. This deep-seated notion, with its roots in the 'cause and effect' everyday experiences of other phenomena, underlies many of the problems which pupils have in understanding the behaviour of electrical circuits. It is this notion which might be considered as the underlying mental model having various expressions.

Popularity of models A, B, C and D with different age-groups

The four models (A, B, C and D) appear to vary in popularity with different age-groups. Usually less than 5 per cent of secondary pupils use the unipolar model A. Osborne and Freyberg[8] found model B thinking in the explanations of less than 10 per cent of 15-year-olds, whilst it was held by nearly 40 per cent of 12-year-olds.

Shipstone found that almost 50 per cent of 12-year-olds in an 11–18 British comprehensive school held a 'current-used-up' model, C. This rose to 60 per cent in 14-year-olds and fell to less than 40 per cent in 17-year-olds. (All the students tested had studied electricity in the year in which they were tested and the sixth-formers had completed 'A' level work.) The scientific model D was held by less than 10 per cent of 12-year-olds and less than 40 per cent of 15-year-olds, only rising to 60 per cent in the 17-year-olds (Figure 15.6).

Gott[5] found that 50 per cent of 15-year-olds had a 'current-used-up'

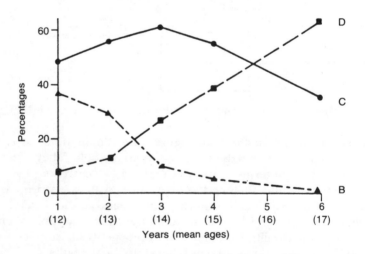

Figure 15.6 Popularity of models B, C and D

Source: D. Shipstone, 'Electricity in simple circuits', pp. 33–51 in R. Driver, E. Guesne and A. Tiberghien (eds), *Children's Ideas in Science*, Open University Press, Milton Keynes, 1985.

model and it appeared that having two bulbs in a circuit reduced the number of pupils conserving current.

Osborne and Freyberg[8] have found the use of two ammeters in a circuit, and also the analogy of the heart and blood circulation, to be effective in moving some pupils' thinking to model D. However, Gauld[12] has shown that pupils tend to hold on to their consumption model, C, even 'remembering' ammeter readings to support that view. Dupin and Johsua[11] have found that pupils try to account for equal ammeter readings on either side of a bulb in terms other than current conservation.

The point of particular concern is that pupils need to be using the model D explanation of a circuit before they can hold the scientifically accepted view of ammeters, voltmeters, potential difference, resistance or series and parallel circuits. Notably Osborne[13] found that, in a small group of 11-year-olds, 86 per cent held model D after a critical lesson in which current measurements were made on either side of a bulb but that only 47 per cent still held it after one year.

Closset[14][15] suggests that it is important to teach pupils what a model is and that any model has limited use. Most of the researchers recognise the value of presenting pupils with a cognitive conflict in which experiences challenge their existing models. However, the point is made that this in itself is not enough – that it is necessary to offer, at the same time, a new model which impresses the learner as having an advantage over the one they hold. Closset recommends taking pupils into our confidence about the purpose of experiences to challenge their existing views.[14] She makes the point that the concepts taught in school were formulated from the formal models of physics, and that we need more simple concepts which relate to simpler models appropriate to pupils.

BATTERY

In their earliest experiences of batteries pupils often think of the battery as a unipolar 'giver' of electricity. It seems that pupils generally think of the battery as a store of electricity or energy.[10] They see it as delivering a constant current in a closed circuit, rather than maintaining a constant voltage or potential difference.[16] Indeed, pupils have very little notion of voltage or potential difference and the battery was seen as storing a certain amount of electricity by 85 per cent of a group of 400 German secondary school pupils.[17]

CURRENT AND VOLTAGE

Osborne and Freyberg,[8] working in New Zealand and in the USA, found that pupils think of current as synonymous with electricity and electrical energy. Likewise, 87 per cent of von Rhoneck's sample of thirty-seven German secondary pupils thought that current is energy.[18] It appears to be envisaged as a quasi-material. Among these pupils voltage was seen as the strength or force of the current.

Current is usually introduced to pupils as the primary concept and they tend to think of voltage as a property of the current rather than as a precondition for a current to flow.[19] Indeed, Maichle[17] found that in a sample of some 300 German secondary pupils 23 per cent thought that voltage and current are the same thing. It follows that pupils expect voltage to increase as current increases. They are very reluctant to believe that, if no current is flowing, there can still be a voltage between two points.[18] Plenty of experience is advised, with both ammeters and voltmeters in simple circuits, in order to erode the 'voltage equals current' idea.

Some researchers[19] [20] have suggested that the usual early focus on current gives rise to the 'voltage equals current' idea and that attempts should be made to make pupils 'voltage-minded' by introducing voltage first as a property of the isolated battery.[10] [16] [18] [19] [20] Von Rhoneck proposes a lot of experience in handling a voltmeter and predicting and then measuring voltages so as to establish the voltage concept.[18] Psillos et al.[10] support this suggestion and propose a lot of measuring of voltage alongside current measurements, so as to establish the independence of these concepts. They advise teaching only about voltage, and not about potential difference or electromotive force. They also advise against pupils measuring the voltage distribution in a circuit on the grounds that it can lead to the idea that voltage is consumed.

CIRCUIT

Problems in the sequential model of a circuit

Pupils usually think of the circuit as a series of happenings as electricity leaves the battery, travels through the components and returns to the battery. Shipstone[1] finds that some 80 per cent of 13-year-olds hold a sequential view. Tiberghien[3] suggests that an emphasis on current is what leads to this sequential reasoning in that it involves tracing flow as though events were sequential, and several researchers suggest an introduction to electricity which focuses upon energy as well as current.[1] [3] [20] [21] [22]

The sequential model is one which is prompted and supported by many life experiences involving cause and effect. However, it prevents pupils from thinking of the circuit as a complete system and it doesn't allow them to think of the interactions when a change in one place affects the whole circuit, and not just that part 'downstream' from the change.[3][15][22] A sequential model allows the idea of electricity standing, but not flowing, in unconnected wires and it does not account for the instantaneous lighting of a bulb when the circuit is completed.

Working with series and parallel circuits

The importance of treating series and parallel circuits separately and at different times before going on to treat them in conjunction is stressed by van Aalst.[23] He proposes separating sessions of electricity work by interposing work on something else as a way of allowing ideas to become established before they have to be related to others.

The use of analogies

Research has been done on the various analogies used to help pupils to take a holistic 'complete system' view of the circuit. It recognises both the value and the problems inherent in these analogies. Of course, not all analogies are introduced by the teacher. Pupils themselves naturally use their own life experiences as analogies to help them to make sense of circuits and many of their mental blocks are formed around their own self-generated analogies. However, hydrodynamic, thermal and mechanical analogies have all been found useful to some extent.[11][24]

Schwedes[25] has drawn attention to the value of water circuit analogies, but only if pupils have sufficient experience and understanding of the way the water circuit itself works. There are issues in rate of flow, seen as velocity or as volume, which present traps in themselves, and students may see the battery as a 'high point' with current (water) running off both sides. Russell[26] found that, among Malaysian pupils using the water analogy, only 33 per cent saw its value, only 27 per cent used the analogy to explain events, and only 6 per cent used it correctly.

Given pupils' difficulties with heat and temperature any teacher is likely to think twice before offering a thermal model as a helpful analogy, and there is the danger of going round in circles, using problem situations to try to shed light on problem situations. Given Osborne's work in using body circulation to help understanding of the circuit, it is interesting to note that there is even a reference in the medical literature[27] to trying to help students to understand the heart and blood circulatory system by offering the analogy of the electric circuit!

However, researchers suggest the use of mechanical analogies[11][28] such as the bicycle chain, a transportation belt or workers pushing a train around a track. The importance of using multiple analogies is also stressed.[29] The analogy of workers pushing a train around a track was found to support the adoption of the model D view of the circuit,[11] and

Hartel[28] recommends the bicycle chain 'stiff ring' analogy because it helps pupils to recognise that all points influence all others. This is one of the critical concepts and it appears to be particularly difficult to establish against pupils' natural inclination to a sequential model.

Representing circuits in drawings and diagrams

Circuit diagrams can be seen either as pictures or as abstractions but it is clear that pupils often find it hard to recognise the circuits in the practical situation of real equipment. Moreover, Caillot[30] found that students retain from their work with diagrams strong images rather than the principles they are intended to establish.

The topological arrangement of a diagram or a drawing presents problems for pupils which are easily overlooked.[22] It seems that pupils' spatial abilities affect their use of circuit diagrams: they sometimes do not regard as identical several circuits, which, though identical, have been rotated so as to have a different spatial arrangement.

Johsua[31] found that diagrams are often interpreted figuratively, as a system of pipes, and that potential differences are rarely recognised. He also found a tendency for pupils to see resistances in the circuit as 'useful'. Likwise, a resistance which was not seen as 'useful' would not be drawn in the circuit.

Niedderer[32] found that pupils, when asked whether a circuit diagram would 'work' in practice, more often judged symmetrical diagrams to be functioning than non-symmetric ones.

ESTABLISHING AND DIFFERENTIATING CRITICAL CONCEPTS: DEVELOPING AN ENERGY VIEW

Pupils tend to start with one concept for electricity in a direct current circuit: a concept labelled 'current', or 'energy' or 'electricity', all interchangeable and having the properties of movement, storability and consumption.[1][10] Understanding an electrical circuit involves first differentiating the concepts of current, voltage and energy before relating them as a system, in which the energy transfer depends upon current, time and the potential difference of the battery.

The notion of current flowing in the circuit is one which pupils often meet in their introduction to a circuit and, because this relates well with their intuitive notions, this concept then becomes the primary concept.[16] The result of this tends to be that when voltage is introduced it is seen as a property of current.

Psillos et al.[10] point to the need for particular effort to introduce voltage initially as a property of the battery, a precondition for current to flow and present even when no current is flowing. In this it could more easily be differentiated from current.

Von Rhoneck[18] found in a group of thirteen pupils that eight of them thought of voltage as a force and that all thirteen of them thought of current as energy. Clearly pupils' notions of the relationship between force and energy can have bearing on their views of electrical energy.

The earliest idea of resistance is of a 'hindrance' – a barrier to the flow of charge. Shipstone[1] explains how pupils think of a resistance affecting only parts of the circuit 'downstream', coupling their idea of hindrance with the notion of the sequential circuit in which the current is influenced by each circuit element in turn.

16

MAGNETISM

MAGNETISM AND GRAVITY

Relatively little research has been published in relation to children's ideas about magnetism, although some studies of ideas about gravity have touched upon it. Researchers studying ideas about gravity have found that pupils are inclined to link magnetism with gravity. They sometimes account for gravity in terms of a magnetic force drawing objects towards the Earth.[1] Conversely, pupils have been found to account for the way magnets act by calling magnetism 'a type of gravity'.[2]

Given that pupils tend to link magnetism with gravity and given that pupils also tend to link gravity with the effects of air, Bar and Zinn[3] looked for pupils' ideas suggesting a link between magnetism and air among the 9–14 age group. These researchers found 40 per cent of their sample of ninety-eight pupils considering that a conducting medium (air) is necessary for a magnet to have an effect. A connection between magnetism and gravity was made by 20 per cent of the sample.

HOW MAGNETS WORK

Barrow[2] investigated awareness of magnets and magnetism among seventy-eight pupils across all age ranges. All were well aware of magnets in their everyday experience, in picking up nails or pins or in 'sticking' notices to refrigerators. Before teaching, most pupils offered no explanation of magnetism. A few referred to 'chemicals making them stick'. After teaching, references were made to a 'type of gravity', to 'energies' and to 'electrons and protons'. Less than 10 per cent of the sample appeared to have the idea of poles, although approximately 25 per cent responded accurately when tested on attraction and repulsion of poles. However, pupils tended to think of poles only at the ends of magnets and Barrow suggests that pupils might be encouraged to focus on the magnetic force and find the part of the magnet where attraction and repulsion are strongest. There was generally a lack of experience of repulsion as distinct from attraction. Barrow[2] stresses the importance of work with two magnets. (In the context of distinguishing between a magnet and magnetic material which is not magnetised, Gagliari[4] stresses the importance of repulsion as the only test for a magnet to distinguish it from magnetic material.)

Barrow's study found that pupils' awareness of the uses of magnets had not been extended by teaching. Barrow raises the possibility that teaching about magnets might dissociate pupils from their everyday awareness of magnetism.[2] With this in mind, approaches which draw in everyday experience and focus upon the uses of magnets would be advisable.

A study of pupils between the ages of 3 and 9 by Selman et al.[5] found two levels of conception of magnetism. The first level appeared to be only linking events. At a more sophisticated level the notion of an unseen force began to emerge and pupils talked of a magnet working by 'pulling on things'.

Finley[6] studied the effect of a television programme about magnets on the ideas of twenty-four pupils. Pupils, prior to the programme, referred to magnets 'sticking' to objects and they recognised specific examples of things affected, such as pins or paper clips. They also thought of big magnets as stronger than small ones. After the programme, magnets were thought of in terms of 'picking up' rather than 'sticking' and there was awareness of action at a distance. Pupils identified a generic group of materials affected by magnets, although they took this to be all metals rather than certain metals. The effect of the programme's presenting a small strong magnet was simply to reverse pupils' prior ideas such that they then thought of all small magnets being stronger than all big ones. In general pupils appeared to have embraced some of the ideas of magnetism without adopting the language and the use of words 'attract', 'repel' or 'magnetise'.

ELECTROMAGNETISM

Pupils in Barrow's study[2] did not generally recognise the magnetic effect of an electric current: only 10 per cent did so. Selman et al.[5] found some pupils in the 3–9 age group focusing on the wire as the active agent whilst others referred to electricity as the explanation of electromagnetism. In a sample of ninety-four 13-year-olds, Andersson[7] found sixty-four who thought that a coil of wire had to be uninsulated in order to create an electromagnet.

17

LIGHT

THE NATURE AND REPRESENTATION OF LIGHT

Ideas about the nature of light are often taken for granted in school science and the only definition given is usually that it is 'a form of energy'. Watts[1] suggested that young people are therefore in the position of having to construct their own understanding of what light is whilst exploring its properties.

Guesne[2] concludes that most 10- and 11-year-old children conceive of light as a source (such as an electric bulb), an effect (such as a patch of light) or a state (such as brightness). She found that children of this age did not recognise light as a physical entity existing in space between the source and the effect that it produced. She also found that at the ages of 13 and 14 many students recognised light as an entity, the majority using this notion to explain shadows but only where the light was intense enough to produce perceptible effects at some point in its path.

Ramadas and Driver[3] report on the findings of a study involving 456 15-year-olds in which various ideas about light were considered. When questioned about light rays many children thought of them as 'long, thin, flashing, unlike ordinary light'. Pupils sometimes associated them with science fiction contexts. The fact that the path light takes is not itself directly visible presented special difficulties for children, especially in representing the presence of light in various situations. Darkness appeared to be as important a part of students' conceptions as light, and in their diagrams it was not uncommon, in certain contexts, for students to shade in the darkness on white paper instead of shading in the light.

Investigating children's understanding of sources of light Osborne *et al.*,[4] found that children between the ages of 7 and 11 showed a knowledge of a wide range of sources but that they talked about primary sources nearly four times as often as they mentioned secondary sources of light. These researchers found no evidence to suggest that the children's ideas about sources developed with age. This study also considered the representations used by children to show light and it found that nearly all children's drawings showed the light around sources represented by short lines. The use of extensive numbers of lines linking source and object was very limited. The representations used by older children became more varied and context dependent. Very few children offered no representation of light, although for many lower juniors it was limited to 'simple lines' surrounding the source.

Andersson and Karrqvist[5] made observations on colloquial speech and they suggest that the everyday concept of light is psychological rather than physical in nature, citing phrases such as 'the light is bad' or 'it is light'. The other meaning of 'light' which they noted in the English language was a 'source of light' such as an electric bulb.

Watts and Gilbert[6] suggest seven frameworks which encompass 'the bulk of youngsters responses' about light:

- ambient light where a distinction is drawn between direct light and normal 'daylight' (on a scale which runs from very bright to dark, daylight would be somewhere near the midpoint and shadows are thought to occur only in bright light);
- composite light in which responses describe the composition of light (although some children treat light as a single entity, many discuss its parts or bits);
- de-coupled light in which the responses describe 'light' as being completely separate from 'seeing' (situations are thought to require light in order that things are lit up but there is no suggestion that light is then reflected to the eyes: rather, eyes simply observe a well-lit scene);
- illuminative light in which responses describe light as intentionally designed to allow us to see and which emphasise the general human purpose of light;
- modal light in which many different kinds of light, derived from different circumstances and giving different effects, are identified;
- obvious light in which light is thought to be a property only of large conspicuous luminous bodies;
- projected light in which responses treat light as a substance that is projected, in some instances transporting colours. (Light might be described as a directed beam which can be stopped or slowed down by obstacles.)

The science view of light does not appear to be common among pupils. In a multiple-choice question about how a lamp brightens a room Anderson and Smith[7] found that more than 75 per cent of the sample of 227 did not choose the scientifically correct answer but preferred a response that specified no mechanism at all by which a lamp brightened a room.

LIGHT TRANSMISSION

When children have a notion of light as an entity they do not necessarily think of light travelling – a point made by Guesne.[2] La Rosa *et al.*[8] suggest that students who talked of light going from point A to point B might have thought of it as like a wire or a road going from A to B.

Watts[1] describes a boy who talked about rays of light as 'strands of a rope making up a beam of light' and also about 'light in different modes' such as natural or electric.

Stead and Osborne[9] used different contexts (such as a candle, a lamp, a TV and a mirror) to test for the idea of light existing in space. They found that most students did not think of light travelling out very far from the source, particularly in daytime. Pupils thought of light as travelling further at night. Fetherstonhaugh and Treagust[10] found that around 40 per cent of the forty-seven 13- to 15-year-olds in their study thought that light travels different distances depending upon whether it is night or day. About 20 per cent believed that light does not travel at all during the day. A smaller proportion thought that light did not travel at night.

Feher and Rice,[11] from their work on children's ideas about shadows, conclude that many younger children think of a shadow as the presence of something that light allows us to see, rather than as the absence of light. The shadow was thought of as existing on its own, hiding in the object, until the light pushes the shadow away from the object on to the wall or ground. These researchers suggest that children tend to expect the shadow of an object to be the same shape as the object. Pupils' explanations of their predictions often referred to the shadow as a 'reflection', or as a 'dark reflection' on the screen.

Guesne[2] found that 10- and 11-year-old children perceived the 'light source' as being responsible for shadows but noticed only the reproduction of the object's form. The majority of 13- and 14-year-olds interpreted shadows in terms of an obstacle blocking the passage of light and they used the notion of 'light entity in space'. Tiberghien *et al.*[12] report that 90 per cent of their sample of ninety-four 10- and 11-year-olds correctly located where their own shadow would fall when the sun was in front or behind them. The same group of children found more difficulty in anticipating where the shadow of a tree would fall, with 60 per cent offering the correct idea of the relative positions of the source, the object and the object's shadow. Pupils did not offer an explanation in terms of the straight path of light.

VISION

Research into children's ideas about vision is summarised in Chapter 4.

LIGHT MEETING SURFACES

About a quarter of the 13- to 15-year-olds in Fetherstonhaugh and Treagust's study[10] thought that light stays on a mirror during reflection. Between a third and a half of the sample felt that images could be in two places. Well over half of the children thought that lenses were not necessary to form images, but nearly all thought that a lens would have to be whole to form an image.

Anderson and Smith[7] found that the majority of students (about 60 per cent) described light as bouncing off mirrors but not off other objects. A few students (less than 20 per cent) never depicted light as bouncing or reflecting off any objects. Though about 20 per cent of the students depicted light as bouncing off opaque objects as well as mirrors, only 2 per cent portrayed the light as being scattered. Many of the students who believed light bounced off opaque objects did not regard that idea as relevant to explaining about how we see.

When asked where the image is located when looking at an object in a mirror, about 25 per cent of the children questioned by Goldberg and McDermott[13] thought it would be on the mirror rather than behind it. When asked if moving their position would alter the position of an image, over half thought that it would. Most (90 per cent) of the children thought that moving back from a mirror would enable them to see more of themselves in the mirror.

Shapiro[14] reports on the ideas suggested by six Canadian 11-year-olds to explain how a pencil standing in a beaker of water appeared to be broken. The most common response, from about 25 per cent of the children, was that the water made it look broken. Other popular answers were that water bends the light rays, that the shape of the beaker makes it look broken or that the combination of water and the beaker made it look bigger. Some children thought the water acted as a magnifier and some related their answers to light rays.

COLOUR

When children were asked why red light is seen to come from a red projector slide, Zylbersztajn and Watts[15] found that only 2 per cent of the sample of 150 13-year-olds gave an answer in terms of transmission of some frequencies of light, despite having recently been taught about colour. About half thought that the white light from the projector had been changed in some way, with a third of this group suggesting a dyeing mechanism. Another 13 per cent of the total offered models in which the white light projected the colour of the filter forward in a kind of knock-on effect.

Anderson and Smith[7] found that 72 per cent of their sample did not think that white light was a mixture of colours of light. Of those who did hold the idea, only 2 per cent also knew all the colours involved in the mixture. Sixty-one per cent of the children thought that colour was an innate property of an object and that light helped our eyes to see the object. They thought that our eyes see the colour of the object rather than the colour of the reflected light.

18

SOUND

SOUND PRODUCTION

Many children's explanations of how sounds are produced are in terms of the physical properties of the material producing the sound. Children suggest that the sound is produced because the object is made of plastic or of rubber, or because it is thick, thin, taut or hard. This idea is noted both by Watt and Russell[1] and by Asoko et al.[2] The latter note that younger children very often link the production of sounds with their own actions or consider the sound to be part of the instrument, 'released' by human action.

Watt and Russell found that pupils often commented upon the action used to generate the sound and attempted to suggest a mechanism for sound production. The proportion (of a group of fifty-seven) suggesting a mechanism for sound production from a drum increased with age, from 13 per cent of infants to 98 per cent of upper juniors. The suggested location of sound generation also changed with age: younger children suggested that sound is generated inside the drum and older children that it is generated on the surface, although some explanations involved both. Mechanisms of sound production offered by the children were context-specific, those proposed for a rubber band being very different from those proposed for the drum. However, there were three main groups of explanations:

- those which involved the physical attributes of the object (for example, the tautness of a drum);
- those referring to the force needed to produce the sound (for example, the human action of beating the drum);
- those which involved vibrations.

Asoko et al.,[2] working with 260 pupils between the ages of 4 and 16, explored ideas about sound production in four contexts: a guitar string being plucked; a toy hooter horn being sounded by squeezing the bulb; stones being clashed together; and a cymbal being struck. Although they found that reference to movement or vibration of the sound source became more common with increasing age, this was context-specific to objects which could very obviously be seen to vibrate, such as the guitar string and the cymbal. (Younger children often indicated vibrations by using words such as 'wobble', or by gesturing with their hands.) No pupils used ideas about vibrations consistently, in all contexts.

With reference to the guitar, there was an increase throughout the infant and junior years of responses which referred to the vibration of the source. At the same time there was a decrease in other ideas, particularly those relating only to personal action and properties of the source, such as tautness. Approximately 80 per cent of the responses of secondary children referred to vibration of the guitar string. However, over the whole age range very few children described the transfer of the vibrations of the string to the surrounding air.

In thinking about the cymbal, almost 40 per cent of reception class children associated the sound with vibration, and the proportion was greater among older children as personal action references decreased. Again there was very little mention, by children of any age, of the vibration being transferred to the air.

In the context of the hooter horn, references to vibrations were far fewer. The younger children explained the hooter horn in terms of personal action but this notion fell away sharply with age as more references were made to the involvement of air and to movement. The number of replies focusing on the involvement of air remained high, with approximately 40 per cent of the secondary aged sample referring to it. There were very few references to the vibration of the source and even fewer to the vibration being passed to the air.

When the students considered how the stones produced sound, the vast majority of answers at all ages referred to personal action and these responses were often complemented by references to the properties of the stones. There were virtually no explanations based on the involvement of air or vibrations.

Asoko *et al.* suggest that, because children do not have a generalised theory of sound production transferable across contexts,

> teachers should plan to give children experience of sound produc-
> tion in less obvious contexts as well as in contexts where the
> vibrations are more clear. It may be useful to allow the children to
> experiment with applying vibration ideas developed in obvious
> contexts to less obvious contexts with a view to developing a
> generalised theory.[2]

They also propose that, because the role of the ear does not appear to be problematic for most children, this may be a useful context for developing ideas about vibrations in air. When explaining how covering a sound affects its volume many children used ideas about 'gaps' or 'stopping the sound', and these ideas may lead to the scientific view of sound as vibrations travelling through air and other materials.

SOUND TRANSMISSION

Watt and Russell[1] found that the idea of sound travelling was not one which children readily expressed. When they did so, they tended to think that the sound needs an unobstructed pathway in order to travel. This idea seems to draw upon everyday experiences of moving among furniture, of umbrellas stopping the rain or of building a dam across a stream, where movement would be impeded by anything in the path. Watt and Russell suggest that children may envisage sound as an invisible object with dimensions, which would need room in order to move. The idea that air is needed as a medium for sound transmission was rarely mentioned, but when it was Watt and Russell concluded that children's notions of air had a bearing on their understanding of sound travel. For example, those children who envisaged air as empty space would be thinking of sound transmission in air as sound travelling through an empty space.

Likewise Asoko *et al.*[2] found that pupils rarely suggested a mechanism for sound travel at any age. Moreover, it was difficult to interpret children's explanations when certain expressions, such as sound 'goes', could have had various meanings. When they were asked how the ticking of a clock is heard, children up to the age of 14 focused their answers either on the mechanism of the clock or on the personal action of the child listening. The role of air was mentioned by only a small number of children. Only among 16-year-olds was the notion of sound travel in air common: it was referred to by 70 per cent of this group.

Difficulties in thinking about sound travelling are not restricted to younger children. In a study of tertiary students, who were shortly to go on to teach secondary school physics, Linder and Erickson[3] observed four conceptualisations of sound:

- as an entity that was carried by individual molecules through a medium;
- as an entity that was transferred from one molecule to another through the medium;
- as a substance which travelled, 'usually in the form of flowing air';
- as a substance in the form of some 'travelling pattern'.

Linder and Erickson describe the first two perspectives as 'microscopic', given that the students explained sound in terms of molecules and tended to portray sound as a 'thing'. They describe the other two perspectives as 'macroscopic', since students explained sound in terms of the bulk properties of the medium.

HEARING

Research into pupils' ideas about hearing is summarised in Chapter 4.

SOUND MEETING SURFACES

Research into children's ideas about sound meeting surfaces has focused on ideas about sound absorption.

There appears to be little understanding by pupils of any age of the process of sound absorption.[2] When an object emitting a sound was covered, most children predicted that the sound would be muffled, offering explanations such as 'the sound is trapped', or 'it comes through more slowly'. Alternatively, children referred to the material from which the cover was made. The fact that some sound can still be heard was often accounted for in terms of leakage through holes or gaps, an explanation used by children of all ages. Very few children explained their ideas in terms of vibrations. The researchers suggest that there is some uncertainty as to what exactly the children are explaining: are they explaining the fact that the sound they hear is less, or that they can still hear it even though the clock has been covered, or both? (Children explaining where the sound has gone may have used different ideas from those explaining how the sound gets out.)

CHARACTERISTICS OF SOUND

Research has not focused upon children's ideas about pitch, loudness or quality of sound. However, the studies suggest that pupils may be confused about the speed/size of vibration: bigger vibrations were thought to be slower than small vibrations and consequently difficulties arose in discussing pitch and volume.

REPRESENTING SOUND

Watt and Russell[1] studied children's representation of sound in diagrams. They found that older children – especially boys – were more likely to represent sound diagrammatically. Children showed sound either as a single entity which travelled to the receiver or as a continuous line. The most common depiction of sound adopted a direction roughly parallel to the direction of the sound travel. However, a quarter of those upper juniors who represented sound used lines perpendicular to the travel and it is suggested that the response had been learned from secondary sources. Some children thought that sound spreads out, but a large number thought that sound goes only to the intended listener. A wide range of notations were used to represent sound: including words, lines, arrows, shading and musical notes.

Watt and Russell also considered the vocabulary used by children in describing sound and found that junior children made frequent use of words such as 'vibration', 'echo', 'travel' and 'sound wave'. Both 'vibrate' and 'echo' were often used to mean 'repeat'.

19

HEATING

HEAT AND TEMPERATURE

Children's ideas about heat have been the subject of a lot of research and studies have taken place in many countries. Certain patterns emerge and it is clear that children have difficulty in understanding this area of science. Harris,[1] as reported by Hewson and Hamlyn,[2] suggests that the subject of heat is one of the most confused in science and that the source of this confusion centres on the use of words like 'heat', 'heat flow' and 'heat capacity'. Harris, referring to students' tendency to think of heat as a 'substance' which flows from place to place, claims that 'many students' conceptions of heat today are, on the whole, not very different from those of Lavoisier (1789), that is, they think calorically'. Indeed, many researchers have found that children think of heat as a substance, and Hewson and Hamlyn have drawn attention to language and cultural influences.

Erickson[3] reported that children think of heat as a 'type of subtle substance, like air, that is capable of flowing into and out of objects'. Other studies have observed a similar notion and that the 'substance' is often thought to flow or have fluid characteristics. Erickson noted that both cold and heat are often associated with air.

Engel Clough and Driver[4] report that pupils up to the age of 16 think of cold as 'an entity which, like heat, has the properties of a material substance'. It appears that children do not necessarily think of hot and cold as part of the same continuum. Rather, they perceive them as two different phenomena, with cold often being thought of as the opposite of heat.

Watts and Gilbert[5] found seven 'alternative frameworks' for thinking about heat which were commonly used by a group of 14- to 17-year-olds:

- conspicuous heat, in which heat is only associated with very hot bodies and large amounts of heat;
- dynamic heat, in which heat is associated with movement;
- motile heat, in which heat is seen as something which spreads out

from one place to another and as 'more insidious and fluid-like than direct (conspicuous) heat';

- normal heat, which is taken as body temperature and humans are seen as the standard for measuring heat;
- product heat, which is taken to be manufactured, deliberately contrived heat as distinct from natural heat;
- standard heat, in which any temperature above 'freezing' represents heat and in which cold is the opposite of heat and applies to any temperature below freezing;
- regional heat, which assumes a static model of heat occupying a particular area, and cooling is seen as a reduction of heat intensity.

Engel Clough and Driver note that certain 'facts' about heat such as 'heat rises', 'hot things expand' and 'heat travels through metals' are 'known' by children but they are not explained. (Erickson[3] reports that children who have an intuitive notion that heat makes things rise may use this to explain water expanding up a tube.)

Erickson reports that distinguishing between the concepts of heat and temperature was one of the most difficult tasks for children. They tend to view temperature as the mixture of heat and cold inside an object, or simply as a measure of the amount of heat possessed by that object, with no distinction between the intensity of heat and the amount of heat possessed. Many children think that the temperature of a body is related to its size, volume or the amount of stuff present. Children also think of temperature as a property of the material, their everyday experience of touching objects supporting a notion that some substances are naturally warmer or colder than others.

When considering pupils' ideas of the difference between 'heat' and 'temperature', Tiberghien[6] reports three categories of response:

- the idea that heat is hot, but temperature can be cold or hot: 'temperature – you can have something freezing, whereas heat – you tend to think of something being hot. Heat . . . it's the warm end of the scale'. (This view was more common among 10- to 12-year-olds.)
- the idea that there is no difference between heat and temperature: 'temperature is heat'. (This type of thinking was found in pupils from age 10–16.)
- the idea that temperature is a means of measuring heat: 'temperature – you can measure heat with, but heat is hot – you can feel heat'.

Tiberghien notes that children do not recognise temperature as a physical parameter that can describe the condition of a material. For them other criteria are more pertinent for describing materials.

There have been several studies of children's ideas about the resultant temperature when volumes of water at different temperatures are mixed. When a quantity of cold water is mixed with an equal quantity of hot water children often say that the mixture will be 'warm'. However, if the initial temperatures of the water are given there are fewer correct answers. Driver and Russell,[7] studying 324 Malaysian and English pupils, found that over 50 per cent of 8- to 9-year-olds and 80 per cent of 13- to 14-year-olds gave correct qualitative judgements but less than 25 per cent of 13- to 14-year-olds predicted an average temperature when numerical values were introduced. They tended to add or subtract the two initial temperatures to find the final one. This pattern was also found by Stavy and Berkovitz[8] in their study of seventy-seven Israeli 9- to 10-year-olds.

Strauss and Stavy[9] report that, when considering the final temperature of a mixture of two beakers of cold water, children aged 4–6 often judged the temperature to be the same. However, older children, aged 5–8, often said that the water would be twice as cold because there was twice as much water. Older children, aged up to 12, again judged the water to have the same temperature as the separate beakers. To explain this, Strauss and Stavy suggest that the youngest children do not consider the amount of water when making their judgement, whereas older children do attend to the amount and judge the temperature as if it were an extensive physical quantity. The oldest children are able to differentiate between intensive and extensive quantities and make judgements accordingly, understanding that the temperature remains unchanged despite changes in the amount of water. Strauss and Stavy also found that children tended to make more correct predictions of temperature when equal amounts of hot and cold water were mixed, than when two equal amounts of cold water were mixed.

A study was carried out by Driver and Russell[7] in which children were shown a beaker of ice with a thermometer reading 0°C. Pupils were asked what would happen to the reading if more ice was added. The majority of the youngest children (aged 8) thought that the temperature would go up when the volume of ice was increased. The older children (aged up to 14) tended to think that the temperature would decrease when more ice was added.

In Appleton's study[10] of twenty-five Australian 8- to 11-year-olds, three children did not recognise a mercury-in-glass thermometer and did not know what it was used for. The majority of the remaining children either said that it told how hot or cold something was or that it told us the temperature of something. The children were asked to speculate on the likely temperatures of some water which had just boiled and of a cold drink with lots of ice in it. Most children seemed very uncertain in their suggestions and many may have simply guessed. Less than half gave an answer in the 0°C to 10°C range for the iced water and less than a quarter suggested a temperature in the 90°C to 100°C range for the boiled water. One child thought that thermometers are 'used for measuring heat' only and therefore gave no temperature for the iced water. When asked how they thought the thermometer worked, roughly a third suggested that the thermometer 'was sensitive to heat', or that it was 'made to go to the right number'. Other suggestions involved pressure, pushing, or were concerned with heat rising. Appleton concluded that 'apparently simple and straightforward activities on temperature with this group of children were found to expose a high level of ignorance regarding relatively basic ideas about temperature and its measurement'.

ENERGY TRANSFER PROCESSES

Research into ideas about energy transfer has concentrated on heat conduction.

Erickson[3] investigated children's ideas about how the whole of a metal rod gets hot when only one end is heated. Children thought of heat accumulating in one spot and then overflowing to another part of the rod and they appeared to be attributing material properties to the heat.

From Engel's study[11] of children's ideas about the conduction of heat, it appears that children use different explanations in different situations. Considering spoons made of different substances and what they would feel like in a jug of hot water, many children explained the differences in terms of heat travelling through different materials at different rates. Explaining the differences experienced when they placed their hands on metal and plastic plates, children tended to refer to some observable property of the material or to suggest that metals let heat in or out more easily than other materials. Most children explained metal parts of a bike feeling colder than the plastic parts in terms of metal attracting or absorbing coldness.

Watts and Gilbert[5] report pupils' ideas about a metal bar which was heated at one end and cooled at the other. Pupils aged 13–17 referred to hot molecules moving along the bar to the cold end, where they cooled and stopped moving. The younger pupils also referred to cold molecules in the water and some suggested an exchange of hot molecules from the bar with cold molecules from the water.

Engel Clough and Driver[4] observed that pupils' answers were influenced by the direction of heat conduction in relation to the pupil. More children used the idea of heat moving towards, as opposed to away from, the hand. Children appeared to find it difficult to think of heat conduction when they felt a cold surface. This finding is supported by Brook et al.[12] who report that children seemed to think that the sensations of hotness and coldness are due to something leaving the hot or cold object and entering the body. Students in their sample of 300

15-year-olds thought of coldness being transferred to the person from the cold object, rather than heat being transferred away from the person to the object. The percentage of students showing an understanding of heat transfer fell from 15 per cent to 6 per cent when heat transfer was away from the body rather than towards it. It appears that very few students understood heat transfer in terms of the behaviour of particles: less than 5 per cent of the sample attempted to describe conduction in terms of particles and only a few of these used the accepted terms. Pupils appeared to be confused as to the heat transfer process in a given situation and conductors and insulators were seen as opposites, having no degrees of conducting ability.

Driver[13] reports that, athough older pupils (aged 11–16) who have been exposed to teaching about the kinetic-molecular theory of matter might attempt to explain phenomena such as conductivity in terms of particulate ideas, these were not used spontaneously by most children. When particle ideas were used there was a tendency to attribute macroscopic properties, such as melting or expanding, to the microscopic particles.

Engel Clough and Driver[4] report that, to explain different conductivities, students drew on the observable properties of the materials, such as hardness or thickness. In their 12-year-old group, 37 per cent referred to such properties in explaining why metal and plastic plates felt as though they were at different temperatures. Some children said that metals were colder substances than plastic. A third of the 12-year-olds explained the different temperatures of four spoons standing in a bowl of hot water in terms of different speeds of movement of heat. Many children referred to metals 'pulling in' heat or to heat being 'released' or 'let out easily' by metals. Five students in the sample suggested that heat did not penetrate metals and stayed on the surface therefore allowing the heat to be conducted well.

20

ENERGY

CONCEPTUALISATIONS OF ENERGY

Across the field of research studies on pupils' ideas about energy, several recurring conceptualisations of energy have emerged. Energy is seen as:

- associated only with animate objects;
- a causal agent stored in certain objects;
- linked with force and movement;
- fuel;
- a fluid, an ingredient or a product.

ENERGY AND LIVING THINGS

The idea that energy is associated with living things, and particularly with human beings, is reported from several studies. Watts and Gilbert[1] describe several frameworks observed among children. One of these involves 'human centred energy' in which energy is associated mainly with human beings or with objects which were treated as if they had human characteristics. Such anthropomorphic views were found to be held by pupils of all ages including 'A' level students.

Solomon[2] examined children's thinking about energy by asking them to write three or four sentences showing how they would use the word 'energy'. Human activities, health, food and fuels all figured prominently in pupils' responses, which showed a movement with age away from the idea of energy associated only with living activities and also a significantly greater interest in living associations on the part of girls than among boys.

Solomon outlined four themes into which responses fell. Two of these were:

- vitalism, in which energy is thought to be needed for life (as in 'When we run out of energy we need medicines and vitamins' and 'Exercise is good for you, it builds up your energy.');

- activity, in which we are thought to need energy to move (as in 'When we run out of energy we need food and rest' and 'Exercises use up energy, then you become tired.').

When Stead[3] asked pupils to talk about energy in particular situations, they suggested that energy was needed to live and be active. They also related energy to fitness and strength, saying that without energy living things were tired, listless, fatigued and less active. Non-living things were thought not to need energy.

'Living' and 'human-centred' energy frames were also noted by Arzi[4] when asking children about energy in, or obtained from, food. In thinking about energy and chocolate some students had difficulty in reconciling the ideas that energy is a good thing to have, but chocolate is not.

When Bliss and Ogborn[5] asked pupils to choose three energy pictures, from ten in which energy was needed or being used, pictures of living things proved to be the most popular.

ENERGY STORES

Watts and Gilbert[1] describe a 'depository' model of energy used by pupils, in which some objects are thought of as having energy and being rechargeable, some as needing energy and expending what they get, and some (whose activities are 'normal') as neutral. Energy is thought of as a causal agent stored in certain objects. This model was also identified by Gilbert and Pope[6] who report many ideas from 10- to 12-year-olds which are within the 'depository' framework. These researchers also found some multiple frameworks in which a depository model was linked to ideas about activity and movement.

Ault et al.[7] also report on pupils using different frameworks, some of which even contradicted each other, in different contexts. Pupils held a notion of a source of energy 'in' some things. Only the things with energy in them were thought capable of making changes happen. Gayford,[8] examining children's ideas about energy in biological contexts, also found that pupils 'often had a notion of energy as something that is stored, rather like a material is stored'.

Solomon[2] found responses in which pupils related machines, or various kinds of work, to an input of energy from electricity or some fuel.

ENERGY, MOVEMENT AND FORCE

Many children appear to link energy with movement and force. Stead[3] found that those children who associated energy with inanimate objects often suggested movement, or the lack of it, as determining whether energy was present or not. Absence of activity was reported by Bliss and Ogborn[5] as an explanation given for energy not being attributed to a situation. Watts and Gilbert[1] found an 'obvious activity' framework among their subjects, in which energy was associated with overt displays of movement. Often the outward display itself was thought of as the energy: energy was thought of as 'doing'.

Duit[9] notes a close association between energy and force in children's responses. Watts and Gilbert[10] also found some students using the words 'force' and 'energy' synonymously and some treating the two concepts as distinct but interconnected.

Ault *et al.*[7] found an undifferentiated view of energy, work, force and power amongst their students, and Barbetta *et al.*[11] suggest that confusion in the use of the words 'force', 'energy' and 'work' is not only terminological but conceptual. The latter group found that two-thirds of the pupils who had not been exposed to the concept of energy in class thought that it was something necessary for movement and/or that it was a type of force. The remaining pupils offered no ideas. The majority of pupils who had been introduced to the concept of energy answered by giving textbook definitions or by quoting 'forms of energy'.

Brook and Driver[10] also found that pupils' notions of energy, movement and force were strongly associated. Almost one in five of their pupils focused on the amount of force which a ball-bearing had at different points on a track and some used the word 'force' in a way similar to that in which a scientist would use 'kinetic energy'. About one in ten children thought that a truck would have energy only when moving, or would have most energy when moving. These researchers suggest that students tend to focus on directly observable features of phenomena, rather than on abstract ideas (such as energy) which are often used by scientists.

Confusion between energy, force, friction, work and gravity was identified by Stead[3] who also noted that 'potential energy' was confused with the potential to have energy.

ENERGY AS A FUEL

Several researchers have found pupils holding ideas of energy as a fuel, with a global perspective and ideas about limited resources. One of the themes which Solomon[2] identified in children's responses relates to shortage of energy in the future and the need for new sources of energy to meet the world's needs. Duit[13] found that German students closely linked energy with fuels and electricity, although this was not the case for students from the Philippines.

Stead[3] found that for pupils, 'energy' was synonymous with 'fuel' and that phrases like 'energy crisis' and 'conserve energy' meant 'fuel crisis' and 'conserve fuel'. Children had the notion that fuel is energy rather than that fuel 'contains' or 'is a source of' energy.

Duit[9] found that approximately 10 per cent of his sample mentioned 'energy crisis' in their word associations, and about one-third mentioned power plants.

Watts and Gilbert[1] describe the 'functional' model of energy in which energy is a very general kind of fuel. Energy is associated mainly with technical applications: it is not seen as essential to all processes but just those which make life comfortable. A similar notion of energy as a fuel was also noted by Ault et al.[7]

ENERGY AS A FLUID, INGREDIENT OR PRODUCT

Watts and Gilbert[1] identified three further models by which pupils envisage energy:

- The 'flow transfer' model in which energy is thought of as a fluid. (It is assumed possible for energy to be 'put in', 'given', 'conducted' or 'transported' and energy is thought to flow out of one thing into another.)
- The model of energy as an 'ingredient'. (Energy is viewed as a reactive agent rather than a causal one, lying dormant within objects until something triggers it. Rather than being thought continuous it is assumed to arise all of a sudden as a result of some combination of ingredients.)
- The model of energy as a 'by-product' of a situation, rather like a waste product. (Energy is not conserved: it is seen as a relatively short-lived product that is generated, is active and then disappears or fades.)

The fluid notion of energy was also noted by Duit[9] and by Gayford.[8] The idea of energy as a physical substance was also noted by Stead.[3]

Duit[13] found that, for students in the Philippines, energy seems to be very process oriented, often linked with strength. In both Germany and the Philippines many students suggested that energy could occur in several forms.

CONSERVATION OF ENERGY

Duit[9] reports that students do not necessarily see a need for the idea of energy conservation. Students aged 12–14 were asked to predict the height or final speed of a ball on a U-shaped track and to explain their predictions. Although up to 43 per cent of students (before instruction) made a correct prediction, at best only 2 per cent explained their prediction in terms of energy transfer and none mentioned energy conservation. After instruction, up to 63 per cent gave correct predictions but only 17 per cent used ideas about energy in their explanations and at best only 10 per cent included energy conservation. Students tended to explain in terms of track geometry or in terms of force or 'drive'. Duit suggests that they preferred to use ideas gained from everyday experience rather than those which they were encouraged to use in science lessons.

Driver and Warrington[14] also found that few students used ideas about energy conservation when they were asked to explain various simple systems. All the students in this study went on to obtain 'O' and 'A' levels in physics, which suggests that they were able to use the idea of energy conservation when required, though most of them chose not to when given a free choice.

Black and Solomon[15] noted the application of ideas about energy conservation in the responses given by forty-six 14-year-olds to a question in which they were asked to describe fully the energy changes for a bouncing ball. Some students recognised the principle of conservation of energy but still intuitively reasoned that energy would be lost. About one-third of the students said that, since it could not be destroyed, the energy must be stored in some way or that it must turn up again in its original form. Relatively few students (15 per cent of the total) used ideas of transformation and dissipation of energy, although 30 per cent said that the form of the energy had changed.

Gayford[8] reported very little understanding of energy as a conserved quality. A large majority of pupils (79 per cent) did not consider that biological processes, such as respiration, involve energy conservation. Pupils thought that these processes actually form energy, which is used in subsequent reactions.

An 'energy gets used up' view, in which things go until energy is used up or fuel is consumed, was found by Ault et al.[7] to appear frequently in children's understanding.

Duit[16] suggests that in order to promote learning about energy 'more time should be devoted to qualitative questions', and that 'students should be advised to explain the physical phenomena in their own words'.

21

FORCES

DESCRIBING FORCES

The development of ideas about forces often takes place in the context of learning about horizontal motion or about gravity and falling. Consequently a lot of the research into pupils' thinking about forces relates to these domains. Research into pupils' ideas about forces causing horizontal motion and about friction is summarised in Chapter 22. Research into pupils' ideas about weight and falling is summarised in Chapter 23.

Some studies, including a developmental study by Piaget,[1] have explored pupils' ideas about forces themselves and how they act, and these are the subject of this summary.

Underlying pupils' ideas about practical experiences of forces are their understandings about the way forces are transmitted through solids, liquids and gases – understandings which also underpin their ideas about pressure. Studies do not appear to have focused upon ideas about the transmission of forces but there has been some work focusing on pupils' ideas about pressure.

The extent to which pupils have a generalised and consistent view of the existence and behaviour of forces has been the subject of much discussion. Many studies suggest that groups of pupils have consistent frameworks of beliefs. However, the work of Finegold and Gorsky[2] indicates that individuals tend not to adhere consistently to frameworks of beliefs.

Pupils' ideas about the nature of forces have been identified from the very substantial body of research into understandings about motion. Younger pupils, between 7 and 9 years, were found to think of force in terms of anger or feeling.[3] [4] Yet, at the same time, some 7- and 8-year-olds held the physicists' view of force as something acting to cause a change in motion, although they tended to talk of forces getting things going rather than making things stop.

Pupils naturally bring to their learning lay meanings of the word 'force' and many studies have reported the word 'force' being associated with coercion or opposing resistance.[5] [6] [7] Forces are frequently associated with living things[8] [9] and Duit[10] found pupils associating forces with physical activity and muscular strength. When pupils do think of inanimate objects as having or exerting forces, they appear to focus on those objects which can cause things to move and so can be regarded as agents not unlike living things.[5] Pupils sometimes suggest, when describing the action of forces, that objects are 'trying to' bring about a particular action.[8]

Many researchers have found that pupils associate forces only with movement, not recognising the 'passive' forces involved in equilibrium situations.[5] [6] [8] [9] [11] Driver[11] reports that pupils are reluctant to accept the presence of force where there is no motion and a study of 1,000 Norwegian upper secondary students supported this finding,[12] with 50 per cent of the sample not recognising such 'passive' forces.

Research shows a widely held view that there is something, often called 'force', within a moving object.[12] [13] [14] [15] [16] This 'force' is thought of as keeping the object moving and it appears to have something in common with physicists' 'momentum'. Moving objects are thought to stop when the 'force' of motion in them runs out – something like fuel getting used up.[17]

Studies of pupils' ideas about the relationship between forces and motion have identified the following main ideas:

- if there is motion, there is a force acting;
- if there is no motion, then there is no force acting;
- there cannot be a force without motion;
- when an object is moving, there is a force in the direction of its motion;
- a moving object stops when its force is used up;
- a moving object has a force within it which keeps it going;
- motion is proportional to the force acting;
- a constant speed results from a constant force.

Learners generally appear to think of force as a property of a single object rather than as a feature of interaction between two objects and this is reflected in Brown and Clement's studies[18] [19] as well as in those of Maloney,[20] Minstrell and Stimpson,[21] and Watts.[5] Minstrell and Stimpson[21] found that pupils think of weight, motion, activity and strength as being important in determining an object's force. Pupils' inclination to think in terms of force as a property of an object leads several researchers to propose introducing the word 'momentum' for this, recognising that in the early secondary years this would mean only a qualitative, intuitive understanding of the term. It is argued that this is readily accepted by younger pupils and it allows them to think about the meaning of force without wanting to attribute it as a property of a single object.[3][4][6][9]

Erickson and Hobbs[22] suggest activities in which pupils are asked to identify pairs of forces in terms of 'What is pushing and what is pulling?'. They propose that these experiences should involve cases with motion and cases where there is no motion.

So far as the different manifestations of forces are concerned, pupils do not necessarily recognise all of them as forces. For example, Shevlin[7] found that primary children did not associate 'kick' or 'throw' with 'push'. Moreover, Erickson and Hobbs[22] studied pupils in the 6–14 age range and found them making a distinction between forces which pull and those which just hold.

Considering forces in terms of their magnitude and direction appears to present problems to pupils. Terry et al[23] found that some pupils at the secondary stage did not generally use arrows effectively to indicate the point of action and the direction of a force.

Pupils' ideas about forces have arisen from their day-to-day experience of motion and of impacts and efforts. Their ideas are also influenced by everyday meanings attributed to the word 'force'. Consequently their ideas are likely to be embedded in a wide range of experiences, and pupils are likely to have a strong commitment which will be hard to influence through teaching strategies. Indeed, many of the research studies refer to the way in which learned ideas are not applied by pupils when they reflect upon experience: they fall back upon their prior, lay ideas which have been retained alongside learned science. Thus any teaching strategies should recognise that the development of ideas about forces and interaction presents very significant problems for pupils and teachers.

Several researchers stress the importance of paying more attention to Newton's Third Law, in order to help pupils appreciate that a force is not a property of an object but forces are characteristic of action between objects. Given pupils' difficulties in recognising a force of reaction, Minstrell[24] proposes offering 'bridges' between prior ideas and science ideas. For example, pupils who did not recognise a reaction between a table and a book resting upon it were led through thinking about a book resting on an outstretched hand, a book resting on a spring and a book on a springy plank, back to a consideration of the book on a table. Such bridging strategies have been found effective in a number of different contexts.

Osborne[3][4] stresses pupils need to grasp the concept of force before they come to thinking about energy or power. Gunstone and Watts[8] refer to pupils' need for ample time for reconstructing their well-established ideas and also for new ideas to be offered in a form both intelligible and plausible. Finegold and Gorsky[2] stress the need for strategies which develop pupils' ability to extract general rules from instances and to apply general rules to instances. Most of the research studies indicate that teachers need to be aware of pupils having firmly established alternative meanings for the words they themselves are using in a strictly scientific sense.

FORCES IN PAIRS

From a scientific point of view forces always 'come in pairs'. For every force there is an equal and opposite reaction: a mug on a table exerts a force on the table – the table exerts an equal and opposite force on the mug; a stone falling off a cliff is pulled down by the weight of the Earth on it (its weight) – the stone pulls the Earth with an equal force. However, from the research studies, it is clear that pupils tend to think of a force as a single entity being a property of a single object. A paired 'reaction' or 'passive' force is not generally recognised. Sjoberg and Lie's study[12] of 1,000 Norwegian pupils highlights this position. Only nine of the sample of twenty-eight 12- to 14-year-olds in Erickson and Hobbs's study[22] recognised forces acting in both directions when a weight is pulling on a fixed string.

Minstrell[24] studied fifty-five high school pupils and their ideas about the forces involved when a book rests on a table, when he developed a teaching strategy for the idea of a force of reaction. Only twelve of a group of twenty-seven pupils initially thought that the table exerts an upward force, although Minstrell's strategy proved effective in raising this number to twenty-five of the twenty-seven. Initially pupils talked of the table merely being 'in the way'. This idea was also found among pre-engineering students by Clement.[15] Among those who recognised an upward force on the book, there was the idea that the downward force must be greater than the upward force 'otherwise the book would float away'.

Stead and Osborne,[25] in their study of forty-seven New Zealand 11- to 16-year-old pupils' understanding of friction, found nine pupils associating friction and the force of 'reaction'.

Erickson and Hobbs's study,[22] investigating pupils' ideas about equilibrium situations, found pupils distinguishing between 'pulling' and 'holding' and they found only six of thirty-two pupils, between the ages of 6 and 14, making reference to a force of reaction.

Brown and Clement,[18] working with seventy-eight high school pupils, found that pupils considering a collision between two objects think of one object as having the more force – namely, the moving or faster-moving object. Terry et al.,[23] from their study of secondary pupils taking a physics course, note the confusion arising from scientists' use of the word 'reaction' and 'opposite' in the context of paired forces. The word 'reaction' appears to suggest to pupils a sequence of events in which one force leads to the second. The word 'opposite' appears to lead some pupils to think of a reaction force acting on the same object rather than of two forces involved in an interaction between two objects.

FORCES ACTING TOGETHER – NETT FORCE AND EQUILIBRIUM

Erickson and Hobbs[22] studied ideas about equilibrium among thirty-two Canadian pupils between the ages of 6 and 14. Pupils appeared to think of several forces engaged in a struggle in which a stronger force would prevail. Equilibrium was seen by ten pupils in a group of twenty-six as the resolution of the struggle, after which all the forces involved would cease to act. Only fourteen of the thirty-two pupils predicted that if a system in equilibrium were displaced, it would stay in the new position.

Osborne[3] also found New Zealand pupils thinking in terms of a stronger force dominating a weaker one.

PRESSURE

Research into pupils' ideas about pressure has focused upon fluid pressures and particularly air pressure. Séré,[26] working with eleven French 11- to 13-year-olds, found pupils thinking that only wind, and not still air, has pressure. Working with eighty-four 12-, 14- and 16-year-olds, Engel Clough and Driver[27] found high proportions (67 per cent, 80 per cent and 87 per cent respectively) thinking that pressure increases with depth. However, pupils were less inclined to think in terms of pressure acting in all directions in air or water (13 per cent, 19 per cent and 34 per cent respectively): they were inclined to think of a greater pressure downwards. This study found frequent references to air or a vacuum 'sucking' in pupils' explanations of changes experienced with straws and syringes. Atmospheric pressure pushing was mentioned but few pupils explained in terms of balancing pressures.

Studying 600 French 11- to 13-year-olds and their ideas about air pressure differences and consequent movement of air, Séré[28] found 85 per cent accurately describing the extent to which air is squashed in a ball before and after blowing it up. However, only 63 per cent of the pupils accurately compared air pressure inside the ball with the air outside. Generally pupils did not readily make pressure comparisons. An important finding from Séré's study is that pupils tend to associate pressure in gases with moving air, assuming pressure acting in the direction of motion. There was less tendency to associate pressure with static gases.

152

TURNING FORCES

From an early age children have an intuitive understanding of moments, as identified by Inhelder and Piaget.[29] When they manipulate a see-saw, for example, they 'know' that a 'weight' further away from the centre has a bigger effect and they 'know' how to achieve a balance using different weights on either side of a beam.

22

HORIZONTAL MOTION

DESCRIBING MOTION

Pupils' and students' understanding of motion (including horizontal motion) has been the subject of considerable research in many countries throughout the world. This area of science has been of particular interest because of the difficulties which learners of all ages seem to have in grasping the physicist's Newtonian view of motion.

Commonly occurring prior ideas about motion include the notions that if an object is pushed with a constant force this produces constant motion; and that if the pushing force ceases there is a 'force' in the moving object which keeps it going but which gradually gets used up and then the object stops.

Everyday experience from birth onwards suggests and reinforces such ideas about the way things move. With such constant reinforcement the ideas become firmly established and have been called 'gut dynamics'.[1] It is argued that 'gut dynamics' underlies most people's ability to interact with moving objects and to play sport. In addition people appear to generate for themselves a set of explanations and rules for why things move the way they do. These rules have been termed 'lay dynamics'.[2]

Throughout history the same everyday experiences have led earlier scientists, like Aristotle and Buridan, to develop theories of motion which have a lot in common with 'gut dynamics' and 'lay dynamics'.

The extent to which students' ideas about motion are coherent and theory-like is a matter of dispute. Some researchers comment on the *ad hoc* and context-dependent nature of students' reasoning.[3] [4] [5] Others argue that there are underlying consistent forms of reasoning about motion which can be identified.[6] [7] [8]

It is clear that understanding motion in Newtonian terms (in which motion at a constant velocity needs no causal explanation, and in which acceleration is the result of a nett force) is a major task for pupils. Students of all ages, including physics undergraduates, fail to grasp the Newtonian conception of motion.[9] They modify rather than abandon

154

their 'gut' and 'lay' dynamics and merely attach new labels to their own theories.[10] In particular, it appears from the work of many researchers that learners do not easily share the physicists' commitment to consistency of explanation in the form of a coherent framework: they may hold independent and even conflicting ideas about related phenomena.

Children's ideas and descriptions of motion tend to be less differentiated than a physicist's. They tend to see objects as either at rest or moving. The period of change, when for example an object speeds up from rest to a steady speed or slows down and stops, is less frequently focused on by children. The term 'acceleration' is not commonly used by school-age pupils prior to its introduction in science lessons. Everyday terms such as 'going faster' are used in ambiguous ways, sometimes referring to the magnitude of the speed of an object and at other times referring to the speed increasing with time. There are many studies which report such problems.

Jung[9] reports pupils leaving time out of their thinking such that they were imagining an object 'getting to a certain velocity' or 'being set into motion' rather than accelerating over a period of time. Among some 300 university students only 40 per cent successfully compared the acceleration of objects,[11] and only 68 per cent of a sample of fifty-two 17-year-olds studying physics recognised that an overtaking object is going faster all the time.[12]

It is common for pupils to think that, if speed is increasing, then acceleration is also increasing. This was the case for 60 per cent of the fifty-two sixth-formers taking physics, and it was the case for 88 per cent of a group of 113 pupils aged 12–14 who were studied by Jones.[12]

It is important to note here the need for proportional reasoning in developing scientific concepts of velocity and acceleration – an aspect studied by Piaget.[13] Following from this Boulanger has found that training in proportional reasoning resulted in improved differentiation of speed, distance and time among a group of seventy-four 9-year-old pupils.[14] There appears to be an important message for science teachers here: that children need to develop the language tools to describe motion appropriately (including vocabulary, graphical representations and numerical formulations, for example $v = d/t$) prior to developing an understanding of dynamical principles.

STATIONARY OBJECTS

The physicists' view of rest, as a special case of motion at a constant speed where the speed is zero, is not held by pupils. They generally regard the state of rest as fundamentally different from the state of motion,[2] although some 13-year-olds were found to recognise a stationary object as having a speed equal to zero.[15]

Rest is widely regarded as a 'natural' state in which no forces are acting on an object.[16][17] Indeed, even pupils who recognised a 'holding' force seemed to think of such a force as quite different from a pushing or a pulling force.[18]

Minstrell[16] records the following ideas pupils have about a stationary book: air pressure keeps the book stationary; gravity keeps the book stationary; the table is 'in the way' of the book falling; an object in contact with the earth, like a book on the ground, no longer experiences the force of gravity; a downward force on the book must be greater than an upward force, otherwise it would float away. The idea of the table being 'in the way' appears to be the most generally held view.

In the context of making a graph to show the movement of an object over time, it has been found that 12- and 14-year-olds tend not to represent time passing for any period when an object is stationary.[15]

FORCES

Research findings on pupils' ideas about forces are summarised in Chapter 21. Those ideas which relate directly to motion are identified here.

The word 'force' has many connotations for children, as it does in everyday discourse. In a study of primary-aged pupils Osborne[19][20] reported many thinking of force in terms of anger or feeling. Yet, at the same time, he found other 7- and 8-year-olds with the physicists' view of force as something acting to cause a change in motion. However, pupils tended to talk of forces getting things going rather than making things stop.

Research shows a very widely held view that there is something, often called 'force', within a moving object.[7][17][21][22][23] This 'force' is thought of as keeping the object moving and it appears to have something in common with the physicists' idea of 'momentum' in that pupils see it as being connected with how big and how fast the object is. In so far as it is seen to 'run out' after a while when a pushed object slows down and stops, it is seen as a kind of fuel.[24]

Pupils have particular difficulty in relating time to forces. They see forces as being 'above' time.[9] Consequently the relationship between an impulse (in which a force is applied for a short time) and a continuous force (in which the force is applied for a long time) is problematic for many pupils.

FORCES CAUSING CHANGES IN MOTION: SPEEDING UP AND SLOWING DOWN

The idea that motion at a constant speed, and in a straight line, is, like rest, a natural state which does not require the application of force, was proposed by Newton. It represented a revolution in thinking from that of earlier scientists who had explained uniform motion in terms of forces in the surrounding air, or in the moving body, which must be there to keep the body moving. Research into learners' prior ideas about motion finds remarkable parallels between pupils' ideas and those of scientists' from Aristotle's time to the fourteenth century, although we are warned against too naïve a labelling of pupils' views as 'Aristotelian'.[25]

Some researchers find pupils distinguishing between different kinds of moving object: those which move 'actively' of their own accord like balls or gliders, and those which are being dragged or pushed and which are seen as passive. Pupils appear to think of actively moving objects as having an impetus within them (which would keep them moving horizontally for a time if they fell off a cliff, for example). They tend to describe 'passive' moving objects as not possessing impetus and therefore likely to fall straight downwards on reaching the edge of a cliff.[7] [10] [24]

Most 15-year-olds appear to expect a moving object to come to a stop even when there is no friction. This indicates the extent of the resistance teachers face when they offer the Newtonian idea that a moving object continues to move at a constant speed unless a force acts upon it.

The work of a large number of researchers has identified the following generally held ideas:

① '*If there is motion, there is a force acting.*' This is a very persistent idea over a wide age range. It was found by Clement in a sample of 150 first-year university students,[23] and it was found in many of the students, including those who had studied physics, described by McCloskey.[10] [26] Studies of school pupils, together covering hundreds of individuals in several countries, indicate a similarly persistent and widespread view.[27] [28]

② '*There cannot be a force without motion*' and '*If there is no motion then there is no force acting.*' Pupils often cannot envisage a force acting without causing, or having the possibility of causing, motion.[29] Thus when an object is at rest on a table the weight of the object is seen as acting downwards (because the object would move downwards were the table not there) but they see no upward force of the table as the table itself cannot move up.

③ '*When an object is moving there is a force in the direction of its motion.*' This impetus view, held by Buridan in the fourteenth century, emerges from many studies, both of school pupils and of university students, including those studying physics.[2] [21] [23] [27] [30] [31] [32] Osborne, in a study of 200 pupils aged 13, 14 and 15 reports an increasing prevalence of the view, held by 46 per cent, 53 per cent and 66 per cent of these age groups respectively.[19] [20]

4 *'A moving object has a force within it which keeps it going.'* This view, which is associated with Buridan's impetus theory, is identified in the studies of McCloskey,[7] Sjoberg and Lie,[17] Viennot,[21] Watts and Zylbersztajn,[22] and Clement.[23] Moreover, 50 per cent of a group of eighty-seven high school pupils, and also 33 per cent of a sample of university students, were found to extend this idea so as to predict that a ball emerging from a curved tube will continue to move on a curved path, as though it possessed a circular impetus determining the curved path.[15 26 33] Pupils talked of the 'force still trying to circle round'.

5 *'A moving object stops when its force is used up.'* This widespread version of the impetus idea has been described in Norwegian as well as American research.[17 30 34]

6 *'Motion is proportional to the force acting'* and *'A constant speed results from a constant force.'* The notion that force determines speed: that a stronger force makes an object go faster, and conversely that making an object go faster needs a bigger force, was found among pupils studied by Champagne *et al.*[29] and by Hewson.[35] Many researchers have found substantial numbers of pupils strongly committed to the idea that a constant speed implies that a constant force is being applied to the moving object.[17 22 27 29 30 35] It is significant that pupils appear to associate force, not with acceleration, but with speed.[2] Thus the physicists' idea of force causing a change in motion is not readily accepted and pupils are likely to think of continuing to apply a force if they want to keep an object moving at constant speed. In fact force was associated with velocity rather than with acceleration by a substantial proportion of some several hundred students between the last year of secondary school and the third year of university.[21]

It may happen that a pupil, believing that a moving object contains a force keeping it going, and not believing that a moving object would tend to continue moving in the same direction, would combine the two misconceptions to make accurate predictions about the movement of an object. Conversely, a pupil who understands that a moving object does not contain a force, whilst not believing that the object would continue moving, would combine a sound view with a misconception to make a wrong prediction about movement. Eckstein and Shemesh describe this situation in a study of 159 9- to 15-year-olds.[33] The percentage of pupils holding both 'misconceptions' remained unchanged over the whole seven-year span of the study and the researchers argue that pupils appear to have reached, by the age of 9, a certain stable maturity in their ideas about motion which is highly resistant to change.

FRICTION

Friction was associated with rubbing by 50 per cent of 13-year-olds in Stead and Osborne's group of thirty-eight 12- to 16-year-olds.[36] Ideas about friction in a group of forty-seven secondary school pupils[37] included the following:

- friction is a force (sixteen pupils);
- friction is the same thing as reaction (nine pupils);
- friction depends upon movement (seventeen pupils);
- friction is associated with energy, especially heat (six pupils);
- friction occurs only between solids (twelve pupils);
- friction occurs with liquids but not with gases (ten pupils);
- friction causes electricity (most pupils);
- friction 'does' this and that, as though it were an object;
- friction is 'trying to' do this and that.

Friction was not recognised as a force by pupils who thought of forces only as 'getting things going' and not as 'stopping things'. Also, some pupils saw friction as a directionless resistance to motion as distinct from a force opposed to motion.

TEACHING APPROACHES

There are clearly particular problems in teaching physicists' dynamics, in that pupils' prior ideas are firmly established from long and continuous reinforcement, and physicists' ideas seem less intelligible, less helpful, and even to fly in the face of common sense.[38] Moreover, pupils do not generally feel the need for the all-embracing unifying theory sought by science.

Perhaps the most helpful message of all to emerge from the research is that difficulties do not betoken either poor teaching or poor learners: difficulties are inevitable in view of the everyday effectiveness of 'gut dynamics' and 'lay dynamics' for coping with the world of force and motion;[21] [39] and some difficulties are a consequence of the well-established, traditional approaches.[7]

Some approaches for more effective teaching of dynamics have been investigated.

Use of analogies

If they are to change their ideas, it is proposed that learners must come to feel that their existing ideas are unsatisfactory.[40] Then they need usable anchoring ideas or intermediate 'bridging' analogies between their prior ideas and those of the physicists' dynamics.[41] Bridging strategies, anchors and analogies are seen by several researchers as a helpful approach to dynamics.[41] [42] [43] [44] For example, if pupils cannot accept the idea of a force of reaction exerted by a table upon a book which rests upon it, they can be offered a bridging analogy in the form of a book resting on a spring and then a book on a flexible, springy, surface. Pupils may find that two intermeshed hairbrushes provide a helpful bridging analogy towards the concept of friction.[41]

Concrete, rather than abstract, anchoring conceptions are recommended[42] and pupils' own evaluation of them is thought to be critically important. It is noted that some anchors have to be acknowledged as 'brittle'. (For example, when two skaters are offered as a bridge towards recognising an equal and opposite force, 97 per cent of pupils acknowledged that the skaters would move apart at equal speeds if the skaters pushed one another, but only 40 per cent of pupils thought that it would be so if only one skater were to push on the other. Clearly this analogy is not a thoroughly reliable bridge.[42]) The development of bridging analogies calls for a careful analysis of dynamics so as to clarify helpful bridging steps such as A, B and C:

Children's dynamics — A — B — C — Newtonian dynamics

Approaches which help children to change their ideas

Pupils' ideas about motion seem to be well established by the age of 9 and hard to change after this age[33] and yet the difficulties of quantitative approaches for younger pupils are acknowledged. Therefore, attempts to teach about motion in a qualitative way at an earlier stage are recommended.

It is widely accepted that pupils need to have opportunities to articulate their own views. It is also suggested that they need to develop the ability to perform thought experiments.[24] Reflection and discussion are recognised as critically important, requiring time and carefully designed tasks for that purpose.[23] [45]

Hewson stresses the need for the new ideas to be offered to pupils in such a way as to appear both intelligible and fruitful.[46] He refers to the strong commitment with which pupils hold certain of their ideas: to pupils being simply angry and unwilling to believe evidence which challenges a deeply held view. Clearly, in such circumstances the plausibility of the new idea and its usefulness for coping with motion will be critically important. Indeed it may often be that a bridging idea stands a greater chance of being accepted as intelligible or plausible than the physicists' idea which is the ultimate aim.

160

Sequencing of teaching

The early introduction of the concept of momentum *in qualitative terms* prior to considering forces is an important proposal with considerable support.[2] [19] [29] [47] Although in traditional courses this has been seen as a mathematical notion to be faced by older pupils, many studies suggest that we need to offer the idea of momentum so that pupils can attach to it their own idea that a moving object has something which keeps it going. The 11- and 12-year-olds studied by di Sessa appeared to have little difficulty with a purely qualitative notion of momentum.[5] (In fact there is a general suggestion that Newtonian ideas about motion become harder to accept as pupils' become firmer in their own dynamics.) Introducing momentum before force then allows force to be seen as that which causes a change in momentum, and it prevents the label 'force' being attached to the pupils' notion of 'something in the object which keeps it moving'.

Pupils' difficulties in relating distance, time and speed have been noted. An early focus upon these is recommended:[5] [46] [48] [49] it is proposed that pupils would then develop a descriptive capability, and a fluency in time, distance and rates as a basis for the causal explanations of physics.

Attention to the time of action of a force is also important such that pupils can relate impulses and continuous forces in terms of the length of time over which they act.

A number of software packages are emerging which are designed to give pupils 'first-hand' experience of frictionless motion.[48] Since it is friction which causes moving objects to slow down, friction can be held responsible for supporting much of gut dynamics, and experience of frictionless motion contributes to making Newtonian ideas more plausible. In the absence of friction, pupils are able to relate force to motion in accordance with physicists' dynamics.[49] Moreover, it is proposed that teaching about friction may be helpful[37] and that this is the concept which allows us to link the principles of physics with the real world.

There is considerable support for allowing pupils to develop their own dynamics – to clarify and label their own ideas. This is seen as a process which could begin early and which should precede any attempts to teach formal physics concepts, and which is better with 11-year-olds than with 14-year-olds.[5] [8] [20] [23]

Alongside this is the call for a more intelligible account of motion,[50] in which 'gut dynamics' and 'lay dynamics' are refined to provide a coherent and usable framework. These approaches would involve extensive experience of motion involving a range of forces and objects, work in friction-free situations, differentiating phases of motion, differentiating impulses and continuous forces, describing, discussing and looking for rules.

Gilbert and Zylbersztajn[51] draw attention to the advantages to be gained from a historical perspective in which pupils can see similarities between their own ideas about motion and those of leading scientists in the past. In particular, the Impetus Theory developed during the Middle Ages offers a link with most pupils' own thinking and it can provide both an approach to learning about forces and motion and also an opportunity for recognising the nature of science.

GRAVITY

THE EARTH'S GRAVITY

Several studies investigating children's ideas about the Earth as a body in space have identified the ways in which 'down' is interpreted[1][2][3][4][5] and these are described in Chapter 24. There appears to be a progression in ideas, from an absolute view of 'down' (not seen as specific to Earth) to an Earth-referenced view of 'down', with most 14-year-olds having an Earth-referenced view.[1] However, Baxter found only about 20 per cent of 15- and 16-year-olds having an Earth-referenced view of 'down' which was based on the centre of the Earth rather than the Earth's surface.[2]

The ideas identified by Nussbaum, by Baxter and by Vosniadou and Brewer are brought together in Figure 24.1.

Selman *et al.*[6] has classified pupils' thinking about unseen forces in general, identifying broad phases in which they perceive unilateral, then multiple and then balanced forces. Others have studied developing ideas about gravity in particular. A detailed study, by Stead and Osborne,[7] of New Zealand pupils aged from 11 to 17 revealed ideas of gravity 'pushing', 'pulling' or 'holding'. 'Holding' appeared to be the most common perception of gravity and this was bound up with ideas of gravity being connected with air pressing down and with an atmospheric shield which prevents things floating away. The notion that there must be air for gravity to act appears to be widespread. It was also found among Italian middle school pupils by Ruggiero *et al.*[8] The idea that gravity is in some way related to air has implications, of course, for the way pupils think about gravity acting in space, on other planets and on the Moon. Relating gravity to air appears to offer an explanation of gravity which lies outside objects rather than in terms of a property of all objects. Stead and Osborne found only one pupil in a sample of forty-two who had the idea that all objects exert a gravitational force.

The Earth's magnetism and its spin are both thought to be connected with gravity.[7][9] Stead and Osborne found references to 'artificial gravity' caused by spinning and Vicentini-Missoni[9] found references to spin linked with gravity among thirty-six 9-year-olds.

A considerable amount of work has been directed towards pupils' ideas about the way gravity changes with height above the Earth's surface. Significant numbers appear to hold the physicist's view that the force of gravity decreases with height above the Earth's surface. Stead and Osborne[7] found one-third of a sample of 257 14-year-olds thinking this way and Ruggiero et al.[8] also found this idea among 12- and 13-year-olds. However, it appears that pupils who hold this view tend to expect a far bigger decrease in the force of gravity with increasing height than is actually the case.

Stead and Osborne[7] also found one-third of their 14-year-old sample holding the view that gravity increases with height above the Earth. This idea was also present among pupils studied by Ruggiero et al.[8] Pupils holding this 'the higher – the stronger' gravity view assume this applies until things get outside the Earth's atmosphere. Watts[10] found that pupils in the 12–17 age range thought that gravity depends upon height, but they appeared to confuse gravity with potential energy in assuming a higher force of gravity at greater heights.

Stead and Osborne[7] found some of their sample thinking of gravity as an upward force which holds us vertical. There were also references to gravity as a kind of 'material' which could be trapped in aeroplanes and which could flow up electricity pylons to keep birds in place on the wires. Pupils' ideas about birds clearly contribute to their thinking about gravity, and some pupils accounted for birds being able to stay up in terms of gravity being present only at the Earth's surface.

Watts[10] found among secondary-age pupils the idea that gravity must be a very large force since it affects so many things at once.

WEIGHT

The physicist's idea that the weight of an object is a force – the force of gravity on that object – does not appear to be a firmly held idea among secondary pupils. Stead and Osborne,[7] Ruggiero et al.,[8] Vicentini-Missoni[9] and Watts[10] all found that their subjects did not generally equate weight with the force of gravity. Indeed, there seems to be a widespread separation of ideas about weight from ideas about gravity. Stead and Osborne found some 15-year-olds thinking that gravity only affects heavy things: some thinking that it is possible to have weight without gravity (saying that astronauts wear moon-boots 'to give them weight where there is no gravity'), and some thinking that it is gravity which keeps birds up. Some 12- and 13-year-olds in the study by Ruggiero et al. thought that gravity does not operate without weight.

Ruggiero et al.[8] found that among a sample of pupils and adults weight was seen as a property of an object, whereas gravity was seen as a property of space. However, within their sample of twenty-two 12- and 13-year-olds, these researchers found pupils relating both gravity and weight to air and atmospheric pressure, with pupils thinking that air is necessary to keep things on the ground and that weight is affected by, or depends upon, air.

Watts[10] found secondary pupils having a very flexible view of gravity, in which it does not act in the same way on all things and in which it does not even act in the same way at all times on a particular thing. They saw gravity as acting in conjunction with weight to hold things down.

Stead and Osborne's work[7] included a study of pupils' ideas about the effect of gravity on objects in water. Among 13-year-olds, they found 30 per cent assuming that there is no force of gravity in water and that this explains why things float. Pupils also suggested that there is less gravity in water or even that there is gravity in water but that it acts upwards. This study also uncovered the idea that gravity would only act on the parts of a body above the surface of the water – the head of a swimmer, for instance.

Research into children's ideas about mass and density is summarised in Chapter 8.

FALLING

Stead and Osborne,[7] and also Ruggiero et al.,[8] found that pupils do not always feel the need to identify a force to account for things falling: they think things 'just fall naturally' or that the person letting the object go causes the fall.

Vicentini-Missoni[9] found, among thirty-six 9-year-olds, a clear distinction between 'falling down' involving a loss of equilibrium, and 'falling' in response to gravity. Pupils did not combine ideas of equilibrium, gravity and falling into the unifying conception of the physicist. There appeared to be a progression from the idea that things fall if nothing holds them up, through the idea that things fall because of their weight (without recognising that weight is the force of gravity on an object), to the idea that weight is a force and that all things fall in the absence of support.

Osborne[11] describes pupils thinking that all things fall, that heavier things fall faster, and that barriers stop things falling. The idea that falling is caused by weight, and that not only the Earth but also heaviness pulls a thing down, was found by Selman et al.[6] in a sample of 105 children from pre-school age onwards.

Watts, in his study of secondary pupils, found some thinking that gravity begins to act when an object begins to fall and that it ceases to act when the object lands on the ground. In fact their explanation amounted more to a description than an explanation of falling. Pupils who recognised gravity as a constant force accounted for the behaviour of a ball thrown in the air in terms of the object trying to counteract gravity and failing. Some pupils talked of objects containing a force which counteracts gravity and which then runs out so that the object falls back to Earth.

It appears to be very common indeed for pupils (and also university physics students) to assume that heavier objects fall to Earth faster, having a bigger acceleration due to gravity. Gunstone and White[12] studied a sample of 176 pre-course first-year physics students and found that 40 per cent believed a bigger weight to have a bigger acceleration in fall. Of Nachtigall's sixty-seven German 10-year-olds, 91 per cent expected a heavier ball to land first.[13] In this study it was notable that 47 per cent of the sample described fall as being with a constant speed on the grounds that the force of gravity is constant. Clearly these pupils were thinking of the force as causing velocity rather than a change in velocity. Champagne et al.,[14] studying twelve American 12- and 13-year-olds, also found pupils linking force with speed. Those who recognised an increasing velocity during free-fall then argued that there must be a gravity gradient, with increasing force of gravity nearer the Earth. (These studies are summarised in McDermott's critical review of research in the domain of mechanics.[15])

Ruggiero et al.,[8] among their 12- and 13-year-old sample, found roughly equal numbers accounting for fall in terms of each of the following ideas:

- gravity operating on the weight of the object to cause fall;
- gravity and the weight of the object acting separately to cause fall;
- natural motion in the absence of support.

The idea of an acceleration due to the force of gravity is often confused with gravitational field. Rogers[16] found that pupils, recognising a negative acceleration ($-g$) as a ball is thrown up and recognising a positive acceleration ($+g$) as it falls, put these together to infer, not zero acceleration, but no gravitational force at the vertex of movement.

GRAVITY IN SPACE

Stead and Osborne[7] found 11-year-olds thinking of gravity as relating only to the Earth. This notion appears to be bound up with pupils' common belief that gravity is associated with air and that where there is no air there is no gravity. This is a view which 12- and 13-year-olds were found to hold and one which Ruggiero et al.[8] and Watts and Gilbert[17] met in the same age group. Watts and Gilbert also found secondary pupils thinking that gravity needs a medium and that there would be no gravity in places without air. Some pupils in Stead and Osborne's sample appeared to think in terms of 'molecules of gravity' in air.

In Stead and Osborne's[7] sample of 258 13-year-olds, 44 per cent said that there is no gravity on the Moon. The idea that not all planets have gravity was common among 14-year-olds, and 81 per cent of 13-year-olds and 75 per cent of 14-year-olds said there is no gravity in space. It may be that science fiction ideas of 'weightlessness' have contributed to this view.

24

THE EARTH IN SPACE

THE EARTH

Several studies have investigated children's ideas about the Earth as a body in space. Nussbaum[1] and Baxter[2] report a possible progression of ideas among American, Israeli and English children, from a flat Earth with limited sky and an absolute view of 'down', to a spherical Earth surrounded by sky with 'down' being towards the centre of the Earth. These findings are supported by the studies of Nepalese children by Mali and Howe[3] and of Californian children by Sneider and Pulos.[4] The work of Vosniadou and Brewer[5] with Greek and American children also cites many similar explanations.

The ideas identified by Nussbaum, Baxter and Vosniadou and Brewer are summarised in Figure 24.1 which shows how similar ideas found by the different studies appear to represent the steps of a developmental sequence.

Vosniadou and Brewer[5] note that some children thought there were two Earths – one flat on which we live and one spherical in space. Moreover, while many children thought the Earth was round, at ages 8 and 9 they thought it was round like a plate and that it has an edge. Nussbaum[1] suggests that conceptual progress takes place with age or with schooling, such that most 8- and 10-year-olds hold the earliest idea N1, most 12-year-olds hold ideas N2 or N3 and most 14-year-olds hold ideas N4 or N5 (Figure 24.1). Baxter[2] suggests that the idea B3 is the one held by most children whilst the accepted science view B4 is used by less than 20 per cent even at the age of 16. When Nussbaum and Sharoni-Dagan[6] evaluated a unit of instruction for 8-year-olds, they observed that, while 12 per cent of the pupils held ideas N4 and N5 before instruction, 42 per cent held them afterwards.

DAY AND NIGHT

Vosniadou and Brewer,[5] Baxter[2] and Klein[7] studied children's ideas about why it gets dark at night. They suggest a development in

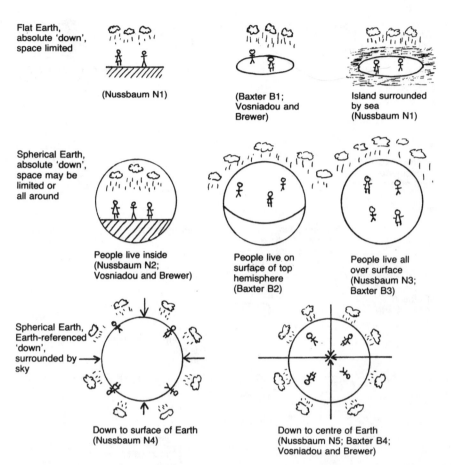

Flat Earth, absolute 'down', space limited

(Nussbaum N1)

(Baxter B1; Vosniadou and Brewer)

Island surrounded by sea (Nussbaum N1)

Spherical Earth, absolute 'down', space may be limited or all around

People live inside (Nussbaum N2; Vosniadou and Brewer)

People live on surface of top hemisphere (Baxter B2)

People live all over surface (Nussbaum N3; Baxter B3)

Spherical Earth, Earth-referenced 'down', surrounded by sky

Down to surface of Earth (Nussbaum N4)

Down to centre of Earth (Nussbaum N5; Baxter B4; Vosniadou and Brewer)

Figure 24.1 Children's notions of the Earth's shape, sky and the direction of 'down'

Key: N1–N5: progression of ideas noted by Nussbaum[1]
B1–B5: progression of ideas noted by Baxter[2]

children's thinking with age, from more directly observable reasons to those involving astronomical movements. (The last two studies also note that many younger children considered the Sun to be animate.) The children's notions of day and night could be seen to fit into four bands of thinking, as shown in Figure 24.2.

Sadler's study of American 14-year-olds[8] identifies the variety of ideas held about the cause of day and night. He notes that, although over half the interviewed students had taken or were taking a one-year course of

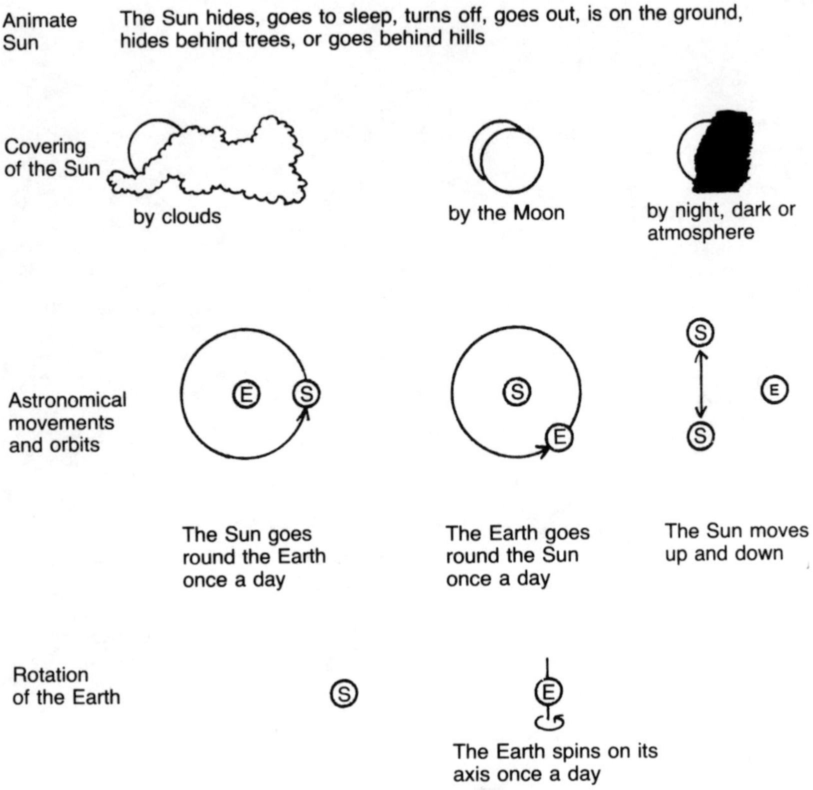

Animate
Sun

The Sun hides, goes to sleep, turns off, goes out, is on the ground, hides behind trees, or goes behind hills

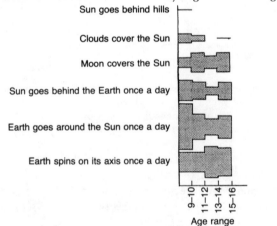

Covering
of the Sun

by clouds   by the Moon   by night, dark or
atmosphere

Astronomical
movements
and orbits

The Sun goes
round the Earth
once a day

The Earth goes
round the Sun
once a day

The Sun moves
up and down

Rotation
of the Earth

The Earth spins on its
axis once a day

Figure 24.2 Children's ideas about why it gets dark at night

Sun goes behind hills

Clouds cover the Sun

Moon covers the Sun

Sun goes behind the Earth once a day

Earth goes around the Sun once a day

Earth spins on its axis once a day

9-10   11-12   13-14   15-16

Age range

Figure 24.3 The prevalence, with age, of pupils' ideas about day and night
Source: J. Baxter, 'Children's understanding of familiar astronomical events', *International Journal of Science Education* 11 (Special Issue): 502–13.

which a quarter was astronomy, these students did not seem to have the correct view any more often than the other pupils but they did use many more scientific terms in their explanations.

Baxter[2] identified six ideas about day and night and the prevalence of these is shown in Figure 24.3. It appears that at the ages of 15 and 16 many still hold covering and orbital theories of day and night.

THE EARTH, MOON AND SUN

Although little work has been done on children's views of the solar system as a whole, three studies have looked at ideas about the relationship between the Earth, the Sun and the Moon. Vosniadou and Brewer[5] observed a move in children's thinking with age from an Earth-centred to a Sun-centred solar system. However, children even at an older age were much less sure of the position of the Moon.

Jones et al.[9] investigated Tasmanian children's ideas about the size, shape and relationships of the Earth, Sun and Moon. They too found evidence of a move from Earth-centred to Sun-centred thinking, noting the five different models shown in Figure 24.4. Children's ideas about the shapes of the Earth, Sun and Moon appeared to change with age: younger children suggested two-dimensional or non-spherical three-dimensional shapes and older children chose spheres. So far as the relative sizes of the Sun, Moon and Earth are concerned, there was no apparent trend towards a correct understanding among older children and far fewer girls than boys chose the correct model.

Sadler[8] observed a lack of understanding both of the relative sizes and the relative distances apart of the Earth, Sun and Moon. Most pupils drew the three the same size or between half or double each other's diameter, and the Sun and Moon were drawn within one to four Earth diameters away from the Earth. These misconceptions, Sadler suggests, may be compounded, or indeed caused, by the models used in classrooms or by the diagrams in books, which do not use the true scale for size and distance.

THE PHASES OF THE MOON AND ECLIPSES

Baxter[2] has investigated ideas about the phases of the Moon. He noted five ideas, including the science view. The four alternative notions involve the covering of (or casting a shadow on) the Moon by increasingly distant objects (Figure 24.5).

Figure 24.6 shows the prevalence, with age, of the ideas Baxter identified and the dominance of the 'shadow of the Earth' idea even among 16-year-olds.

Baxter's findings are supported by Sadler[8] who found that 37 per cent

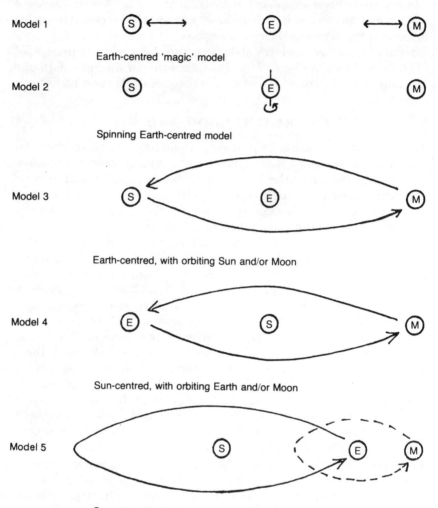

Figure 24.4 Models of children's thinking about the relationship of the Sun, Moon and Earth

Source: B.L. Jones, P.P. Lynch and C. Reesink, 'Children's conception of the Earth, Sun and Moon', *International Journal of Science Education* 9 (1): 43–53.

of his sample attributed the phases of the Moon to the Earth's shadow covering the Moon..

Targon[10] found that 65 per cent of his sample of university students had no knowledge, and a further 23 per cent only fragmentary knowledge, of the phases of the Moon; 6 per cent held the correct notion and 8 per cent had an 'alternative' eclipse notion.

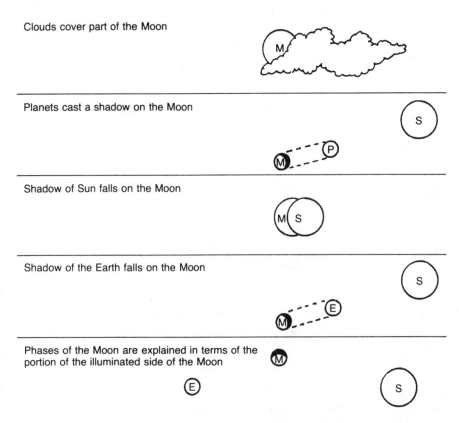

Clouds cover part of the Moon

Planets cast a shadow on the Moon

Shadow of Sun falls on the Moon

Shadow of the Earth falls on the Moon

Phases of the Moon are explained in terms of the portion of the illuminated side of the Moon

Figure 24.5 Children's ideas about the causes of the phases of the Moon
Source: J. Baxter, 'Children's understanding of familiar astronomical events', *International Journal of Science Education* 11 (Special Issue): 502–13.

THE CHANGING YEAR

Investigating explanations of the cold in winter, Baxter[2] observed an age-related trend in children's thinking: from explanations involving nearer and more familiar objects to explanations involving more distant and less tangible objects, and also the movement of astral bodies. However, by far the most common suggestion, at all ages, was that the distance of the Earth from the Sun is the cause of the seasons. Many children believed the Earth is nearer the Sun in the summer than in the winter and that this accounts for hotter weather in summer. This idea was also observed by Sadler.[8] The prevalence with age of ideas about the cause of the seasons which Baxter identified is shown in Figure 24.7

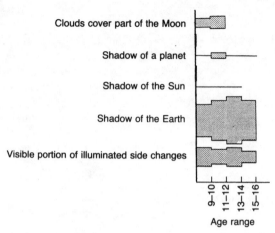

Figure 24.6 The prevalence, with age, of pupils' explanations of the phases of the Moon

Source: J. Baxter, 'Children's understanding of familiar astronomical events', *International Journal of Science Education* 11 (Special Issue): 502–13.

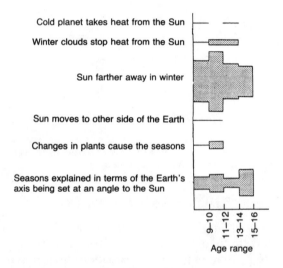

Figure 24.7 The prevalence, with age, of pupils' explanations of the seasons

Source: J. Baxter, 'Children's understanding of familiar astronomical events', *International Journal of Science Education* 11 (Special Issue): 502–13.

THE SOLAR SYSTEM AND BEYOND

Lightman *et al.*[11] found that only 55 per cent of adults thought of the Sun as a star and that 25 per cent thought it was a planet. These researchers note that astronomical literacy is 'entwined with social institutions and values, as well as with education', with younger people, males and better-educated people having more astronomical knowledge.

REFERENCES

INTRODUCTION

1 Nussbaum, J. and Novak, J.D. (1976) 'An assessment of children's concepts of the Earth utilising structured interviews', *Science Education* 60(4): 535–50.
2 Mali, G.B. and Howe, A. (1979) 'Development of Earth and gravity concepts among Nepali children', *Science Education* 63(5): 685–91.
3 Howe, C., Rogers, C. and Tolmie, A. (1990) 'Physics in the primary school: peer interaction and the understanding of floating and sinking', *European Journal of Psychology of Education* 5(4): 459–75.
4 Scott, P. (1987) 'A constructionist view of teaching and learning', and Needham, R. (1987) 'Teaching strategies for developing and understanding science', *Children's Learning in Science Project: CLIS in the Classroom*, Centre for Studies in Science and Mathematics Education, University of Leeds.

1 LIVING THINGS

1 Piaget, J. (1929) *The child's conception of the world*, Routledge & Kegan Paul, London.
2 Carey, S. (1985) *Conceptual change in childhood*, MIT Press, Cambridge, Mass.
3 Looft, W.R. and Bartz, W.H. (1969) 'Animism revived', *Psychological Bulletin* 71: 1–19.
4 Inagaki, K. and Hatano, G. (1987) 'Young children's spontaneous person-ification as analogy', *Child Development* 58: 1013–21.
5 Smeets, P.M. (1974) 'The influence of mental ability and cognitive ability on the attribution of life and life traits to animate and inanimate objects', *Journal of Genetic Pyschology* 124: 17–27.
6 Looft, W.R. (1974) 'Animistic thought in children: understanding 'living' across its associated attributes', *Journal of Genetic Psychology* 124: 235–40.
7 Stead, B.F. (1980) *Living*, LISP Working Paper 15, Science Education Research Unit, University of Waikato, Hamilton, New Zealand.
8 Bell, B.F. (1981) *Animal, plant, living: Notes for teachers*, LISP Working Paper 30, Science Education Research Unit, University of Waikato, Hamilton, New Zealand.
9 Bell, B. and Barker, M. (1982) 'Towards a scientific concept of "animal"', *Journal of Biological Education* 16(3): 197–200.
10 Arnold, B. and Simpson, M. (1979) 'The concept of living things', Aberdeen College of Education *Biology Newsletter* 33: 17–21.

11 Leach, J., Driver, R., Scott, P. and Wood-Robinson, C. (1992) *Progression in conceptual understanding of ecological concepts by pupils aged 5–16*, Centre for Studies in Science and Mathematics Education, University of Leeds.

12 Stavy, R. and Wax, N. (1989) 'Children's conceptions of plants as living things', *Human Development* 32: 88–94.

13 Tamir, P., Gal-Chappin, R. and Nussnovitz, R. (1981) 'How do intermediate and junior high school students conceptualise living and non-living?', *Journal of Research in Science Teaching* 18(3): 241–8.

14 Sedgwick, P.P., Linke, R.D. and Lucas, A.M. (1978) 'A comparison in changes in children's concept of life with the development of relevant criteria in Australian science curriculum materials', *Research in Science Education* 8 185–203.

15 Lucas, A.M., Linke, R.D. and Sedgwick, P.P. (1979) 'Schoolchildren's criteria for "alive": a content analysis approach', *Journal of Psychology* 103: 103–12.

16 Brumby, M.N. (1982) 'Students' perceptions of the concept of life', *Science Education* 66(4): 613–22.

17 Sequeira, M. and Freitas, M. (1986) '"Death" and "Decomposition" of living organisms: children's alternative frameworks', Paper presented at the 11h Conference of the Association for Teacher Education in Europe (ATEE), Toulouse, France, 1–5 September.

18 Bell, B.F. (1981) 'When is an animal, not an animal?', *Journal of Biological Education* 15(3): 213–18.

19 Trowbridge, J.E. and Mintzes, J.J. (1985) 'Students' alternative conceptions of animal classification', *School Science and Mathematics* 85(4): 304–16.

20 Tema, B.O. (1989) 'Rural and urban African pupils' alternative conceptions of "animal"', *Journal of Biological Education* 23(3): 199–207.

21 Stead, B. (1980) *Plants*, LISP Working Paper 24, Science Education Research Unit, University of Waikato, Hamilton, New Zealand.

22 Ryman, D. (1974) 'Children's understanding of the classification of living organisms', *Journal of Biological Education* 8: 140–4.

23 Schofield, B., Black, P., Head, J. and Murphy, P. (1984) *Science in Schools: Age 13: Research Report No 2, Assessment of Performance Unit*, Department of Education and Science, HMSO, London.

24 Askham, L.R. (1976) 'The effects of plants on classification behaviour in an outdoor environment', *Journal of Research in Science Education* 13(1): 49–54.

25 Braund, M. (1991) 'Children's ideas in classifying animals', *Journal of Biological Education* 25(2): 103–10.

26 Arnold, B. (1983) 'Beware the molecell!', Aberdeen College of Education *Biology Newsletter* 42: 2–6.

27 Dreyfus, A. and Jungwirth, E. (1989) 'The pupil and the living cell: a taxonomy of dysfunctional ideas about an abstract idea', *Journal of Biological Education* 23(1): 49–55.

28 Dreyfus, A. and Jungwirth, E. (1988) 'The cell concept of 10th graders: curricular expectations and reality', *International Journal of Science Education* 10(2): 221–9.

29 Deadman, J.A. and Kelly, P.J. (1978) 'What do secondary school boys understand about evolution and heredity before they are taught the topics?', *Journal of Biological Education* 12(1): 7–15.

30 Engel Clough, E. and Wood-Robinson, C. (1985) 'How secondary school students interpret instances of biological adaptation', *Journal of Biological Education* 19(2): 125–30.

31 Engel Clough, E. and Wood-Robinson, C. (1985) 'Children's understanding of inheritance', *Journal of Biological Education* 19(4): 304–10.
32 Brumby, M.N. (1984) 'Misconceptions about the concept of natural selection by medical biology students', *Science Education* 68(4): 493-503.
33 Lawson, A.E. and Thompson, L.D. (1988) 'Formal reasoning ability and misconceptions concerning genetics and natural selection', *Journal of Research in Science Teaching* 25(9): 733–46.
34 Brumby, M.N. (1979) 'Problems in learning the concept of natural selection', *Journal of Biological Education* 13(2): 119–22.
35 Caravita, S., Tonucci, F., Consoli, V. and Rusca, G. (1987) 'Investigating pupils' conceptualization in the biological domain: structure–function relationships', Paper presented at the Second European Conference for Research on Learning and Instruction, 19–22 September, Tübingen, FRG.
36 Caravita, S. and Tonucci, F. (1987) 'How children know biological structure–function relationships', Paper presented at the Second International Seminar: Misconceptions and Educational Strategies in Science and Mathematics, 26–29 July, Cornell University, Ithaca, N.Y.

2 NUTRITION

1 Children's Learning in Science (1987) *CLIS in the classroom: approaches to teaching energy, particulate theory of matter, plant nutrition* (a pack of teaching materials with teacher's guide), Centre for Studies in Science and Mathematics Education, University of Leeds.
2 Eisen, Y. and Stavy, R. (1988) 'Students' understanding of photosynthesis', *The American Biology Teacher* 50(4): 208–12.
3 Stavy, R., Eisen, Y. and Yaakobi, D. (1987) 'How students aged 13–15 understand photosynthesis', *International Journal of Science Education* 9(1): 105–15.
4 Barker, M. (1985) *Teaching and Learning about Photosynthesis*, Science Education Research Unit, Working Papers 220–9, University of Waikato, Hamilton, New Zealand.
5 Carey, S. (1985) *Conceptual Change in Childhood*, MIT Press, Cambridge, Mass.
6 Wellman, H.M. and Johnson, C.N. (1982) 'Children's understanding of food and its functions: a preliminary study of the development of concepts of nutrition', *Journal of Applied Development Psychology* 3: 135–48.
7 Contento, I. (1981) 'Children's thinking about food and eating: a Piagetian-based study', *Journal of Nutrition Education* 13: 86–90.
8 Lucas, A. (1987) 'Public knowledge of biology', *Journal of Biological Education* 21(1): 41–5.
9 Wandersee, J.H. (1983) 'Students' misconceptions about photosynthesis: a cross-age study', in Helm, H. and Novak, J.D. (eds) *Proceedings of the International Seminar: Misconceptions in Science and Mathematics*, 20–22 June, Cornell University, Ithaca, N.Y., pp. 441–6.
10 Arnold, B. (1983) 'Beware the molecell', Aberdeen College of Education *Biology Newsletter* 42: 2–6.
11 Simpson, M. (1983) 'The molecell rules, OK?', Aberdeen College of Education *Biology Newsletter* 42: 7–11.
12 Pascoe, H.T. (ed.) (1982) *Pupils' Learning Problems in Certificate Biology*, Course Proceedings, National Inservice Course 1981: Biology Department, Aberdeen College of Education.
13 Fraiberg, S. (1959) *The Magic Years*, Scribners, New York.

REFERENCES

14 Mintzes, J.J. (1984) 'Naïve theories in biology: children's concepts of the human body', *School Science and Mathematics* 84(7): 548–55.

15 Brinkman, F. and Boschhuizen, R. (1989) 'Preinstructional ideas in biology: a survey in relation with different research methods on concepts of health and energy', in Voorbach, M.T. and Prick, L.G.M., *Teacher education 5, Research and developments in teacher education in the Netherlands*, pp. 75–90.

16 Gellert, E. (1962) 'Children's conceptions of the content and functions of the human body', *Genetic Psychology Monographs* 65: 293–405.

17 Simpson, M. (1984) 'Digestion – the long grind', Aberdeen College of Education *Biology Newsletter* 43, May: 12–16.

18 Bell, B. (1985) 'Students' ideas about plant nutrition: what are they?', *Journal of Biological Education* 19(3): 213–18.

19 Simpson, M. (1984) 'Teaching about digestion and getting the system to work', Aberdeen College of Education *Biology Newsletter* 44, November: 15–22

20 Roth, K.J. and Anderson, C.W. (1985) *The Power Plant: Teachers' Guide*, Institute for Research on Teaching, Michigan State University, East Lansing, Michigan.

21 Arnold, B. and Simpson, M. (1980) 'The concept of photosynthesis at 'O' grade – why pupil difficulties occur', Scottish Association for Biological Education *Newsletter* 5, p. 4.

22 Barker, M. and Carr, M. (1989) 'Photosynthesis – can our pupils see the wood for the trees?', *Journal of Biological Education* 23(1): 41–4.

23 Simpson, M. and Arnold, B. (1982) 'The inappropriate use of subsumers in biology learning', *European Journal of Science Education* 4(2): 173–82.

24 Simpson, M. and Arnold, B. (1982) 'Availability of prerequisite concepts for learning biology at certificate level', *Journal of Biological Education* 16(1): 65–72.

25 Roth, K.J., Smith, E.L. and Anderson, C.W. (1983) *Students' conceptions of photosynthesis and food for plants*, Report from the Institute for Research on Teaching, Michigan State University, East Lansing, Michigan.

26 Driver, R., Child, D., Gott, R., Head, J., Johnson, S., Worsley, C. and Wylie, F. (1984) *Science in Schools at age 15: Report No 2, Assessment of Performance Unit*, Department of Education and Science, HMSO, London.

27 Bell, B. (1985) 'Students' understanding of plant nutrition', in Bell, B., Watts, M. and Ellington, K. (eds), *Learning, Doing and Understanding in Science*, The Proceedings of a Conference, 11–13 July 1984, Woolley Hall, Nr. Wakefield, SSCR, London, pp. 36–9.

28 Bell, B.F. and Brook, A. (1984) *Aspects of secondary students' understanding of plant nutrition*, Children's Learning in Science Project, Centre for Studies in Science and Mathematics Education, University of Leeds.

29 Stavy, R., Eisen, Y. and Yaakobi, D. (1987) 'How Israeli students aged 13–15 understand photosynthesis', Unpublished manuscript, Tel Aviv University.

30 Barker, M. and Carr, M. (1989) 'Teaching and learning about photosynthesis', *International Journal of Science Education* 11(1): 48–56.

31 Tamir, P. (1989) 'Some issues related to the use of justifications to multiple choice answers', *Journal of Biological Education* 23(4): 285–92.

32 Bell, B., in collaboration with Barron, J. and Stephenson, E. (1985) *The construction of meaning and conceptual change in classroom settings. Case studies on plant nutrition*, Centre for Studies in Science and Mathematics Education, University of Leeds.

33 Barker, M. (1986) *Where does the wood come from? An introduction to photosynthesis for third and fourth formers*, Science Education Research Unit, University
of Waikato, Hamilton, New Zealand.

34 Adeniyi, E.O. (1985) 'Misconceptions of selected ecological concepts held by some Nigerian students', *Journal of Biological Education* 19(4): 311–16.

35 Arnold, B. and Simpson, M. (1980) *An investigation of the development of the concept of photosynthesis to SCE 'O' Grade*, Aberdeen College of Education.

36 Haslam, F. and Treagust, D.F. (1987) 'Diagnosing secondary students' misconceptions of photosynthesis and respiration in plants using a two-tier multiple choice instrument', *Journal of Biological Education* 21(3): 203–11.

37 Simpson, M. and Arnold, B. (1979) 'The concept of photosynthesis at 'O' Grade – what are the pupils' difficulties?', Scottish Association for Biological Education *Newsletter* 4: 38–40.

38 Smith, E.L. and Anderson, C.W. (1984) 'Plants as producers: a case study of elementary science teaching', *Journal of Research in Science Teaching* 21(7): 685–98.

39 Gayford, C.G. (1986) 'Some aspects of the problems of teaching about energy in school biology', *European Journal of Science Education* 8(4): 443–50.

40 Brumby, M.N. (1982) 'Students' perceptions of the concept of life', *Science Education* 66(4): 613–22.

41 Boschhuizen, R. and Brinkman, F.G. (1989) 'The concept of photosynthesis and pupils' ideas on the concept of "cycles"', in Michaelsson, P.E. (ed.), *Perspectives for Teacher Education in an Open Europe*, Proceedings of the 14th Annual Conference of the Association for Teacher Education in Europe held in Kristianstad, Sweden, 3–8 September.

42 Griffiths, A.K. and Grant, B.A.C. (1985) 'High school students' understanding of food webs: identification of a learning hierarchy and related misconceptions', *Journal of Research in Science Teaching* 22(5): 421–36.

43 Smith, E.L. and Anderson, C.W. (1986) 'Alternative student conceptions of matter cycling in ecosystems', Paper presented to National Association of Research in Science Teaching.

44 Leach, J., Driver, R., Scott, P. and Wood-Robinson, C. (1992) *Progression in conceptual understanding of ecological concepts by pupils aged 5–16*, Centre for Studies in Science and Mathematics Education, University of Leeds.

45 Eisen, Y., Stavy, R. and Barak-Regev, M. (1989) 'Is it possible to study photosynthesis without misconceptions?', Paper presented at ATEE Conference, Limerick.

46 Wandersee, J.H. (1985) 'Can the history of science help science educators anticipate student misconceptions?', *Journal of Research in Science Teaching* 23(7): 581–97.

3 GROWTH

1 Carey, S. (1985) *Conceptual Change in Childhood*, MIT Press, Cambridge, Mass.

2 Bell, B.F. (1981) *Animal, plant, living: notes for teachers*, LISP Working Paper 30, Science Education Research Unit, University of Waikato, Hamilton, New Zealand.

3 Tamir, P., Gal-Chappin, R. and Nussnovitz, R. (1981) 'How do intermediate and junior high school students conceptualise living and non-living?', *Journal of Research in Science Teaching* 18(3): 241–8.

4 Schaefer, G. (1979) 'Concept formation in biology: the concept of "growth"', *European Journal of Science Education* 1(1): 87–101.
5 Barker, M. (1985) *Teaching and learning about photosynthesis*, LISP, Working papers 220–9, Science Education Research Unit, University of Waikato, Hamilton, New Zealand.
6 Okeke, E.A.C. and Wood-Robinson, C. (1980) 'A study of Nigerian pupils' understanding of selected biological concepts', *Journal of Biological Education* 14(4): 329–38.
7 Driver, R., Child, D., Gott, R., Head, J., Johnson, S., Worsley, C. and Wylie, F. (1984) *Science in Schools at age 15: Report No 2. Assessment of Performance Unit*, Department of Education and Science, HMSO, London.
8 Hackling, M.W. and Treagust, D.F. (1982) 'What lower secondary students should understand about the mechanisms of inheritance, and what they do understand following instruction', *Research in Science Education 12: 78–88*.
9 Smith, E.L. and Anderson, C.W. (1986) 'Alternative student conceptions of matter cycling in ecosystems', Paper presented to National Association of Research in Science Teaching.
10 Russell, T. and Watt, D. (1989) *Growth*, Primary SPACE Project, Research Report, Liverpool University Press.
11 Roth, K.J., Smith, E.L. and Anderson, C.W. (1983) *Students' conceptions of photosynthesis and food for plants*, Report from the Institute for Research on Teaching, Michigan State University, East Lansing, Michigan.
12 Wandersee, J.H. (1983) 'Students' misconceptions about photosynthesis: a cross-age study', in Helm, H. and Novak, J.D. (eds), *Proceedings of the International Seminar: Misconceptions in Science and Mathematics*, 20–22 June, Cornell University, Ithaca, N.Y., pp. 441–6.
13 Leach, J., Driver, R., Scott, P. and Wood-Robinson, C. (1992) *Progression in conceptual understanding of ecological concepts by pupils aged 5–16*, Centre for Studies in Science and Mathematics Education, University of Leeds.
14 Dreyfus, A. and Jungwirth, E. (1988) 'The cell concept of 10th graders: curricular expectations and reality', *International Journal of Science Education* 10(2): 221–9.

4 RESPONDING TO THE ENVIRONMENT

1 Bell, B.F. (1981) *Animal, plant, living: notes for teachers*, LISP Working Paper 30, University of Waikato, Hamilton, New Zealand.
2 Leach, J., Driver, R., Scott, P. and Wood-Robinson, C. (1992) *Progression in conceptual understanding of ecological concepts by pupils aged 5–16*, Centre for Studies in Science and Mathematics Education, University of Leeds.
3 Stavy, R. and Wax, N. (1989) 'Children's conceptions of plants as living things', *Human Development* 32: 88–94.
4 Piaget, J. (1974) *Understanding Causality*, W.W. Norton, New York.
5 Guesne, E. (1985) 'Light', in Driver, R., Guesne, E. and Tiberghien, A. (eds), *Children's ideas in science*, Open University Press, Milton Keynes.
6 Andersson, B. and Karrqvist, C. (1981) *Light and its properties*, EKNA Report 8, Institutionen for Praktisk Pedagogik, University of Gothenburg, Sweden.
7 Andersson, B. and Karrqvist, C. (1983) 'How Swedish pupils aged 12–15 years understand light and its properties', *European Journal of Science Education* 5(4): 387–402.
8 Ramadas, J. and Driver, R. (1989) *Aspects of secondary students' ideas about light*, Children's Learning in Science Project, Centre for Studies in Science and Mathematics Education, University of Leeds.

REFERENCES

9 Fetherstonhaugh, T. and Treagust, D.F. (1990) 'Students' understanding of light and its properties following a teaching strategy to engender conceptual change', Paper presented to the annual meeting of the American Educational Research Association, Boston 16–20 April.

10 Osborne, J., Black, P., Smith, S. and Meadows, J. (1990) *Light*, Primary SPACE Project Research Report, Liverpool University Press.

11 Jung, W. (1981) *Conceptual frameworks in elementary optics*, Working paper presented at the International Workshop of Problems Concerning Students' Representation of Physics and Chemistry Knowledge, 14–16 September, Pedagogische Hochshule, Ludwigsburg.

12 Watts, D.M. (1985) 'Student conceptions of light: A case study', *Physics Education* 20(4): 183–7.

13 Shapiro, B.L. (1989) 'What children bring to light: Giving high status to learners' views and actions in science', *Science Education* 73(6): 711–33.

14 Ramadas, J. (1981) 'Evolving and testing a strategy for curriculum development in science relevant to the Indian school system', Unpublished Ph.D. thesis, University of Poona.

15 Crookes, J. and Goldby, G. (1984) *How we see things: An introduction to light*, Science Process Curriculum Group, Secondary Science Curriculum Review in Leicestershire.

16 De Souza Barros, S. (1985) 'Spontaneous concepts about light phenomena in children: qualitative analysis', Paper presented to the ICPE conference 'Communicating Physics', Duisberg, West Germany.

17 Anderson, C.W. and Smith, E.L. (1983) 'Children's conceptions of light and colour: developing the concept of unseen rays', Paper presented to the Annual Meeting of American Research Association, Montreal, Canada.

18 Boyes, E. and Stanisstreet, M. (1991) 'Development of pupils' ideas of hearing and seeing – the path of light and sound', *Research in Science and Technology Education* 9: 223–44.

19 Johnson, C.N. and Wellman, H.M. (1982) 'Children's developing conceptions of mind and brain', *Child Development* 53: 222–34.

20 Watt, D. and Russell, T. (1990) *Sound*, Primary SPACE Project, Research Report, Liverpool University Press.

21 Asoko, H.M., Leach, J. and Scott, P.H. (1992) 'Sounds interesting: working with teachers to find out how children think about sound', NFER–Nelson, *Topic* 8:1–7.

22 Gellert, E. (1962) 'Children's conceptions of the content and functions of the human body', *Genetic Psychology Monographs* 65: 293–405.

23 Carey, S. (1985) *Conceptual change in childhood*, MIT Press, Cambridge, Mass.

24 Caravita, S., Tonucci, F., Consoli, V. and Rusca, G. (1987) 'Investigating pupils' conceptualization in the biological domain: structure–function relationships', Paper presented at the Second European Conference for Research on Learning and Instruction, 19–22 September, Tübingen, FRG.

25 Caravita, S. and Tonucci, F. (1987) 'How children know biological structure–function relationships', Paper presented at the Second International Seminar: Misconceptions and Educational Strategies in Science and Mathematics, 26–29 July, Cornell University, Ithaca, N.Y.

26 Wandersee, J.H. (1983) 'Students' misconceptions about photosynthesis: a cross-age study', in Helm, H. and Novak, J.D. (eds), *Proceedings of the International Seminar: Misconceptions in Science and Mathematics*, 20–22 June, Cornell University, Ithaca, N.Y., pp. 441–6.

5 REPRODUCTION AND INHERITANCE

1 Carey, S. (1985) *Conceptual Change in Childhood*, MIT Press, Cambridge, Mass.
2 Tamir, P., Gal-Chappin, R. and Nussnovitz, R. (1981) 'How do intermediate and junior high school students conceptualise living and non-living?', *Journal of Research in Science Teaching* 18(3): 241–8.
3 Bell, B.F. (1981) *Animal, plant, living: notes for teachers*, LISP Working Paper 30, Science Education Research Unit, University of Waikato, Hamilton, New Zealand.
4 Bernstein, A.C. and Cowan, P.A. (1975) 'Children's concepts of how people get babies', *Child Development* 46: 77–91.
5 Goldman, R.J. and Goldman, J.D.G. (1982) 'How children perceive the origin of babies and the roles of mothers and fathers in procreation: a cross-national study', *Child Development* 53: 491–504.
6 Nagy, M.H. (1953) 'Children's birth theories', *Journal of Genetic Psychology* 83: 217–26.
7 Okeke, E.A.C. and Wood-Robinson, C. (1980) 'A study of Nigerian pupils' understanding of selected biological concepts', *Journal of Biological Education* 14(4): 329–38.
8 Barker, M. (1985) *Teaching and learning about photosynthesis*, Science Education Research Unit, Working Papers 220–9, University of Waikato, Hamilton, New Zealand.
9 Gott, R., Davey, A., Gamble, R., Head, J., Khaligh, N., Murphy, P., Orgee, T., Schofield, B. and Welford, G. (1985) *Science in Schools: Ages 13 and 15. Report No 3*, Assessment of Performance Unit, Department of Education and Science, HMSO, London.
10 Hampshire Education Authority (1986) *Children's preconceptions in biology*, Secondary Science Curriculum Review in Hampshire.
11 Engel Clough E. and Wood-Robinson, C. (1985) 'Children's understanding of inheritance', *Journal of Biological Education* 19(4): 304–10.
12 Hackling, M.W. and Treagust, D.F. (1982) 'What lower secondary students should understand about the mechanisms of inheritance, and what they do understand following instruction', *Research in Science Education* 12: 78–88.
13 Deadman, J.A. and Kelly, P.J. (1978) 'What do secondary school boys understand about evolution and heredity before they are taught the topics?', *Journal of Biological Education* 12(1): 7–15.
14 Kargbo, D.B., Hobbs, E.D. and Erickson, G.L. (1980) 'Student beliefs about inherited characteristics', *Journal of Biological Education* 14(2): 137–46.
15 Lucas, A. (1987) 'Public knowledge of biology', *Journal of Biological Education* 21(1): 41–5.
16 Hickman, F.M., Kennedy, M.H. and McInerny, J.D. (1978) 'Human genetics education: results of BSCS needs assessment surveys', *American Biology Teacher* 40(5): 285–303.
17 Engel Clough, E. and Wood-Robinson, C. (1985) 'How secondary school students interpret instances of biological adaptation', *Journal of Biological Education* 19(2): 125–30.
18 Brumby, M.N. (1984) 'Misconceptions about the concept of natural selection by medical biology students', *Science Education* 68(4): 493–503.
19 Lawson, A.E. and Thompson, L.D. (1988) 'Formal reasoning ability and misconceptions concerning genetics and natural selection', *Journal of Research in Science Teaching* 25(9): 733–46.

20 Brumby, M.N. (1979) 'Problems in learning the concept of natural selection', *Journal of Biological Education* 13(2): 119–22.

6 MICROBES

1 Maxted, M.A. (1984) 'Pupils' prior beliefs about bacteria and science processes: their interplay in school science laboratory work', Unpublished MA thesis, University of British Columbia.
2 Prout, A. (1985) 'Science, health and everyday knowledge', *European Journal of Science Education* 7(4): 399–406.
3 Sequira, M. and Freitas, M. (1987) 'Children's alternative conceptions about "mold" and "copper oxide"', in Novak, J.D. (ed.), *Proceedings of the 2nd International Seminar: Misconceptions and Educational Strategies in Science and Mathematics*, 26–29 July, Cornell University, Ithaca, N.Y.
4 Nagy, M.H. (1953) 'The representation of germs by children', *Journal of General Psychology* 83: 227–40.
5 Wallace, V. (1986) *Children's understanding of microorganisms: Pupils' understanding of science*, College of St Paul and St Mary, Cheltenham, now Cheltenham and Gloucester College of Higher Education.
6 Campbell, J.D. (1975) 'Illness is a point of view', *Child Development* 46: 92–100.
7 Gochman, D. (1978) 'Some correlates of children's health beliefs and behaviour', *Journal of Health and Social Behaviour* 12: 148–54.
8 Natapoff, J.N. (1978) 'Children's views of health', *American Journal of Public Health* 68: 995.
9 Brumby, M., Garrard, J. and Auman, J. (1985) 'Students' perceptions of the concept of health', *European Journal of Science Education* 7(3): 307–23.
10 Barenholz, H. and Tamir, P. (1987) 'The design, implementation and evaluation of a microbiology course with special reference to misconceptions and concept maps', in Novak, J.D. (ed.), *Proceedings of the 2nd International Seminar: Misconceptions and Educational Strategies in Science and Mathematics*, 26–29 July, Cornell University, Ithaca, N.Y., pp. 32–45.
11 Helman, C.G. (1978) 'Feed a cold, starve a fever', *Culture, Medicine and Psychiatry* 2: 107–37.
12 Lucas, A. (1987) 'Public knowledge of biology', *Journal of Biology Education* 21(1): 41–5.
13 Brumby, M. (1984) 'Misconceptions about the concept of natural selection by medical biology students', *Science Education* 68(4) 493–503.
14 Brinkman, F. and Boschhuizen, R. (1989) 'Preinstructional ideas in biology: a survey in relation with different research methods on concepts of health and energy', in Voorbach, M.T. and Prick, L.G.M., *Teacher education 5, Research and developments in teacher education in the Netherlands*, pp. 75–90.
15 Leach, J., Driver, R., Scott, P. and Wood-Robinson, C. (1992) *Progression in conceptual understanding of ecological concepts by pupils aged 5–16*, Centre for Studies in Science and Mathematics Education, University of Leeds.

7 ECOSYSTEMS

1 Leach, J., Driver, R., Scott, P. and Wood-Robinson, C. (1992) *Progression in conceptual understanding of ecological concepts by pupils age 5–16*,

REFERENCES

Centre for Studies in Science and Mathematics Education, University of Leeds.

2 Piaget, J. (1929) *The Child's Conception of the World*, Routledge & Kegan Paul, London.

3 Barker, M. (1985) *Teaching and learning about photosynthesis*, LISP Working papers 220–9, Science Education Research Unit, University of Waikato, Hamilton, New Zealand.

4 Pascoe, H.T. (ed.) (1982) *Pupils' learning problems in certificate biology*, Course Proceedings, National Inservice Course 1981: Biology Department, Aberdeen College of Education.

5 Smith, E.L. and Anderson, C.W. (1986) 'Alternative student conceptions of matter cycling in ecosystems', Paper presented to National Association of Research in Science Teaching.

6 Bell, B.F. and Brook, A. (1984) *Aspects of secondary students' understanding of plant nutrition*, Children's Learning in Science Project, Centre for Studies in Science and Mathematics Education, University of Leeds.

7 Barker, M. and Carr, M. (1989) 'Teaching and learning about photosynthesis', *International Journal of Science Education* 11(1): 48–56.

8 Simpson, M. and Arnold, B. (1982) 'Availability of prerequisite concepts for learning biology at certificate level', *Journal of Biological Education* 16(1): 65–72.

9 Roth, K.J. and Anderson, C.W. (1985) *The Power Plant: Teachers' Guide*, Institute for Research on Teaching, Michigan State University, East Lansing, Michigan.

10 Simpson, M. (1983) 'The molecell rules, OK?', Aberdeen College of Education *Biology Newsletter* 42: 7–11.

11 Gayford, C.G. (1986) 'Some aspects of the problems of teaching about energy in school biology', *European Journal of Science Education* 8(4): 443–50.

12 Senior, R. (1983) 'Pupils' understanding of some aspects of interdependency at age fifteen', unpublished M.Ed. thesis, University of Leeds.

13 Schollum, B. (1983) 'Arrows in science diagrams: help or hindrance for pupils?', *Research in Science Education* 13: 45–9.

14 Brumby, M.N. (1982) 'Students' perceptions of the concept of life', *Science Education* 66(4): 613–22.

15 Eisen, Y. and Stavy, R. (1988) 'Students' understanding of photosynthesis', *The American Biology Teacher* 50(4): 208–12.

16 Adeniyi, E.O. (1985) 'Misconceptions of selected ecological concepts held by some Nigerian students', *Journal of Biological Education* 19(4): 311–16.

17 Bell, B. and Barker, M. (1982) 'Towards a scientific concept of animal', *Journal of Biological Education* 16: 197–200.

18 Webb, P. and Boltt, G. (1990) 'Food chain to food web: a natural progression?', *Journal of Biological Education* 24(3): 187–90.

19 Boschhuizen, R. (1990) 'The concept of photosynthesis and pupils' ideas on the concept of 'cycles'', in Voorbach, M.T. and Prick, L.G.M., *Teacher Education 6, Research and Developments in Teacher Education in the Netherlands* (in press).

20 Griffiths, A.K. and Grant, B.A.C. (1985) 'High school students' understanding of food webs: identification of a learning hierarchy and related misconceptions', *Journal of Research in Science Teaching* 22(5): 421–36.

21 Jungwirth, E. (1975) 'Preconceived adaptation and inverted evolution (a case study of distorted concept formation in high school biology)', *Australian Science Teaching Journal* 21: 95–100.

REFERENCES

22 Engel Clough, E. and Wood-Robinson, C. (1985) 'How secondary students interpret instances of biological adaptation', *Journal of Biological Education* 19: 125–30.

23 Caravita, S. and Tonucci, F. (1987) 'How children know biological structure–function relationships', Paper presented at the Second International Seminar: Misconceptions and Educational Strategies in Science and Mathematics, 26–29 July, Cornell University, Ithaca, N.Y.

24 Caravita, S. and Tonucci, F. (1987) 'Investigating pupils' conceptualisation in the biological domain: structure–function relationships', Paper presented at the European Conference for Research on Learning and Instruction.

25 Sequeira, M. and Freitas, M. (1986) 'Death and decomposition of living organisms: children's alternative frameworks', Paper presented at the 11th Conference of the Association for Teacher Education in Europe (ATEE).

26 Helden, G. (1992) 'Pupils' understanding of ecological processes', Learning in Science and Mathematics Group Working Paper, Kristianstad University College, Sweden.

27 Stavy, R., Eisen, Y. and Yaakobi, D. (1987) 'How Israeli students aged 13–15 understand photosynthesis', Unpublished manuscript, Tel Aviv University.

28 Wandersee, J.H. (1983) 'Students' misconceptions about photosynthesis: a cross-age study', in Helm, H. and Novak, J.D. (eds), *Proceedings of the International Seminar: Misconceptions in Science and Mathematics*, 20–22 June, Cornell University, Ithaca, N.Y., pp. 441–6.

29 Haslam, F. and Treagust, D.F. (1987) 'Diagnosing secondary students' misconceptions of photosynthesis and respiration in plants using a two-tier multiple choice instrument', *Journal of Biological Education* 21(3): 203–11.

30 Gellert, E. (1962) 'Children's conceptions of the content and functions of the human body', *Genetic Psychology Monographs* 65: 293–405.

31 Nagy, M.H. (1953) 'Children's conceptions of some bodily functions', *Journal of Genetic Psychology* 83: 199–216.

32 Arnaudin, M.W. and Mintzes, J.J. (1985) 'Students' alternative conceptions of the human circulatory system: A cross age study', *Science Education* 69(5): 721–33.

33 Anderson, C.W. and Sheldon, T.H. (1990) 'The effects of instruction on college non-majors' conceptions of respiration and photosynthesis', *Journal of Research in Science Teaching* 27(6).

34 Arnold, B. and Simpson, M. (1980) *An investigation of the development of the concept of photosynthesis to SCE 'O' grade*, Aberdeen College of Education.

35 Driver, R., Child, D., Gott, R., Head, J., Johnson, S., Worsley, C. and Wylie, F. (1984) *Science in schools at age 15: Report No 2, Assessment of Performance Unit*, Department of Education and Science, HMSO, London.

36 Smith, E.L. and Anderson, C.W. (1984) 'Plants as producers: a case study of elementary science teaching', *Journal of Research in Science Teaching* 21(7): 685–98.

37 Brody, M.J. (1992) 'Student science knowledge related to ecological crises', Paper presented to AERA, San Francisco.

38 Boyes, E. and Stanisstreet, M. 'The "greenhouse effect": children's perceptions of causes, consequences and cures', University of Liverpool, Submitted for publication 1992.

39 Boyes, E. and Stanisstreet, M. 'Students' perceptions of global warming', University of Liverpool, Submitted for publication 1992.

40 Francis, C., Boyes, E., Qualter, A. and Stanisstreet, M., 'Ideas of elementary

students about reducing the "greenhouse effect"', University of Liverpool, Submitted for publication 1992.

8 MATERIALS

1 Smith, C., Carey, S. and Wiser, M.(1984) 'A case study of the development of size, weight, and density', *Cognition* 21(3): 177–237.
2 Jones, B.L. and Lynch, P.P. (1989) 'Children's understanding of the notions of solid and liquid in relation to some common substances', *International Journal of Science Education* 11(4): 417–27.
3 Vogelezang, M.J. (1987) 'Development of the concept of "chemical substance" – some thoughts and arguments', *International Journal of Science Education* 9(5): 519–28.
4 Bouma, H., Brandt, I. and Sutton, C. (1990) *Words as Tools in Science Lessons*, Chemiedidactiek, University of Amsterdam.
5 Ben-Zvi, R., Eylon, B. and Silberstein, J. (1986) 'Is an atom of copper malleable?', *Journal of Chemical Education* 63(1): 64–6.
6 Holding, B. (1987) 'Investigation of schoolchildren's understanding of the process of dissolving with special reference to the conservation of mass and the development of atomistic ideas', unpublished Ph.D. thesis, University of Leeds.
7 Pfundt, H. (1981) 'The atom – the final link in the division process or the first building block? Pre-instructional conceptions about the structure of substances', *Chemica Didactica* 7: 75–94.
8 Bouma, J. and Brandt, L. (1990) 'A simple method for the teacher to obtain information on pupils' preconceptions', *Journal of Chemical Education* 67(1): 24–5.
9 Ryan, C. (1990) 'Student teachers' concepts of purity and of states of matter', *Research in Science and Technological Education* 8(2): 171–84.
10 Briggs, H. and Holding, B. (1986) *Aspects of secondary students' understanding of elementary ideas in chemistry*, Centre for Studies in Science and Mathematics Education, University of Leeds.
11 Cosgrove, M. (1983) *Mixtures, an introduction to chemistry*, LISP Working Paper 209, Science Education Research Unit, University of Waikato, Hamilton, New Zealand.
12 Meheut, M., Saltiel, E. and Tiberghien, A. (1985) 'Pupils' (11–12 year olds) conceptions of combustion', *European Journal of Science Education* 7(1): 83–93.
13 Laverty, D.T. and McGarvey, J.E.B. (1991) 'A "constructivist" approach to learning', *Education in Chemistry* 28(4): 99–102.
14 Ben-Zvi, R., Eylon, B. and Silberstein, J. (1988) 'Theories, principles and laws', *Education in Chemistry* 25: 89–92.
15 Ben-Zvi, R., Eylon, B. and Silberstein, J. (1987) 'Students' visualisation of chemical reactions', *Education in Chemistry* 24(3): 117–20.
16 Herron, J.D., Cantu, L.L., Ward, R. and Srinivasan, V. (1977) 'Problems associated with concept analysis', *Science Education* 61: 185–99.
17 Driver, R. (1985) 'Beyond appearances: the conservation of matter under physical and chemical transformations', in Driver, R., Guesne, E. and Tiberghien, A. (eds), *Children's Ideas in Science*, Open University Press, Milton Keynes, pp. 145–69.
18 Andersson, B. (1984) *Chemical Reactions*, EKNA Report 12, Institutionen For Pedagogik, University of Gothenburg, Sweden.

19 Piaget, J. and Inhelder, B. (1974) *The Child's Construction of Quantities: Conservation and atomism*, Routledge & Kegan Paul, London.
20 Mullet, E. and Gervais, H. (1990) 'Distinction between the concepts of weight and mass in high school students', *International Journal of Science Education* 12(2): 217–26.
21 Piaget, J. (1973) *The child's conception of the world*, Paladin, London.
22 Hewson, M.G. (1986) 'The acquisition of scientific knowledge: analysis and representation of student conceptions concerning density', *Science Education* 70(2): 159–70.
23 Rowell, J.A., Dawson, C.J. and Lyndon, H. (1990) 'Changing misconceptions: a challenge to science educators', *International Journal of Science Education* 12(2): 167–75.
24 James, H.J. and Nelson, S.L. (1981) 'A classroom learning cycle: using diagrams to classify matter', *Journal of Chemical Education* 58(6): 476–7.

9 SOLIDS, LIQUIDS AND GASES

1 Stavy, R. and Stachel, D. (1984) *Children's ideas about 'solid' and 'liquid'*, Israeli Science Teaching Centre, School of Education, Tel Aviv University.
2 Jones, B.L. and Lynch, P.P. (1989) 'Children's understanding of the notions of solid and liquid in relation to some common substances', *International Journal of Science Education* 11(4): 417–27.
3 Jones, B. (1984) 'How solid is a solid: does it matter?', *Research in Science Education* 14: 104–13.
4 Osborne, R.J. and Cosgrove, M.M. (1983) 'Children's conceptions of the changes of state of water', *Journal of Research in Science Teaching* 20(9): 825–38.
5 Brook, A., Driver, R., in collaboration with Hind, D. (1989) *Progression in science: the development of pupils' understanding of physical characteristics of air across the age range 5–16 years*, Centre for Studies in Science and Mathematics Education, University of Leeds.
6 Séré, M.G. (1985) 'The gaseous state', in Driver, R., Guesne, E. and Tiberghien, A. (eds), *Children's Ideas in Science*, Open University Press, Milton Keynes, pp. 105–23.
7 Séré, M.G. (1986) 'Children's conceptions of the gaseous state, prior to teaching', *European Journal of Science Education* 8(4): 413–25.
8 Mas, C.J.F., Perez, J.H. and Harris, H. (1987) 'Parallels between adolescents' conceptions of gases and the history of chemistry', *Journal of Chemical Education* 64(7): 616–18.
9 Piaget, J. (1973) *The Child's Conception of the World*, Paladin, London.
10 Stavy, R. (1988) 'Children's conception of gas', *International Journal of Science Education* 10(5): 552–60.
11 Leboutet-Barrell, L. (1976) 'Concepts of mechanics among young people', *Physics Education* 20: 462–5.
12 Stavy, R. (1987) 'Acquisition of conservation of matter', Paper presented at the Second Conference on Misconceptions, July. Cornell University, Ithaca, N.Y.
13 Nussbaum, J. (1985) 'The particulate nature of matter in the gaseous phase', in Driver, R., Guesne, E. and Tiberghien, A. (eds), *Children's Ideas in Science*, Open University Press, Milton Keynes, pp. 124–44
14 Longden, K.A. (1984) 'Understanding of dissolving shown by 11–12-year-old children', Unpublished M.Sc. thesis, University of Oxford.
15 Cosgrove, M. and Osborne, R. (1980) *Physical change*, LISP Working Paper

REFERENCES

26, Science Education Research Unit, University of Waikato, Hamilton, New Zealand.

16 Bar, V. and Travis, A.S. (1991) 'Children's views concerning phase changes', *Journal of Research in Science Teaching* 28(4): 363–82.

17 Bar, V. (1986) *The development of the conception of evaporation*, The Amos de Shalit Science Teaching Centre, The Hebrew University of Jerusalem, Israel.

18 Beveridge, M. (1983) 'Negative and positive evidence in the development of children's understanding of the process of evaporation', Mimeograph, Department of Education, University of Manchester.

19 Beveridge, M. (1985) 'The development of young children's understanding of the process of evaporation', *British Journal of Educational Psychology* 55: 84–90.

20 Russell, T., Harlen, W. and Watt, D. (1989) 'Children's ideas about evaporation', *International Journal of Science Education* 11(5): 566–76.

21 Russell, T. and Watt, D. (1989) *Evaporation and condensation*, Primary SPACE Project, Research Report. Liverpool University Press.

22 Stavy, R. (1990) 'Children's conception of changes in the state of matter: from liquid (or solid) to gas', *Journal of Research in Science Teaching* 27(3): 247–66.

23 Andersson, B. (1980) 'Some aspects of children's understanding of boiling point', in Archenhold, W.F., Driver, R., Orton, A. and Wood-Robinson, C. (eds), *Cognitive Development Research in Science and Mathematics*, Proceedings of an International Seminar, 17–21 September 1979, University of Leeds.

24 Dow, W.M., Auld, J. and Wilson, D. (1978) *Pupils concepts of gases, liquids and solids*, Dundee College of Education.

25 Holding, B. (1987) 'Investigation of schoolchildren's understanding of the process of dissolving with special reference to the conservation of matter and the development of atomistic ideas', unpublished Ph.D. thesis, University of Leeds.

26 Comber, M. (1983) 'Concept development in relation to the particulate theory of matter in the middle school', *Research in Science and Technological Education* 1(1): 27–39.

27 Friedman, E. (1982) 'Investigating children's ideas about some chemistry concepts', unpublished M.Ed. Studies project, Monash University, Victoria, Australia.

28 Pfundt, H. (1981) 'The atom – the final link in the division process or the first building block? Pre-instructional conceptions about the structure of substances', *Chemica Didactica* 7: 75–94.

29 Piaget, J. and Inhelder, B. (1974) *The Child's Construction of Quantities: Conservation and Atomism*, Routledge & Kegan Paul, London.

30 Driver, R. and Russell, T. (1982) *An investigation of the ideas of heat, temperature and change of state of children aged between eight and fourteen years*, Centre for Studies in Science and Mathematics Education, University of Leeds.

31 Andersson, B. and Renstrom, L. (1982) *How Swedish pupils, aged 12–15, explain the 'sugar in water' problem*, The EKNA Project, Institutionen for Praktisk Pedagogik, University of Gothenburg, Sweden.

32 Schollum, B. (1980) *Chemical change*, LISP Working Paper 27, Science Education Research Unit, University of Waikato, Hamilton, New Zealand.

33 Cosgrove, M.M. (1983) *Mixtures, an introduction to chemistry*, LISP Working Paper 209, Science Education Research Unit, University of Waikato, Hamilton, New Zealand.

34 Pieto, J., Blanco, A. and Rodriguez, A. (1989) 'The ideas of 11–14-year-old

students about the nature of solutions', *International Journal of Science Education* 11(4): 451–63.

35 Fensham, N. and Fensham, P. (1987) 'Descriptions and frameworks of solutions and reaction in solutions', *Research in Science Education* 17: 139–48.

36 Meheut, M., Saltiel, E. and Tiberghien, A. (1985) 'Pupils' (11–12-year-olds) conceptions of combustion', *European Journal of Science Education* 7(1): 83–93.

10 CHEMICAL CHANGE

1 Bouma, H., Brandt, L. and Sutton, C. (1990) *Words as Tools in Science Lessons*, Chemiedidactiek, University of Amsterdam.

2 Bouma, J. and Brandt, L. (1990) 'A simple method for the teacher to obtain information on pupils' preconceptions', *Journal of Chemical Education* 67(1): 24–5.

3 Briggs, H. and Holding, B. (1986) *Aspects of secondary students' understanding of elementary ideas in chemistry*, Centre for Studies in Science and Mathematics Education, University of Leeds.

4 Ryan, C. (1990) 'Student teachers' concepts of purity and of states of matter', *Research in Science and Technological Education* 8(2): 171–84.

5 Pella, M.O. and Voelker, A.M. (1967) 'Teaching the concepts of physical and chemical change to elementary school children', *Journal of Research in Science Teaching* 5: 311–23.

6 Schollum. B.F. (1982) 'Chemical change', *New Zealand Science Teacher* 33: 5–9.

7 Gensler, W.J. (1970) 'Physical versus chemical change', *Journal of Chemical Education* 47: 154.

8 Strong, L.E. (1970) 'Differentiating physical and chemical changes', *Journal of Chemical Education* 47: 689.

9 Voelker, A.M. (1975) 'Elementary school children's attainment of the concepts of physical and chemical change – a replication', *Journal of Research in Science Teaching* 12: 5–14.

10 Vogelezang, M.J. (1987) 'Development of the concept of "chemical substance" – some thoughts and arguments', *International Journal of Science Education* 9(5): 519–28.

11 Andersson, B. (1986) 'Pupils' explanations of some aspects of chemical reactions', *Science Education* 70(5): 549–63.

12 Andersson, B. (1991) 'Pupils' conceptions of matter and its transformations (age 12–16)', *Studies in Science Education* 18: 53–85.

13 Pfundt, H. (1981) 'Pre-instructional conceptions about substances and transformations of substances', in Jung, W., Pfundt, H. and von Rhoneck, C. (eds), *Proceedings of the International Workshop on Problems Concerning Students' Representation of Physics and Chemistry Knowledge*, 14–16 September, Pedagogische Hochschule, Ludwigsburg, pp. 320–41.

14 Stavridou, H. and Solomonidou, C. (1989) 'Physical phenomena – chemical phenomena: do pupils make the distinction?'. *International Journal of Science Education* 11(1): 83–92.

15 Novick, S. and Nussbaum, J. (1978) 'Junior high school pupils' understanding of the particulate nature of matter: An interview study', *Science Education* 62(3): 273–81.

16 Laverty, D.T. and McGarvey, J.E.B. (1991) 'A "constructivist" approach to learning', *Education in Chemistry* 28(4): 99–102.

17 Andersson, B. and Renstrom, L. (1982) *Oxidation of steel wool*, EKNA Report 7, Institutionen for Praktisk Pedagogik, University of Gothenburg, Sweden.

REFERENCES

18 Donnelly, J.F. and Welford, A.G. (1988) 'Children's performance in chemistry', *Education in Chemistry* 25: 7–10.

19 Schollum, B. (1980) *Burning. A resource unit for teachers*, LISP Working Paper 36, Science Education Research Unit, University of Waikato, Hamilton, New Zealand.

20 Schollum, B. (1980) *Reactions. A resource unit for teachers*, LISP Working Paper 37, Science Education Research Unit, University of Waikato, Hamilton, New Zealand.

21 De Vos, W. and Verdonk, A.H. (1985) 'A new road to reactions: Part 1 and Part 2', *Journal of Chemical Education* 62(3): 239–40; 648–9.

22 Knox, J. (1985) 'A study of secondary school students' ideas about the process of burning', unpublished M.Ed. thesis, University of Leeds.

23 Meheut, M., Saltiel, E. and Tiberghien, A. (1985) 'Pupils' (11–12-year-olds) conceptions of combustion', *European Journal of Science Education* 7(1): 83–93.

24 Driver, R. (1985) 'Beyond appearances: The conservation of matter under physical and chemical transformations', in Driver, R., Guesne, E. and Tiberghien, A. (eds), *Children's ideas in science*, Open University Press, Milton Keynes, pp. 145–69.

25 De Vos, W. and Verdonk, A.H. (1987) 'A new road to chemical reactions: the element and its atoms', *Journal of Chemical Education* 64: 1010–13.

26 Holding, B. (1987) 'Investigation of school children's understanding of the process of dissolving with special reference to the conservation of matter and the development of atomistic ideas', unpublished Ph.D. thesis, University of Leeds.

27 Andersson, B. (1984) *Chemical reactions*, EKNA Report 12, Institutionen for Praktisk Pedagogik, University of Gothenburg, Sweden.

28 Piaget, J. and Inhelder, B. (1974) *The Child's Construction of Quantities: conservation and atomism*, Routledge & Kegan Paul, London.

29 De Vos, W. and Verdonk, A.H. (1986) 'A new road to reactions: teaching the heat effect of reactions', *Journal of Chemical Education* 63: 972–4.

30 Holman, J. (1986) 'Teaching about energy – the chemical perspective', in Driver, R. and Millar, R. (eds), *Energy Matters*, Proceedings of an invited conference: Teaching about Energy within the Secondary School Curriculum, Centre for Studies in Science and Mathematics Education, University of Leeds.

31 Johnston, K. (1987) 'CLIS in the classroom: constructivist approaches to teaching', *Education in Science* 121: 29–30.

32 Kruger, C. and Summers, R. (1989) 'An investigation of some primary teachers' understanding of changes in materials', *School Science Review* 71(255): 17–27.

33 Carr, M. (1984) 'Model confusion in chemistry', *Research in Science Education* 14: 97–103.

34 Hand, B.M. and Treagust, D.F. (1988) 'Application of a conceptual conflict teaching strategy to enhance student learning of acids and bases', *Research in Science Education* 18: 53–63.

35 Hand, B. (1989) 'Student understanding of acids and bases: a two year study', *Research in Science Education* 19: 133–44.

36 Cros, D., Maurin, M., Amouroux, R., Chastrette, M., Leber, J. and Fayol, M. (1986) 'Conceptions of first-year university students of the constituents of matter and the notions of acids and bases', *European Journal of Science Education* 8(3): 305–13.

191

REFERENCES

11 PARTICLES

1 Piaget, J. and Inhelder, B. (1974) *The Child's Construction of Quantities: conservation and atomism*, Routledge & Kegan Paul, London.
2 Ben-Zvi, R., Eylon, B. and Silberstein, J. (1986) 'Is an atom of copper malleable?', *Journal of Chemical Education* 63(1): 64–6.
3 Holding, B. (1987) 'Investigation of school children's understanding of the process of dissolving with special reference to the conservation of matter and the development of atomistic ideas', unpublished Ph.D. thesis, University of Leeds.
4 Pfundt, H. (1981) 'The atom – the final link in the division process or the first building block? Pre-instructional conceptions about the structure of substances', *Chemica Didactica* 7: 75–94.
5 Kircher, E. (1981) 'Research in the classroom about the particle nature of matter (grades 4–6)', in Jung, W., Pfundt, H. and von Rhoneck, C. (eds), *Proceedings of the International Workshop of Problems Concerning Students' Representation of Physics and Chemistry Knowledge*, 14–16 September, Pedagogische Hochshule, Ludwigsburg, pp. 342–64.
6 Mitchell, A.C. and Kellington, S.H. (1982) 'Learning difficulties associated with the particulate theory of matter in the Scottish Integrated Science course', *European Journal of Science Education* 4(4): 429–40.
7 De Vos, W. and Verdonk, A.H. (1987) 'A new road to reactions: the substance and its molecules', *Journal of Chemical Education* 64: 692–4.
8 Dow, W.M., Auld, J. and Wilson, D. (1978) *Pupils' concepts of gases, liquids and solids*, Dundee College of Education.
9 Novick, S. and Nussbaum, J. (1978) 'Junior high school pupils' understanding of the particulate nature of matter: An interview study', *Science Education* 62(3): 273–81.
10 Driver, R. (1983) 'An approach to documenting the understanding of fifteen year old British children about particulate theory of matter', in *Research on Physics Education*, Proceedings of the First International Workshop, 26 June– 13 July, La Londe les Maures, France, Editions du Centre National de la Recherche Scientifique 1984, pp. 339–46.
11 Gabel, D.L. and Samuel, K.V. (1987) 'Understanding the particulate nature of matter', *Journal of Chemical Education* 64(8): 695–7.
12 Happs, J. (1980) *Particles*, LISP Working Paper 18, Science Education Research Unit, University of Waikato, Hamilton, New Zealand.
13 Nussbaum, J. (1985) 'The particulate nature of matter in the gaseous phase', in Driver, R., Guesne, E. and Tiberghien, A. (eds), *Children's Ideas in Science*, Open University Press, Milton Keynes, pp. 124–44.
14 Novick, S. and Nussbaum, J. (1981) 'Pupils' understanding of the particulate nature of matter: a cross-age study', *Science Education* 65(2): 187–96.
15 Nussbaum, J. and Novick, S. (1982) 'Alternative frameworks, conceptual conflict and accommodation: Toward a principled teaching strategy', *Instructional Science* 11: 183–200.
16 Ben-Zvi, R., Eylon, B. and Silberstein, J. (1987) 'Students' visualisation of chemical reactions', *Education in Chemistry* 24(3): 117–20.
17 Osborne, R.J. and Cosgrove, M.M. (1983) 'Children's conceptions of the changes of state of water', *Journal of Research in Science Teaching* 20(9): 825–38.
18 Ben-Zvi, R., Eylon, B. and Silberstein, J. (1988) 'Theories, principles and laws', *Education in Chemistry* 25: 89–92.
19 Briggs, H. and Holding, B. (1986) *Aspects of secondary students' understanding*

of elementary ideas in chemistry, Centre of Studies in Science and Mathematics Education, University of Leeds.

20 Selley, N.J. (1978) 'The confusion of molecular particles with substances', *Education in Chemistry* 15(5): 144–5.

21 Laverty, D.T. and McGarvey, J.E.B. (1991) 'A "constructivist" approach to learning', *Education in Chemistry* 28(4): 99–102.

22 Butts, B. and Smith, R. (1987) 'HSC chemistry students' understanding of the structure and properties of molecular and ionic compounds', *Research in Science Education* 17: 192–201.

23 Peterson, R., Treagust, D. and Garnett, P. (1986) 'Identification of secondary students' misconceptions of covalent bonding and structure concepts using a diagnostic instrument', *Research in Science Education* 16: 40–8.

12 WATER

1 Stavy, R. and Stachel, D. (1984) *Children's ideas about 'solid' and 'liquid'*, Israeli Science Teaching Centre, School of Education, Tel Aviv University.

2 Dow, W.M., Auld, J. and Wilson, D. (1978) *Pupils' concepts of gases, liquids and solids*, Dundee College of Education.

3 Osborne, R.J. and Cosgrove, M.M. (1983) 'Children's conceptions of the changes of state of water', *Journal of Research in Science Teaching* 20(9): 825–38.

4 Stavy, R. (1987) 'Acquisition of conservation of matter', Paper presented at the Second Conference on Misconceptions, July, Cornell University, Ithaca, N.Y.

5 Andersson, B. (1980) 'Some aspects of children's understanding of boiling point', in Archenhold, W.F., Driver, R., Orton, A. and Wood-Robinson, C. (eds), *Cognitive Research in Science and Mathematics*, Proceedings of an International Seminar, 17–21 September 1979, University of Leeds.

6 Bar, V. and Travis, A.S. (1991) 'Children's views concerning phase changes', *Journal of Research in Science Teaching* 28(4): 363–82.

7 Bar, V. (1986) *The development of the conception of evaporation*, The Amos de-Shalit Science Teaching Centre in Israel, The Hebrew University of Jerusalem, Israel.

8 Beveridge, M. (1983) 'Negative and positive evidence in the development of children's understanding of the process of evaporation', Mimeograph, Department of Education, University of Manchester.

9 Beveridge, M. (1985) 'The development of young children's understanding of the process of evaporation', *British Journal of Education Psychology* 55: 84–90.

10 Russell, T., Harlen, W. and Watt, D. (1989) 'Children's ideas about evaporation', *International Journal of Science Education* 11(5): 566–76.

11 Russell, T. and Watt, D. (1989) *Evaporation and condensation*, Primary SPACE Project Research Report, Liverpool University Press.

12 Stavy, R. (1990) 'Children's conception of changes in the state of matter: from liquid (or solid) to gas', *Journal of Research in Science Teaching* 27(3): 247–66.

13 Longden, K.A. (1984) 'Understanding of dissolving shown by 11–12-year-old children', unpublished M.Sc. thesis, University of Oxford.

14 Cosgrove, M. and Osborne, R. (1980) *Physical change*, LISP Working Paper 26, Science Education Research Unit, University of Waikato, Hamilton, New Zealand.

15 Holding, B. (1987) 'Investigation of school children's understanding of the process of dissolving with special reference to the conservation of matter and the development of atomistic ideas', unpublished Ph.D. thesis, University of Leeds.

16 Comber, M. (1983) 'Concept development in relation to the particulate theory of matter in the middle school', *Research in Science and Technology Education* 1(1): 27–39.

17 Friedman, E. (1982) 'Investigating children's ideas about some chemistry concepts', unpublished M.Ed. Studies project, Monash University, Victoria, Australia.

18 Pfundt, H. (1981) 'The atom – the final link in the division process or the first building block? Pre-instructional conceptions about the structure of substances', *Chemica Didactica* 7: 75–94.

19 Piaget, J. and Inhelder, B. (1974) *The child's construction of quantities: conservation and atomism*, Routledge & Kegan Paul, London.

20 Driver, R. and Russell, T. (1982) *An investigation of the ideas of heat, temperature and change of state of children aged between eight and fourteen years*, University of Leeds.

21 Andersson, B. and Renstrom, L. (1982) *How Swedish pupils, aged 12–15, explain the 'sugar in water' problem*, The EKNA Project, Institutionen for Praktisk Pedagogik, University of Gothenburg, Sweden.

22 Schollum, B. (1980) *Chemical change*, LISP Working Paper 27, Science Education Research Unit, University of Waikato, Hamilton, New Zealand.

23 Cosgrove, M. (1983) *Mixtures, an introduction to chemistry*, LISP Working Paper 209, Science Education Research Unit, University of Waikato, Hamilton, New Zealand.

24 Prieto, J., Blanco, A. and Rodriguez, A. (1989) 'The ideas of 11–14-year-old students about the nature of solutions', *International Journal of Science Education* 11(4): 451–63.

25 Fensham, N. and Fensham, P. (1987) 'Descriptions and frameworks of solutions and reactions in solutions', *Research in Science Education* 17: 139–48.

26 Wood-Robinson, C. (1991) 'Young people's ideas about plants', *Studies in Science Education* 19: 119–35.

27 Wellman, H.M. and Johnson, C.N. (1982) 'Children's understanding of food and its functions: A preliminary study of the development of concepts of nutrition', *Journal of Applied Development Psychology* 3: 135–48.

28 Biddulph, F. and Osborne, R. (1984) 'Pupils' ideas about floating and sinking', Paper presented to Australian Science Education Research Association Conference, May, Melbourne, Australia.

29 Grimellini Tomasini, N., Gandolfi, E. and Pecori Balandi, B. (1990) 'Teaching strategies and conceptual change: Sinking and floating at elementary school level', Paper presented at the 1990 Annual Meeting of the American Educational Research Association, 16–20 April, Boston, Massachusetts.

13 AIR

1 Séré, M.G. (1985) 'The gaseous state', in Driver, R., Guesne, E. and Tiberghien, A. (eds), *Children's Ideas in Science*, Open University Press, Milton Keynes, pp. 105–23.

2 Miller, S., Robinson, D. and Driver, R. (1985) 'Secondary students' ideas

about air and air pressure', in Bell, B., Watts, M. and Ellington, K. (eds), *Learning, Doing and Understanding in Science*, Proceedings of a Conference, 11–13 July, Woolley Hall, Near Wakefield. SSCR, London, pp. 58–63.

3 Séré, M.G. (1986) 'Children's conceptions of the gaseous state, prior to teaching', *European Journal of Science Education* 8(4): 413–25.

4 Brook, A. and Driver, R. (in collaboration with Hind, D.) (1989) *Progression in science: the development of pupils' understanding of physical characteristics of air across the age range 5–16 years*, Centre for Studies in Science and Mathematics Education, University of Leeds.

5 Mas, C.J.F., Perez, J.H. and Harris, H. (1987) 'Parallels between adolescents' conceptions of gases and the history of chemistry', *Journal of Chemical Education* 64(7): 616–18.

6 Piaget, J. (1973) *The Child's Conception of the World*, Paladin, London.

7 Stavy, R. (1988) 'Children's conception of gas', *International Journal of Science Education* 10(5): 552–60.

8 Leboutet-Barrell, L. (1976) 'Concepts of mechanics among young people', *Physics Education* 20: 462–5.

9 Ruggiero, S., Cartelli, A., Dupré, F. and Vincentini-Missoni, M. (1985) 'Weight, gravity and air pressure: mental representations by Italian middle school pupils', *European Journal of Science Education* 7(2): 181–94.

10 Séré, M. (1982) 'A study of some frameworks of the field of mechanics, used by children (aged 11–13) when they interpret experiments about air pressure', *European Journal of Science Education* (4): 299–309.

11 Engel Clough, E. and Driver, R. (1985) 'What do children understand about pressure in fluids?' *Research in Science and Technology Education* 3(2): 133–4.

12 Meheut, M., Saltiel, E. and Tiberghien, A. (1985) 'Pupils' (11–12-year-olds) conceptions of combustion', *European Journal of Science Education* 7(1): 83–93.

13 Driver, R. (1985) 'Beyond appearances: the conservation of matter under physical and chemical transformations', in Driver, R., Guesne, E. and Tiberghien, A. (eds), *Children's Ideas in Science*, Open University Press, Milton Keynes, pp. 145–69.

14 Gellert, E. (1962) 'Children's conceptions of the content and functions of the human body', *Genetic Psychology Monographs* 65: 291–411.

15 Nagy, M.H. (1953) 'Children's conceptions of some bodily functions', *Journal of Genetic Psychology* 83: 199–216.

16 Arnaudin, M.W. and Mintzes, J.J. (1985) 'Students' alternative conceptions of the human circulatory system: a cross age study', *Science Education* 69(5): 721–33.

17 Stavy, R., Eisen, Y. and Yaakobi, D. (1987) 'How students aged 13–15 understand photosynthesis', *International Journal of Science Education* 9(1): 105–15.

18 Bell, B. (1985) 'Students' ideas about plant nutrition: what are they?', *Journal of Biological Education* 19(3): 213–18.

19 Adeniyi, E.O. (1989) 'Misconceptions of selected ecological concepts held by some Nigerian students', *Journal of Biological Education* 19(4): 311–16.

20 Wandersee, J.H. (1983) 'Students' misconceptions about photosynthesis: a cross-age study', in Helm, H. and Novak, J.D. (eds), *Proceedings of the International Seminar: Misconceptions in Science and Mathematics*, 20–22 June, Cornell University, Ithaca, N.Y., pp. 441–6.

21 Arnold, B. and Simpson, M. (1980) *An investigation of the development of the concept of photosynthesis to SCE 'O' grade*, Aberdeen College of Education.

22 Driver, R., Child, D., Gott, R., Head, J., Johnson, S., Worsley, C. and Wylie,

F. (1984) *Science in Schools at Age 15: Report No 2*, Assessment of Performance Unit, Department of Education and Science, HMSO, London.
23 Eisen, Y. and Stavy, R. (1988) 'Students' understanding of photosynthesis', *American Biology Teacher* 50(4): 208–12.
24 Moyle, R. (1980) *Weather*, LISP Working Paper 21, Science Education Research Unit, University of Waikato, Hamilton, New Zealand.

14 ROCKS

3

1 Happs, J.C. (1982) *Rocks and minerals*, LISP Working Paper 204, Science Education Research Unit, University of Waikato, Hamilton, New Zealand.
2 Happs, J.C. (1985) 'Regression in learning outcomes: some examples from Earth sciences', *European Journal of Science Education* 7(4): 431–43.
3 Happs, J.C. (1985) 'Cognitive learning theory and classroom complexity', *Research in Science and Technological Education* 3(2): 159–74.
4 Happs, J.C. (1982) *Mountains*, LISP Working Paper 202, Science Education Research Unit, University of Waikato, Hamilton, New Zealand.
5 Happs, J.C. (1982) 'Some aspects of student understanding of soil', *Australian Science Teacher's Journal* 28(3): 25–31.
6 Cosgrove, M.M. and Osborne, R.J. (1983) 'Children's conceptions of the changes of state of water', *Journal of Research in Science Teaching* 20(9): 825–38.

15 ELECTRICITY

1 Shipstone, D.M. (1984) 'A study of children's understanding of electricity in simple DC circuits', *European Journal of Science Education* 6(2): 185–98.
2 Shipstone, D. (1985) 'Electricity in simple circuits', in Driver, R., Guesne, E. and Tiberghien, A. (eds), *Children's Ideas in Science*, Open University Press, Milton Keynes, pp. 33–51.
3 Tiberghien, A. (1983) 'Critical review of research concerning the meaning of electric circuits for students aged 8 to 20 years', in *Research on Physics Education*, Proceedings of the First International Workshop, 26 June–13 July, La Londe les Maures, France, Editions du Centre National de la Recherche Scientifique, Paris (1984), pp. 109–23.
4 Osborne, R. (1981) 'Children's ideas about electric current', *New Zealand Science Teacher* 29: 12–19.
5 Gott, R. (1984) *Electricity at Age 15: Science Report for Teachers. No 7*, Assessment of Performance Unit, Department of Education and Science, HMSO London.
6 Solomon, J., Black, P., Oldham, V. and Stuart, H. (1985) 'The pupils' view of electricity', *European Journal of Science Education* 7(3): 281–94.
7 Licht, P. (1985) 'Concept development in electricity: a strategy and some preliminary results', Paper prepared for the International Symposium on Physics Teaching organised by the Université Libre de Bruxelles/Vrije Universiteit Brussel, 11–13 November.
8 Osborne, R. and Freyberg, P. (1985) *Learning in science: the implications of children's science*, Heinemann, Auckland and London.
9 Butts, W. (1985) 'Children's understanding of electric current in three countries', *Research in Science Education* 15: 127–30.
10 Psillos, D., Koumaras, P. and Tiberghien, A. (1988) 'Voltage presented as a

REFERENCES

primary concept in an introductory teaching sequence on DC circuits', *International Journal of Science Education* 10(1): 29–43.

11 Dupin, J.J. and Johsua, S. (1984) 'Teaching electricity: interactive evolution of representations, models and experiments in a class situation', in Duit, R., Jung, W. and von Rhoneck, C. (eds), *Aspects of Understanding Electricity*, Proceedings of the International Workshop. 10–14 September, Ludwigsburg (Schmidt and Klaunig, Kiel, 1985); *IPN-Arbeitsberichte* 59: 331–41.

12 Gauld, C.F. (1985) *Teaching about electric circuits or meters, models and memory*, LISP Working Paper 209, Science Education Research Unit, University of Waikato, Hamilton, New Zealand.

13 Osborne, R. (1983) 'Children's ideas meet scientists' science', *Lab Talk* 28(1): 2–7 (Victoria, Australia).

14 Closset, J.L. (1984) 'Using cognitive conflict to teach electricity', in Duit, R., Jung, W. and von Rhoneck, C. (eds), *Aspects of Understanding Electricity*, Proceedings of the International Workshop, 10–14 September, Ludwigsburg (Schmidt and Klaunig, Kiel, 1985); *IPN-Arbeitsberichte* 59: 267–73.

15 Closset, J.L. (1983) 'Sequential reasoning in electricity', in *Research on Physics Education*, Proceedings of the First International Workshop, 26 June–13 July, La Londe les Maures, France, Editions du Centre National de la Recherche Scientifique, Paris (1984), pp. 313–19.

16 Cohen, R., Eylon, B. and Ganiel, U. (1983) 'Potential difference and current in simple electric circuits: a study of students' concepts', *American Journal of Physics* 51(5): 407–12.

17 Maichle, U. (1981) 'Representation of knowledge in basic electricity and its use for problem solving', in Jung, W., Pfundt, H. and Rhoneck, C. von (eds), *Proceedings of the International Workshop on Problems concerning students' representation of physics and chemistry knowledge*, 14–16 September, Pedagogische Hochschule, Ludwigsburg, pp. 174–93.

18 von Rhoneck, C. (1981) 'Students' conceptions of the electric circuit before physics instruction', in Jung, W., Pfundt, H. and Rhoneck, C. von (eds), *Proceedings of the International Workshop on Problems concerning students' representation of physics and chemistry knowledge*, 14–16 September, Pedagogische Hochschule, Ludwigsburg, pp. 194–213.

19 von Rhoneck, C. (1984) 'The introduction of voltage as an independent variable – the importance of preconceptions, cognitive conflict and operating rules', in Duit, R., Jung, W. and Rhoneck, C. von (eds), *Aspects of Understanding Electricity*, Proceedings of the International Workshop, 10–14 September, Ludwigsburg (Schmidt and Klaunig, Kiel, 1985); *IPN-Arbeitsberichte* 59: 275–86.

20 Cohen, R. (1984) 'Causal relations in electric circuits: students' concepts', in Duit, R., Jung, W. and Rhoneck, C. von (eds), *Aspects of Understanding Electricity*, Proceedings of the International Workshop, 10–14 September, Ludwigsburg (Schmidt and Klaunig, Kiel, 1985); *IPN-Arbeitsberichte* 59: 107–13.

21 Arnold, M. and Millar, R. (1988) 'Teaching about electric circuits: a constructivist approach', *School Science Review* 70(251): 149–51.

22 Duit, R. (1984) 'The meaning of current and voltage in everyday language and its consequences for understanding the physical concepts of the electric circuit', in Duit, R., Jung, W. and Rhoneck, C. von (eds), *Aspects of Understanding Electricity*, Proceedings of the International Workshop, 10–14 September, Ludwigsburg (Schmidt and Klaunig, Kiel, 1985); *IPN-Arbeitsberichte* 59: 205–14.

23 Aalst, H.F. van (1984) 'The differentiation between connections in series and in parallel from cognitive mapping: implications for teaching', in Duit, R., Jung, W. and Rhoneck, C. von (eds), *Aspects of Understanding Electricity*, Proceedings of the International Workshop, 10–14 September, Ludwigsburg (Schmidt and Klaunig, Kiel, 1985); *IPN-Arbeitsberichte* 59: 115–28.

24 Black, D. and Solomon, J. (1987) 'Can pupils use taught analogies for electric current?', *School Science Review* 69 (December): 249–54.

25 Schwedes, H. (1984) 'The importance of water circuits in teaching electric circuits', in Duit, R., Jung, W. and Rhoneck, C. von (eds), *Aspects of Understanding Electricity*, Proceedings of the International Workshop, 10–14 September, Ludwigsburg (Schmidt and Klaunig, Kiel, 1985); *IPN-Arbeitsberichte* 59: 319–29.

26 Russell, T.J. (1980) 'Children's understanding of simple electrical circuits', in Russell, T.J. and Sia, A.P.C. (eds), *Science and Mathematics, Concept Learning of South East Asian Children: Second Report on Phase II*, Glugor Malaysia; SEAMEO-RECSAM, pp. 67–91.

27 Segre, G. and Gagliardi, M. (1984) 'Models, paradigms and misconceptions in transport processes', Seminar at the University of Naples, Italy.

28 Hartel, H. (1984) 'The electric circuit as a system', in Duit, R., Jung, W. and Rhoneck, C. von (eds), *Aspects of Understanding Electricity*, Proceedings of the International Workshop, 10–14 September, Ludwigsburg (Schmidt and Klaunig, Kiel, 1985); *IPN-Arbeitsberichte* 59: 343–52.

29 Tenney, Y.J. (1984) 'What makes analogies accessible: experiments on the water-flow analogy for electricity', in Duit, R., Jung, W. and Rhoneck, C. von (eds), *Aspects of Understanding Electricity*, Proceedings of the International Workshop, 10–14 September, Ludwigsburg (Schmidt and Klaunig, Kiel, 1985); *IPN-Arbeitsberichte* 59: 311–18.

30 Caillot, M. (1984) 'Problem representations and problem-solving procedures in electricity', in Duit, R., Jung, W. and Rhoneck, C. von (eds), *Aspects of Understanding Electricity*, Proceedings of the International Workshop, 10–14 September, Ludwigsburg (Schmidt and Klaunig, Kiel, 1985); *IPN-Arbeitsberichte* 59: 139–51.

31 Johsua, S. (1984) 'Students' interpretation of simple electrical diagrams', *European Journal of Science Education* 6(3): 271–5.

32 Niedderer, H. (1972) 'Sachstrucktur und schüler – Fähigkeiten beim einfachen elecktrischen stromkeis', Dissertation, University of Kiel.

16 MAGNETISM

1 Bar, V. and Goldmuntz, (1987) *Why things fall*, Scientific Report, Hebrew University Press, Jerusalem.

2 Barrow, L.H. (1987) 'Magnet concepts and elementary students' misconceptions', in Noval, J. (ed.), *Proceedings of the Second International Seminar on Misconceptions and Educational Strategies in Science and Mathematics*, Cornell University, Ithaca, N.Y., 3: 17–22.

3 Bar, V. and Zinn, B. (1989) *Does a magnet act on the moon?*, Scientific Report, The Amos de Shalit Teaching Centre, Hebrew University, Jerusalem.

4 Gagliari, L. (1981) 'Something missing in magnetism?', *Science and Children* 18: 24–5.

5 Selman, R.L., Krupa, M.P., Stone, C.R. and Jacquette, D.S. (1982) 'Concrete operational thought and the emergence of the concept of unseen force in children's theories of electromagnetism and gravity', *Science Education* 66(2): 181–94.

6 Finley, F.N. (1986) 'Evaluating instruction: the complementary use of clinical interviews', *Journal of Research in Science Teaching* 23(17): 635–50.
7 Andersson, B. (1985) *The experiential gestalt of causation – a common core to pupils' preconceptions in science*, Department of Education and Educational Research, University of Gothenburg, Sweden.

17 LIGHT

1 Watts, D.M. (1984) 'Learners' alternative frameworks of light', in Bell, B., Watts, M. and Ellington, K. (eds), *Learning, Doing and Understanding in Science*, The proceedings of a conference, Woolley Hall, England, 11–13 July, SSCR, London, pp. 69–72.
2 Guesne, E. (1985) 'Light', in Driver, R., Guesne, E. and Tiberghien, A. (eds), *Children's Ideas in Science*, Open University Press, Milton Keynes.
3 Ramadas, J. and Driver, R. (1989) *Aspects of secondary students' ideas about light*, Children's Learning in Science Project, Centre for Studies in Science and Mathematics Education, University of Leeds.
4 Osborne, J., Black, P., Smith, S. and Meadows, J. (1990) *Light Research Report*, Primary SPACE Project, Liverpool University Press.
5 Andersson, B. and Karrqvist, C. (1981) *Light and its properties* EKNA Report 8, Institutionen for Praktisk Pedagogik, University of Gothenburg, Sweden.
6 Watts, D.M. and Gilbert, J.K. (1985) *Appraising the understanding of science concepts: light*, Department of Educational Studies, University of Surrey, Guildford.
7 Anderson, C.W. and Smith, E.L. (1983) 'Children's conceptions of light and colour: developing the concept of unseen rays', Paper presented to the annual meeting of the American Educational Research Association, Montreal, Canada.
8 La Rosa, C., Mayer, M., Patrizi, P. and Vincentini, M. (1984) 'Commonsense knowledge in optics: preliminary results of an investigation of the properties of light', *European Journal of Science Education* 6(4): 387–97.
9 Stead, B.F. and Osborne, R.J. (1980) 'Exploring students' concepts of light', *The Australian Science Teachers' Journal* 26(3): 84–90.
10 Fetherstonhaugh, T. and Treagust, D.F. (1990) 'Students' understanding of light and its properties following a teaching strategy to engender conceptual change', Paper presented to the annual meeting of the American Educational Research Association, 16–20 April, Boston.
11 Feher, E. and Rice, K. (1985) 'Showing shadow shapes: activities to elicit and dispel some preconceptions', Paper submitted to *Science and Children*.
12 Tiberghien, A., Delacote, G., Ghiglione, R. and Metalon, B. (1980) 'Conceptions de la lumière chez l'enfant de 10–12 ans', *Revue Française de Pedagogie* 50: 24–41.
13 Goldberg, F.M. and McDermott, L.C. (1986) 'Student difficulties in understanding image formation by a plane mirror', *The Physics Teacher* 24(8): 472–80.
14 Shapiro, B.L. (1989) 'What children bring to light: giving high status to learners' views and actions in science', *Science Education* 73(6): 711–33.
15 Zylbersztajn, A. and Watts, D.M. (1982) 'Throwing some light on colour', Mimeograph, University of Surrey, Guildford.

18 SOUND

1 Watt, D. and Russell, T. (1990) *Sound*, Primary SPACE Project Research Report, Liverpool University Press.

2 Asoko, H.M., Leach, J. and Scott, P.H. (1991) 'A study of students' understanding of sound 5–16 as an example of action research', Paper prepared
for the Symposium, 'Developing Students' Understanding in Science' at the
Annual Conference of the British Educational Research Association at
Roehampton Institute, 2 September 1990, London.
3 Linder, C.J. and Erickson, G.L. (1989) 'A study of tertiary physics students'
conceptualizations of sound', *International Journal of Science Education* 11,
Special Issue, 491–501.

19 HEATING

1 Harris, W.F. (1981) 'Heat in undergraduate education, or isn't it time
we abandoned the theory of caloric?', *International Journal of Mechanical
Engineering Education*, vol. 9: 317–21.
2 Hewson, M.G. and Hamlyn, D. (1984) 'The influence of intellectual environment on conceptions of heat', *European Journal of Science Education* 6(3): 245–62.
3 Erickson, G. (1977) 'Children's conceptions of heat and temperature
phenomena', Paper presented as part of the symposium on 'Patterns of
student beliefs – implications for science teaching' at the CCSE convention,
June, Fredericton.
4 Engel Clough, E. and Driver, R. (1985) 'Secondary students' conceptions of
the conduction of heat: bringing together scientific and personal views',
Physics Education 20: 176–82.
5 Watts, D.M. and Gilbert, J.K. (1985) *Appraising the understanding of science
concepts: heat*, Department of Educational Studies, University of Surrey,
Guildford.
6 Tiberghien, A. (1983) 'Critical review on the research aimed at elucidating
the sense that the notions of temperature and heat have for students aged
10 to 16 years', *Research on Physics Education*, Proceedings of the first
international workshop, 26 June–13 July, La Londe les Maures, France,
Editions du Centre National de la Recherche Scientifique, Paris, 1984, pp.
75–90.
7 Driver, R. and Russell, T. (1982) *An investigation of the ideas of heat temperature
and change of state of children aged between 8 and 14 years*, Centre for Studies
in Science and Mathematics Education, University of Leeds.
8 Stavy, R. and Berkovitz, B. (1980) 'Cognitive conflict as a basis for teaching
quantitative aspects of the concept of temperature', *Science Education* 64(5):
679–92.
9 Strauss, S. and Stavy, R. (1982) 'U-shaped behavioural growth: implications
for theories of development', in Hartup, W. (ed.), *Review of child development
research*, Volume 6, University of Chicago Press.
10 Appleton, K. (1985) 'Children's ideas about temperature', *Research in Science
Education* 15: 122–6.
11 Engel, M.E.T. (1982) 'The development of understanding of selected aspects
of pressure, heat, and evolution in pupils aged 12 to 16 years', unpublished
Ph.D. thesis, University of Leeds.
12 Brook, A., Briggs, H., Bell, B. and Driver, R. (1984) *Aspects of secondary
students' understanding of heat*, Centre for Studies in Science and Mathematics
Education, University of Leeds.
13 Driver, R. (1984) 'Cognitive psychology and pupils' frameworks about heat',
Prepared for Convengo 1984 del Gruppo Nazionale Didattica della Fisica,
San Miniato, Italy.

REFERENCES

20 ENERGY

1 Watts, D.M. and Gilbert, J.K. (1985) *Appraising the understanding of science concepts: energy*, Department of Educational Studies, University of Surrey, Guildford.
2 Solomon, J. (1983) 'Messy, contradictory and obstinately persistent: a study of children's out of school ideas about energy', *School Science Review* 65(231): 225–33.
3 Stead, B. (1980) *Energy*, LISP Working Paper 17, Science Education Research Unit, University of Waikato, Hamilton, New Zealand.
4 Arzi, H.J. (1988) 'On energy in chocolate and yogurt, or: on the applicability of school science concepts to real life', Paper presented at the Annual Meeting of the American Educational Research Association, April, New Orleans.
5 Bliss, J. and Ogborn, J. (1985) 'Children's choices of uses of energy', *European Journal of Science Education* 7(2): 195–203.
6 Gilbert, J.K. and Pope, M. (1982) *School children discussing energy*, Report of the Institute of Educational Development, University of Surrey, Guildford.
7 Ault, C.R., Novak, J.D. and Gowin, D.B. (1988) 'Contructing vee maps for clinical interviews on energy concepts', *Science Education* 72(4): 515–45.
8 Gayford, C.G. (1986) 'Some aspects of the problems of teaching about energy in school biology', *European Journal of Science Education* 8(4): 443–50.
9 Duit, R. (1981) 'Students' notions about energy concept – before and after physics instruction', in Jung, W., Pfundt, H. and Rhoneck, C. von (eds), *Proceedings of the International Workshop on Problems Concerning Students' Representation of Physics and Chemistry Knowledge*, 14–16 September, Pedagogische Hochschule, Ludwigsburg, pp. 268–319.
10 Watts, D.M. and Gilbert, J.K. (1983) 'Enigmas in school science: students' conceptions for scientifically associated words', *Research in Science and Technological Education* 1(2): 161–71.
11 Barbetta, M.G., Loria, A., Mascellani, V. and Michellini, M. (1984) 'An investigation on students' frameworks about motion and the concepts of force and energy', in Lijnse, P. (ed.), *The Many Faces of Teaching and Learning Mechanics in Secondary School and Early Tertiary Education, Proceedings of a Conference on Physics Education*, 20–25 August, Utrecht.
12 Brook, A. and Driver, R. (1984) *Aspects of secondary students' understanding of energy: full report*, Centre for Studies in Science and Mathematics Education, University of Leeds.
13 Duit, R. (1984) 'Learning the energy concept in school – empirical results from the Philippines and West Germany', *Physics Education* 19(2): 59–66.
14 Driver, R. and Warrington, L. (1985) 'Students' use of the principle of energy conservation in problem situations', *Physics Education* 20(4): 171–6.
15 Black, P. and Solomon, J. (1985) 'Life world and science world – pupils' ideas about energy', in Hodgson, B. and Scanlon, E. (eds), *Approaching Primary Science*, Hooper Education Series, Open University, Milton Keynes.
16 Duit, R. (1983) 'Energy conceptions held by students and consequences for science teaching', in Helm, H. and Novak, J.D. (eds), *Proceedings of the International Seminar: Misconceptions in Science and Mathematics*, 20–22 June 1983, Cornell University, Ithaca, N.Y., pp. 316–23.

REFERENCES

21 FORCES

1 Piaget, J. (1973) *La Formation de la notion de force, Etudes d'épistemologie génétique* (Vol XXX), Paris Presses, Université de France.

2 Finegold, M. and Gorsky, P. (1991) 'Students' concepts of force as applied to related physical systems: a search for consistency', *International Journal of Science Education* 13(1): 97–113.

3 Osborne, R. (1980) *Force*, LISP Working Paper 16, Science Education Research Unit, University of Waikato, Hamilton, New Zealand.

4 Osborne, R. (1985) 'Building on children's intuitive ideas', in Osborne, R. and Freyberg, P. *Learning in Science*, Heinemann, Auckland, New Zealand.

5 Watts, D.M. (1983) 'A study of school children's alternative frameworks of the concept of force', *European Journal of Science Education* 5(2): 217–30.

6 Osborne, R., Schollum, B. and Hill, G. (1981) *Force, Friction, Gravity: Notes for teachers*, LISP Working Paper 33, Science Education Research Unit, University of Waikato, Hamilton, New Zealand.

7 Shevlin, J. (1989) 'Children's prior conceptions of force aged 5–11 and their relevance to Attainment Target 10 of the National Curriculum of Science', Unpublished M.Ed. thesis, University of Leeds.

8 Gunstone, R. and Watts, D.M. (1985) 'Force and motion', in Driver, R., Guesne, E. and Tiberghien, A. (eds), *Children's Ideas in Science*, Open University Press, Milton Keynes, pp. 85–104.

9 Watts, D.M. and Gilbert, J.K. (1985) *Appraising the understanding of science concepts: force*, Department of Educational Studies, University of Surrey, Guildford.

10 Duit, R. (1984) 'Work, force and power – words in everyday language and terms in mechanics', in Lijnse, P. (ed.), *The Many Faces of Teaching and Learning Mechanics in Secondary and Early Tertiary Education*, Proceedings of a conference on physics education, 20–25 August, Utrecht; GIREP/SVO/UNESCO, WCC, Utrecht, 1985: 221–33.

11 Driver, R. (1984) 'Cognitive psychology and pupils' frameworks in mechanics', in Ljinse, P. (ed.), *The many faces of teaching and learning mechanics in secondary and early tertiary education*, Proceedings of a conference on physics education, 20–25 August, Utrecht; GIREP/SVO/UNESCO,WCC, Utrecht, 1985: 227–33.

12 Sjoberg, S. and Lie, S. (1981) *Ideas about force and movement among Norwegian pupils and students*, Institute of Physics Report Series: Report 81-11, University of Oslo.

13 Viennot, L. (1979) 'Spontaneous reasoning in elementary dynamics', *European Journal of Science Education* 1(2): 205–21.

14 Watts, D.M. and Zylbersztajn, A. (1981) 'A survey of some children's ideas about force', *Physical Education* 16: 360–5.

15 Clement, J. (1982) 'Students' preconceptions in introductory mechanics', *American Journal of Physics* 50(1): 66–71.

16 McCloskey, M. (1983) 'Intuitive physics', *Scientific American* 248(4): 114–22.

17 Fischbein, E., Stavy, R. and Ma-Naim, H. (1988) 'The psychological structure of naïve impetus conceptions', *International Journal of Science Education* 11(1): 71–81.

18 Brown, D.E. and Clement, J. (1987) 'Misconceptions concerning Newton's law of action and reaction: the underestimated importance of the third law', in Novak, J.D. (ed.), *Proceedings of the Second International Seminar: Misconceptions and Educational Strategies in Science and Mathematics* (Volume III), Ithaca, N.Y., pp. 39–53.

REFERENCES

19 Brown, D.E. (1989) 'Students' concept of force: the importance of understanding Newton's third law', *Physics Education* 24: 353–8.
20 Maloney, D.P. (1985) 'Rule governed physics: some novice predictions', *European Journal of Science Education* 7(3): 295.
21 Minstrell, J. and Stimpson, G. (1986) 'Students' belief in mechanics: cognitive process frameworks', Paper presented to the Fifth Conference on Reasoning and Higher Education, Centre for the Study of Thinking, 14–15 March, Boise, Idaho.
22 Erickson, G. and Hobbs, E. (1978) 'The developmental study of student beliefs about force concepts', Paper presented to the 1978 Annual Convention of the Canadian Society for the Study of Education. 2 June, London, Ontario, Canada.
23 Terry, C., Jones, G. and Hurford, W. (1985) 'Children's conceptual understanding of force and equilibrium', *Physics Education* 20(4): 162–5.
24 Minstrell, J. (1982) 'Explaining the "at rest" condition of an object', *The Physics Teacher* 20:10–14.
25 Stead, K.E. and Osborne, R.J. (1981) 'What is friction: some children's ideas', *New Zealand Science Teacher* 27: 51–7.
26 Séré, M. (1982) 'A study of some frameworks of the field of mechanics, used by children (aged 11 to 13) when they interpret experiments about air pressure', *European Journal of Science Education* (4): 299–309.
27 Engel Clough, E. and Driver, R. (1985) 'What do children understand about pressure in fluids?', *Research in Science and Technology Education* 3(2): 133–4.
28 Séré, M. (1986) 'Children's conceptions of the gaseous state, prior to teaching', *European Journal of Science Education* (8): 413–25.
29 Inhelder, B. and Piaget, J. (1958) *The Growth of Logical Thinking from Childhood to Adolescence*, Routledge & Kegan Paul, London.

22 HORIZONTAL MOTION

1 Claxton, G.L. (1984) 'Teaching and acquiring scientific knowledge', in Keen, T. and Pope, M. (eds), *Kelly in the classroom: educational application of personal construct psychology*, Cyberssystems Inc., Montreal, Canada.
2 Osborne, R. (1984) 'Children's dynamics', *The Physics Teacher* 22(8): 504–8.
3 McClelland, J.A.G. (1984) 'Alternative frameworks: interpretation of evidence', *European Journal of Science Education* 6(1):1–6.
4 Yates, J., Bessman, M., Dunne, M., Jertson, D., Sly, K. and Wendelboe, B. (1988) 'Are conceptions of motion based on naïve theory or on prototypes?', *Cognition* 29: 251–75.
5 Di Sessa, A. (1982) 'Unlearning Aristotelian physics: a study of knowledge-based learning', *Cognitive Science* 6: 37–75.
6 Ogborn, J. and Bliss, J. (1982) 'Steps towards a formalisation of a psycho-logic of motion', in Tiberghien, A. and Mandl, H. (eds), *Knowledge Acquisition in Physics Learning Environments*, NATO ASI Series Berlin, Springer-Verlag.
7 McCloskey, M. (1983) 'Intuitive physics', *Scientific American* 248(4): 114–22.
8 Clement, J. (1983) 'Students' alternative conceptions in mechanics: a coherent system of preconceptions?', in Helm, H. and Novak, J.D. (eds), *Proceedings of the International Seminar: Misconceptions in Science and Mathematics*, 20–22 June, Cornell University, Ithaca, N.Y., pp. 310–15.
9 Jung, W. (1981) 'Some methods of inquiry into knowledge structures in mechanics', in Jung, W., Pfundt, H. and Rhoneck, C. von (eds), *Proceedings*

REFERENCES

of the International Workshop on Problems Concerning Students' Representation of Physics and Chemistry Knowledge, 14–16 September, Pedagogische Hochschule, Ludwigsburg, pp. 254–67.

10 Jira, D.K. and McCloskey, M. (1980) *Students' misconceptions about physical motion*, The Johns Hopkins University.

11 Trowbridge, D.E. and McDermott, L.C. (1981) 'Investigation of student understanding of the concept of acceleration in one dimension', *American Journal of Physics* 49: 242.

12 Jones, A.T. (1983) 'Investigation of students' understanding of speed, velocity and acceleration', *Research in Science Education* 13: 95–104.

13 Piaget, J. (1979) *Children's conceptions of the world*, Routledge & Kegan Paul, London.

14 Boulanger, F.D. (1976) 'The effects of training in the proportional reasoning associated with the concept of speed', *Journal of Research in Science Teaching* 13(2): 145–54.

15 Bliss, J., Morrison, I. and Ogborn, J. (1988) 'A longitudinal study of dynamics concepts', *International Journal of Science Education* 10(1): 99–110.

16 Minstrell, J. (1982) 'Explaining the "at rest" condition of an object', *The Physics Teacher* 20: 10–14.

17 Sjoberg, S. and Lie, S. (1981) *Ideas about force and movement among Norwegian pupils and students*, Institute of Physics Report Series: Report 81-11, University of Oslo.

18 Erickson, G. and Hobbs, E. (1978) 'A developmental study of student beliefs about force concepts', Paper presented to the 1978 Annual Convention of the Canadian Society for the Study of Education, 2 June, London, Ontario, Canada.

19 Osborne, R. (1980) *Force*, LISP Working Paper 16, Science Education Research Unit, University of Waikato, Hamilton, New Zealand.

20 Osborne, R. (1985) 'Building on children's intuitive ideas', in Osborne, R. and Freyberg, P., *Learning in Science*, Heinemann, Auckland, New Zealand.

21 Viennot, L. (1980) 'Spontaneous reasoning in elementary dynamics', in Archenhold, W.F., Driver, R., Orton, A. and Wood-Robinson, C. (eds), *Cognitive Development Research in Science and Mathematics*, Proceedings of an International Seminar, 17–21 September 1979, University of Leeds, pp. 273–4.

22 Watts, D.M. and Zylbersztajn, A. (1981) 'A survey of some children's ideas about force', *Physical Education* 16: 360–5.

23 Clement, J. (1982) 'Students' preconceptions in introductory mechanics', *American Journal of Physics* 50(1): 66–71.

24 Fischbein, E., Stavy, R. and Ma-Naim, H. (1988) 'The psychological structure of naïve impetus conceptions', *International Journal of Science Education* 11(1): 71–81.

25 Lythott, J. (1983) '"Aristotelian" was given as the answer, but what was the question?', in Helm, H. and Novak, J.D. (eds), *Proceedings of the International Seminar: Misconceptions in Science and Mathematics*, 20–22 June, Cornell University, Ithaca, N.Y., pp. 257–65.

26 Caramazza, A., McCloskey, M. and Green, B. (1981) 'Naïve beliefs in "sophisticated" subjects: misconceptions about trajectories of objects', *Cognition* 9: 117–23.

27 Watts, D.M. (1983) 'A study of schoolchildren's alternative frameworks of the concept of force', *European Journal of Science Education* 5(2): 217–30.

28 Bliss, J., Ogborn, J. and Whitelock, D. (1989) 'Secondary school pupils'

REFERENCES

commonsense theories of motion', *International Journal of Science Education* 11(3): 261–72.

29 Champagne, A.B., Klopfer, L.E. and Anderson, J.H. (1980) 'Factors influencing the learning of classical mechanics', *American Journal of Physics* 48(12): 1074–79.

30 Lie, S., Sjoberg, S., Ekeland, P.R. and Enge, M. (1984) 'Ideas in mechanics. A Norwegian study', in Lijnse, P. (ed.), *The Many Faces of Teaching and Learning Mechanics in Secondary and Early Tertiary Education, Proceedings of a Conference on Physics Education.* 20–25 August, Utrecht; GIREP/SVO/UNESCO, WCC, Utrecht 1985, pp. 255–76.

31 Gunstone, R. and Watts, D.M. (1985) 'Force and motion', in Driver, R., Guesne, E. and Tiberghien, A. (eds), *Children's Ideas in Science*, Open University Press, Milton Keynes, pp. 85–104.

32 Gilbert, J.K., Watts, D.M. and Osborne, R.J. (1982) 'Students' conceptions of ideas in mechanics', *Physics Education* 17: 62–6.

33 Eckstein, S.G. and Shemesh, M. (1989) 'Development of children's ideas on motion: intuition vs logical thinking', *International Journal of Science Education* 11(3): 327–36.

34 Langford, J.M. and Zollman, D. (1982) 'Conceptions of dynamics held by elementary and high school students', Paper presented at the Annual Meeting of the American Association of Physics Teachers, 25–28 January, San Francisco.

35 Hewson, P. (1985) 'Epistemological commitments in the learning of science: examples from dynamics', *European Journal of Science Education* 7(2): 163–72.

36 Stead, K.E. and Osborne, R.J. (1981) 'What is friction: some children's ideas', *New Zealand Science Teacher* 27: 51–7.

37 Stead, K. and Osborne, R. (1980) *Friction*, LISP Working Paper 19, Science Education Research Unit, University of Waikato, Hamilton, New Zealand.

38 McDermott, L.C. (1983) 'Critical review of research in the domain of mechanics', in *Research on Physics Education*, Proceedings of the First International Workshop. 26 June-13 July, La Londe les Maures, France, Editions du Centre National de la Recherche Scientifique, Paris, 1984, pp. 139–82.

39 McDermott, L.C. (1984) 'Research on conceptual understanding in mechanics', *Physics Today*, July: 2–10.

40 Posner, G.J., Strike, K.A., Hewson, P.W. and Gertzog, G. (1982) 'Accommodation of a scientific conception: toward a theory of conceptual change', *Science Education* 66: 21.

41 Brown, D.E. and Clement, J. (1989) 'Overcoming misconceptions via analogical reasoning: abstract transfer versus explanatory model construction', Paper presented at the Annual Meeting of the American Educational Research Association, San Francisco.

42 Clement, J., Brown, D.E. and Zietsmann, A. (1989) 'Not all preconceptions are misconceptions: finding "anchoring conceptions" for grounding instruction on students' intuitions', *International Journal of Science Education* 11 (Special Issue): 554–65.

43 Clement, J. (1988) 'Observed methods for generating analysis in scientific problem solving', *Computer Science* 12(4): 563.

44 Minstrell, J. and Stimpson, G. (1986) 'Students' beliefs in mechanics: cognitive process frameworks', Paper presented to the Fifth Conference on Reasoning and Higher Education, Centre for the Study of Thinking, 14–15 March, Boise, Idaho.

REFERENCES

45 Watts, D.M. and Gilbert, J.K. (1985) *Appraising the understanding of science concepts: 'Force'*, Department of Educational Studies, University of Surrey, Guildford.

46 Hewson, P.W. (1984) 'Microcomputers, conceptual change and the design of science instruction: examples from kinematics and dynamics', *South African Journal of Science* 80, January: 15–20.

47 Schollum, B., Hill, G. and Osborne, R. (1981) *Teaching about force*, LISP Working Paper 34, Science Education Research Unit, University of Waikato, Hamilton, New Zealand.

48 Di Sessa, A. (1989) 'A child's science of motion: overview and first results', Draft paper, Graduate School of Education, University of California, Berkeley.

49 Saltiel, E. and Malgrange, J.L. (1980) '"Spontaneous" ways of reasoning in elementary kinematics', *European Journal of Physics* 1: 73–80.

50 Kilmister, C.W. (1982) 'Newton's laws of motion – rules or discoveries?', *Physics Education* 17(2): 58–61.

51 Gilbert, J.K. and Zylbersztajn, A. (1985) 'A conceptual framework for science education: the case study of force and movement', *European Journal of Science Education* 7(2): 107–20.

23 GRAVITY

1 Nussbaum, J. (1985) 'The Earth as a cosmic body', in Driver, R., Guesne, E. and Tiberghien, A. (eds), *Children's Ideas in Science*, Open University Press, Milton Keynes, Chapter 9.

2 Baxter, J. (1989) 'Children's understanding of familiar astronomical events', *International Journal of Science Education* 11 (Special Issue): 502–13.

3 Mali, G.B. and Howe, A. (1979) 'Development of Earth and gravity concepts among Nepali children', *Science Education* 63(5): 685–91.

4 Sneider, C. and Pulos, S. (1983) 'Children's cosmographics: understanding the Earth's shape and gravity', *Science Education* 67(2): 205–22.

5 Vosniadou, S. and Brewer, W.F. (1990) 'A cross cultural investigation of children's conceptions about the Earth, the Sun and the Moon: Greek and American data', in Mandl, H., De Corte, E., Bennett, N. and Friedrid, H.F. (eds), *Learning and Instruction. European Research in an International Context*, Volume 2.2, Papers of the second conference of the European Association for Research on Learning and Instruction held at the University of Tübingen, 1987, Pergamon Press, Oxford.

6 Selman, R.L., Krupa, M.P., Stone, C.R. and Jacquette, D.S. (1982) 'Concrete operational thought and the emergence of the concept of unseen force in children's theories of electromagnetism and gravity', *Science Education* 66(2): 181–94.

7 Stead, K. and Osborne, R. (1980) *Gravity*, LISP Working Paper 20, Science Education Research Unit, University of Waikato, Hamilton, New Zealand.

8 Ruggiero, S., Cartielli, A., Dupre, F. and Vicentini-Missoni, M. (1985) 'Weight, gravity and air pressure: mental representations by Italian middle-school pupils', *European Journal of Science Education* 7(2): 181–94.

9 Vicentini-Missoni, M. (1981) 'Earth and gravity: comparison between adults' and children's knowledge', in Jung, W., Pfundt, H. and Rhoneck, C. von (eds), *Proceedings of the International Workshop on Problems Concerning Students' Representation of Physics and Chemistry Knowledge*, 14–16 September, Pedagogische Hochschule, Ludwigsburg, pp. 223–53.

10 Watts, D.M. (1982) 'Gravity – don't take it for granted!', *Physics Education* 17: 116–21.
11 Osborne, R. (1984) 'Children's dynamics', *The Physics Teacher* 22(8): 504–8.
12 Gunstone, R.F. and White, R.T. (1980) 'A matter of gravity', Paper given at a meeting of the Australian Science Education Research Association, May, Melbourne, Australia.
13 Nachtigall, D. 'Concepts of fifth-grade students concerning freely falling objects', Unpublished paper, University of Dortmund, Germany.
14 Champagne, A., Klopfer, L., Solomon, C. and Cohen, A. (1980) *Interactions of students' knowledge with their comprehension and design of science experiments*, Technical Report, University of Pittsburgh.
15 McDermott, L.C. (1983) 'Critical review of research in the domain of mechanics', in *Research on Physics Education*, Proceedings of the First International Workshop, 26 June–13 July, La Londe les Maures, France, Editions du Centre National de la Recherche Scientifique, Paris, 1984, pp. 139–82.
16 Rogers, E.M. (1984) 'Gravity, the new Cinderella in elementary mechanics teaching', in Lijnse, P.L. (ed.), *The Many Faces of Teaching and Learning Mechanics in Secondary and Early Tertiary Education, Proceedings of a Conference on Physics Education*. 20–25 August, Utrecht; GIREP/SVO/ UNESCO, WCC, Utrecht 1985, pp. 625–30.
17 Watts, D.M. and Gilbert, J.K. (1985) *Appraising the understanding of science concepts: 'Gravity'*, Department of Educational Studies, University of Surrey, Guildford.

24 EARTH IN SPACE

1 Nussbaum, J. (1985) 'The Earth as a cosmic book', in Driver, R., Guesne, E. and Tiberghien, A. (eds), *Children's Ideas in Science*, Open University Press, Milton Keynes, Chapter 9.
2 Baxter, J. (1989) 'Children's understanding of familiar astronomical events', *International Journal of Science Education* 11 (Special Issue): 502–13.
3 Mali, G.B. and Howe, A. (1979) 'Development of Earth and gravity concepts among Nepali children', *Science Education* 63(5): 685–91.
4 Sneider, C. and Pulos, S. (1983) 'Children's cosmographics: understanding the Earth's shape and gravity', *Science Education* 67(2): 205–22.
5 Vosniadou, S. and Brewer, W.F. (1990) 'A cross cultural investigation of children's conceptions about the Earth, the Sun and the Moon: Greek and American data', in Mandl, H., De Corte, E., Bennett, N. and Friedrid, H.F. (eds), *Learning and Instruction. European Research in an International Context*, Volume 2.2, Papers of the second conference of the European Association for Research on Learning and Instruction held at the University of Tübingen, 1987, Pergamon Press, Oxford.
6 Nussbaum, J. and Sharoni-Dagan, N. (1983) 'Changes in second grade children's preconceptions about the Earth as a cosmic body resulting from a short series of audio tutorial lessons', *Science Education* 67(1): 99–114.
7 Klein, C.A. (1982) 'Children's concepts of the Sun, a cross cultural study', *Science Education* 65(1): 95–107.
8 Sadler, P.M. (1987) 'Misconceptions in astronomy', Paper presented at the Second International Seminar: Misconceptions and Educational Strategies in Science and Mathematics, 26–29 July, Cornell University, Ithaca, N.Y.
9 Jones, B.L., Lynch, P.P. and Reesink, C. (1987) 'Children's conception of

the Earth, Sun and Moon', *International Journal of Science Education* 9(1): 43–53.

10 Targon, D. (1987) 'A study of conceptual change in the content domain of the lunar phases', Paper presented at the Second International Seminar: Misconceptions and Educational Strategies in Science and Mathematics, 26–29 July, Cornell University, Ithaca, N.Y.

11 Lightman, A.P., Miller, J.D. and Leadbetter, J.B. 'Contemporary cosmological beliefs', Paper presented to the Second International Seminar: Misconceptions and Educational Strategies in Science and Mathematics, 26–29 July, Cornell University, Ithaca, N.Y.

INDEX